Stealing from
Each Other

Stealing from Each Other

How the Welfare State Robs
Americans of Money and Spirit

Edgar K. Browning

Westport, Connecticut
London

Library of Congress Cataloging-in-Publication Data

Browning, Edgar K.
  Stealing from each other : how the welfare state robs Americans of
money and spirit / Edgar K. Browning.
      p. cm.
  Includes bibliographical references and index.
  ISBN 978–0–313–34822–8 (alk. paper)
  1. Public welfare—United States.   2. Welfare state.   3. United
States—Social policy.   I. Title.
  HV91.B713   2008
  361.6′50973—dc22   2007042511

British Library Cataloguing in Publication Data is available.

Library of Congress Catalog Card Number: 2007042511
ISBN: 978–0–313–34822–8

First published in 2008

Praeger Publishers, 88 Post Road West, Westport, CT 06881
An imprint of Greenwood Publishing Group, Inc.
www.praeger.com

Printed in the United States of America

The paper used in this book complies with the
Permanent Paper Standard issued by the National
Information Standards Organization (Z39.48–1984).

10   9   8   7   6   5   4   3   2   1

Contents

Acknowledgments

This book has grown out of my teaching "Poverty, Inequality, and Social Policy" at Texas A&M University for the past 20 or so years. I was fortunate to be allowed to structure the course according to my own interests and priorities, and it evolved over time to include the topics discussed in this book. My students in this course have contributed in many ways to the final product, and should any of them read this volume they will probably be relieved to find that all the graphs cluttering the classroom blackboard are absent here.

A number of people provided valuable comments and criticisms of earlier drafts of some or all the chapters. For selflessly providing this assistance I am grateful to John Allen, John Browning, Patricia Griffin, and Lucas Rentschler. Since I, perhaps unwisely, did not incorporate all their suggestions, any remaining defects are solely my responsibility.

Special thanks to my wife, Deborah Bay, who put up with my preoccupation with this project for more than three years. In addition, she created the beautiful and apposite photograph shown on the cover. You can see some of her other work at her Web site, http://www.deborahbay.com.

Finally, thanks to Stan Wakefield for helping me find the right publisher. I also want to thank the people at Greenwood Publishing, and especially my editor Jeff Olson, who helped to make the completion of the project relatively painless.

Introduction

In 1986, the economics department at Texas A&M University asked me to develop a course for the University Honors program. The course, "Poverty, Inequality, and Social Policy," soon became a regular course in the economics curriculum, and I have now taught it for more than 20 years. I learned a great deal about the modern welfare state from teaching this course, and it became apparent that news media coverage of this topic was woefully inadequate. This book evolved as a result of my conviction that informed citizens need to know how welfare-state policies affect them and that it is difficult for them to acquire the relevant information from conventional sources.

The foundational question related to welfare-state policies is: When is it justified for the government to take the resources that belong to some people and use them to provide benefits to other people? It is no exaggeration to say that most of what modern governments do falls into this category of redistributive policies. Are these welfare-state policies good for our society? I argue in this book that most are decidedly harmful to the well-being of Americans.

When I began studying economics in the 1960s, the conventional wisdom was that welfare-state policies had very little net economic cost. In other words, it was thought that a government policy providing a dollar benefit to one person involved a cost of not much more than a dollar for another person—the *net* cost for the two people together was close to zero because what one lost the other gained. Of course, it was recognized that there were some real costs, such as administrative costs and what economists call "deadweight losses," but these costs were largely dismissed as being of negligible size.

Economic research over the past 40 years has shown this view to be tragically mistaken. To give but one example of the evolution in economic research: In 1969, the prominent economist Richard Musgrave suggested that the real cost to taxpayers of raising a dollar in tax revenue was about $1.02.[1]

That two-cent hidden cost was due to the estimated efficiency loss of taxation resulting from its effect on labor supply. In sharp contrast, the President's Council of Economic Advisers has pointed out, based on recent research, that it costs Americans from $1.40 to $1.60 to raise a dollar in tax revenue. In other words, the hidden real cost of the government acquiring a dollar in revenue is at least 20 times as large as Musgrave suggested in 1969. (The costs of the federal tax system are discussed in chapter 9.)

As with taxation, so too with other policies of the welfare state: It is now well known to professional economists that policies of the welfare state impose large costs on Americans. Unfortunately, these costs are not easy to see as they involve consequences like saving and investment not undertaken, labor effort not supplied, new businesses not started, and so on. Nonetheless, these costs are very real and well documented in the technical literature.

It is ironic that over the period when economics was confirming the heavy damages imposed by the welfare state, these policies were becoming more politically entrenched. In 1964, Barry Goldwater, along with a large part of the Republican party, was openly critical of the entire welfare-state edifice, but at that time the evidence did not support such a strong position. Conversely, the Republican party today has made its peace with the welfare state and has become the party of big-government conservatism,[2] at a time when the best evidence suggests these policies are hugely harmful and a threat to our future prosperity. Of course, the more egalitarian Democratic party just ignores this evidence altogether.

How harmful are the welfare-state policies discussed in this volume? We cannot know with certainty the exact magnitude, but the research discussed in this book suggests that *the welfare state lowers the income of the average American by about 25 percent.* Note that this does not refer to the direct tax burden of supporting these policies; the 25 percent loss is in before-tax income and is in addition to any taxes paid. Put somewhat differently, gross domestic product (GDP) is a quarter lower than it would have been without the welfare state. The loss ultimately reflects the reduced productivity of the economy that results from the myriad effects of welfare-state policies.

This is a huge total loss, more than $4 *trillion* annually.

In order to appreciate what is at stake here, I would like to draw an analogy between the welfare state and global warming. It might be thought that global warming has little in common with welfare programs or Social Security, but in fact the similarities are striking.

First of all, both issues involve *long-term* consequences of our present actions. In the case of global warming, we are urged to bear costs today with the prospect of achieving benefits that will occur many years or decades in the future. Similarly, reforming the welfare state also involves present costs that will be repaid by later benefits. In both cases, the more importance you attach to our future prosperity the more important it is to change policies in a way that involves costs in the present.

A second similarity is that in both cases scientific research is necessary to identify and measure the costs and benefits of alternative courses of action. The average citizen is unlikely to even be aware of the relevant costs and benefits, much less their magnitudes, unless informed by the news media. Unfortunately, the news media have not done a very good job in communicating what the best evidence indicates about the consequences of the welfare state and potential reform options. One of the purposes of this book is to attempt to repair that omission.

The news media have, of course, been filled with stories about the potential damages that global warming may produce, to the point that many people think it is the most pressing issue confronting humanity. But is it? How large are the costs we will bear if nothing is done and global warming occurs as predicted by the various computer climate models? Several researchers have taken the climate predictions and used them to estimate the monetary value of the costs (and benefits, because a warmer climate carries with it some benefits). What is the result?

According to R. Tol and G. Yohe, the peer-reviewed estimates of the net cost of unabated global warming over the next century range from about minus 2 percent (a net benefit!) to plus 5 percent of world income, or world GDP. The midpoint estimate seems to be between 1 and 2 percent of world income.[3] Consequently, all of the hyperventilating of Al Gore and other environmental crusaders is over a future cost that will be equivalent to losing less than 2 percent of our income. That does not necessarily mean we should not be concerned; 2 percent of GDP is a large cost and worth avoiding—at least if it can be accomplished at a cost that is even lower.

But the point of the comparison is that the evidence indicates that the cost of welfare-state policies is about 10 times larger than the future (and uncertain) cost of global warming. If global warming is a serious threat to our well-being, on the evidence it is hard to avoid the conclusion that the modern welfare state is an even greater danger, and we are already bearing its costs. Nor should the estimated 25 percent loss in our income due to the welfare state be dismissed as highly conjectural. The science supporting this estimate is at least as well established as that dealing with global warming.

The major policies constituting our welfare state are discussed in chapters 6 through 11. The first five chapters deal with the underpinnings of the welfare state, in particular the issues of inequality and poverty. It is little exaggeration to say that the egalitarian belief that social justice is promoted by the redistributive policies of the welfare state is the reason we have these policies. That belief is based on the claim that free markets generate an unacceptable degree of inequality and poverty, so I begin with an examination of issues related to that claim. However, the chapters can be read in almost any order. If you have a particular interest in, say, Social Security, by all means start with chapter 7.

Regardless of the order in which you read these chapters, my hope is that you will come away from reading this book with a greater understanding of the costs we bear as a result of our redistributive welfare-state policies. For far too long, politicians have sacrificed our long-term interests for short-term political and economic benefits. It is not too late to change course, though it becomes more difficult with each passing year. A first step is to appreciate the harmful consequences of stealing from each other.

Egalitarianism and the Market

When the definitive history of the twentieth century is written, one of its major themes will be the rise of the modern welfare state. The twenty-first century will have to decide whether this great experiment with redistributive government was a success or a failure. I argue in this volume that it has been largely a failure.

In 1900, government played a very small role in the day-to-day activities of American citizens. There was no income tax, no Social Security, no federal welfare programs, no minimum-wage laws, no federal involvement in education, no affirmative action. Government was truly small and limited, spending well under 10 percent of our incomes in total, with the federal government spending only about 3 percent.

No one today would describe our government as either small or limited. Government now spends more than a third of our incomes, with the federal government alone spending more than 20 percent. Most of this spending is on welfare-state programs, that is, programs that have as a major goal or consequence the transfer of income earned by some people to other people. Roughly two-thirds of federal spending is of this type.

Welfare-state policies have both benefits and costs. The benefits are generally obvious, as they take the form of government providing goods, services, and cash to people. Many of the costs are not so obvious. While the taxes required to pay for these programs are often apparent, many hidden costs go largely unrecognized. A major purpose of this book is to explain and document these hidden costs.

For example, are you aware that your *before-tax* income is substantially lower as a result of the welfare state? The research cited later in this book suggests that the average American has a before-tax income that is about 25 percent lower today as a direct result of the redistributive policies adopted in the twentieth century. That is a substantial cost, and it is not the only cost we bear in paying for the welfare state.

THE EGALITARIAN MENACE

Why has government grown so much over the past century? The answer is simple: The rise of egalitarian ideology. *Business Week* had it right when, after a decade of particularly rapid growth in welfare-state policies, it noted in 1975: "The greatest single force changing and expanding the role of the federal government in the United States today is the push for equality."[1] That force did not dissipate after 1975; if anything, it is stronger today than ever. As Thomas Sowell has recently pointed out, "The reigning dogma of our time is equality."[2]

Egalitarianism has been defined by Aaron Wildavsky as "the belief in the moral virtue of diminishing differences among people of varying incomes, genders, races, sexual preferences, and (especially) power."[3] To this I would only add that egalitarians look to government as the means to reduce these differences. In short, egalitarians believe that it is the duty and responsibility of government to equalize incomes (among other things) through the policies of the welfare state.

Equality has always been a cherished value in America, but it is susceptible to different interpretations that are important to keep distinct. "Equality under the law" is the concept enshrined in the Constitution, and it is compatible with, and indeed required for, a society of free people. "Equality of opportunity" is another meaning, and it too, within reason, is compatible with free people living in a regime of limited government.

Modern-day egalitarians have usurped the term *equality* and extended it to an illogical extreme to mean "equality of result." When people's free choices and actions produce different outcomes—such as different incomes, schooling, housing, or jobs—as they invariably do, egalitarians view these results as morally objectionable and call on government to rectify the so-called problem. It is this brand of egalitarianism that is a threat to our prosperity and to our freedom.

Most Americans are unaware of the extent to which big government is the result of egalitarian ideology. That is because they mostly do not share this ideology and believe it is limited to the radical fringe. Unfortunately, it is not just a fringe phenomenon. As the Friedmans noted more than a quarter century ago, egalitarianism has become "almost an article of religious faith among the intellectuals."[4] Today we could probably drop the qualifier "almost," as the overwhelming majority of academics, the news media, and the political elites are committed egalitarians. And they wield vast influence over how public-policy issues are framed and debated.

They have succeeded in framing the debate to the point that the very word *unequal* is interpreted as synonymous with an injustice requiring government amelioration. In fact, my thesaurus gives as synonyms for *equal* the words *fair, just,* and *equitable,* implying that *unequal* now has the opposite connotation. Try this test: Look for the words *unequal* or *inequality* in media discussions, and see if the writer doesn't clearly intend you the reader to recoil in disgust at some injustice in society.

The political left has always been more closely associated with egalitarianism than the political right. That was most apparent during the conflict between communism and capitalism in the last century. Communism made two great promises: It would produce greater prosperity (higher average incomes) and greater equality through the means of a centrally planned economy. It was no secret that those on the left had sympathies with communism because they approved of both goals, particularly the goal of greater equality.

Communism failed to produce either prosperity or equality, as we will see in chapter 4. Capitalism convincingly demonstrated its overwhelming superiority in delivering the goods, and one rarely finds people openly advocating any version of central planning or socialism today. One might think that this experience would lead egalitarians to rethink their basic positions because egalitarianism and communism were so inextricably linked. But instead egalitarians now just promote different ways (welfare-state policies) to achieve equality; it rarely occurs to them that empowering government to aggressively pursue equality may be dangerous regardless of whether the methods are called central planning or redistribution of income.

It is not only the political left, as exemplified by the Democratic party in the United States, that promotes egalitarian policies. The Republican party has made its peace with the welfare state and today supports redistributive policies with a fervor that differs only marginally from the Democrats. Consider that it was a Republican president and Congress that recently enacted the largest expansion in the welfare state in three decades—the inclusion of prescription drug benefits in the Medicare program. Although Democrats and Republicans differ in which groups they wish to favor with tax-supported largesse and in how far they will expand redistributive policies, the Republican party no longer has any principled objection to big government, that is, redistributive government.

This is a perilous situation. While Americans are understandably preoccupied with the issue of international terrorism, the more relentless threat to our quality of life may be the continuing expansion of the welfare state. There is no doubt that the war on terror will be resolved in our favor sooner or later, but the threats posed by the radical egalitarians in our midst will not be so easily vanquished.

This book is a critical examination of the underpinnings and consequences of the modern welfare state. Egalitarians have a great advantage in any debate over redistributive policies, for they need only appeal to the emotions. Some of these emotions are admirable, such as compassion and sympathy, but they are often susceptible to manipulation; others are less admirable, such as envy and greed, but they are useful in promoting the egalitarians' objectives; and still other emotions are misplaced, such as guilt. Anti-egalitarians, among whose ranks I count myself, must rely on a patient and often lengthy examination of the multitude of adverse consequences produced by the welfare state to make our case.

For that reason, it is difficult to make a concise statement of the case against the egalitarian ideology that permeates policy debate in America today, but perhaps another quotation from Aaron Wildavsky may communicate part of what is at stake: "I believe that rising egalitarianism will lower our standard of living, decrease our health, debase public discourse, lower the quality of public officials, weaken democracy, make people more suspicious of one another, and (if it is possible) worse. Worse is the constant denigration of American life—our polity, economy, and society—with no viable alternative to take its place."[5]

Our examination of the underpinnings and consequences of the welfare state will show that there is much truth in Wildavsky's statement. But our first task is to explain how and why inequality emerges in a free and capitalistic society. Then we will be in a better position to evaluate whether egalitarians are justified in their antipathy to the results produced in a free society.

HOW THE FREE MARKET DETERMINES INCOMES

The most widespread criticism of capitalism is undoubtedly that it generates an unconscionable degree of inequality in incomes. In evaluating whether this criticism is warranted, we must first understand how markets function to determine personal incomes.

But before considering individual incomes, let's think about the income of society as a whole—that is, the combined incomes of all people in the society. That aggregate income is equal to the total value of all final goods and services produced by the economy, or the economy's gross domestic product (GDP). The value of total production equals the value of incomes received because what is paid for goods and services produced exactly equals what is received as income by someone else. From a society's viewpoint, its output constitutes its real income. That is why so much attention is paid to how GDP changes over time; this tells us (after adjusting for inflation, of course) whether our combined income is growing or declining.

Most economics textbooks emphasize that the equality between aggregate output and income is one of the "Big Ideas"[6] that students should take away from a study of economics. It is important because it tells us that the true source of prosperity for a society lies in its productivity. For a society, and the people comprising it, to become richer, it must increase its production of goods and services. Countries that are poor are poor precisely because their outputs, or GDPs, are small (relative to the size of their population). Countries like the United States are rich because our economy produces a high level of output per capita.

There is, therefore, an inescapable link between productivity and incomes at the aggregate level, but how is this aggregate income divided up among people? That is what egalitarians are obsessed about. As we will see, there is also a link between individual productivity and income at the personal level, but that link is not so obvious as at the aggregate level, where it is in effect a tautology.

People receive their incomes in a variety of forms: wages and salaries, dividends, interest income, capital gains, land rents, profits, and so on. I will focus my discussion on how labor earnings (wages and salaries) are determined in a market economy. The same general principles apply to other types of income, but it is appropriate to focus on labor earnings because for most people, and for the economy as a whole, the bulk of total income is in the form of labor earnings. In the aggregate, labor earnings are typically 70 to 75 percent of all income, so it is clear that a large part of inequality in total incomes must stem from inequality in labor earnings.

Actually, labor earnings are even more important in influencing overall income inequality than this 70–75 percent share suggests. This is because most of the other types of income results from the way people used their labor earnings in prior years. For example, a large part of my current total income is in the form of investment, or capital, income, but that reflects to a large degree savings out of my labor earnings over the past 40 years. Inherited wealth is an important contributor to current incomes in some instances (think Kennedy or Rockefeller), but it is much less significant than most people think. For example, a study found that four-fifths of those with net worths of more than a million dollars had earned (accumulated) their fortunes within their own lifetimes.[7]

Thus, it is appropriate to think of most current income inequality as resulting from differences in labor earnings, past and present. What, then, determines the wage rate received by a worker? Economists believe that each worker's wage is also linked to productivity, but it is what is called the worker's *marginal productivity* that matters. Workers contribute to the output of the companies that employ them, and it is the additional (marginal) contribution to the value of output that will be reflected in the worker's wage. People receive different wages because the values of their (marginal) contributions to the value of the economy's output differ. As Gregory Mankiw expresses it in his textbook: "Put simply, highly productive workers are highly paid, and less productive workers are less highly paid."[8]

We economists believe businesses pay workers wages that equal the value of their contribution to the economy's output. Firms do not do this out of altruism. On the contrary, they would like to pay as little as possible to workers, so why is it that we think they end up compensating workers in line with their productive contribution? The answer is that businesses compete with one another for workers' services, and it is the process of competition that bids wages up to the level of their actual (marginal) productivity.

Suppose Mary is a worker who would, if employed by firm X, add $1,000 a week to the sales revenue of the business. Firm X would be willing to pay a *maximum* of $1,000 a week to hire Mary (a break-even arrangement), but it would certainly be happier if it gets her services for $750, for that would add $250 to its profits. Why do economists believe she will receive a $1,000 salary? Because there are other businesses that would also find their profits enhanced by the addition of Mary's services. If Mary's services are worth $1,000 to firm Y, for example, it might offer Mary a salary of $900 (which would add $100 to its profits). But firm X could then counter with an offer of $950, for it would be better to have only a $50 added profit rather than a zero added profit if it goes without Mary's contribution. This process of bidding among businesses culminates in Mary getting a salary close or equal to $1,000, which is the value of her economic productivity.

Competition among firms for employees is what ensures that workers will receive wages commensurate with their productivities. Of course, workers compete with one another for jobs, and the more workers there are seeking jobs in a given market (other things equal), the lower the wages will be in that market—because if workers are more plentiful the value of their marginal contribution to output will be lower. As economists say, (labor) supply and demand both matter in the determination of market wages. The essential point is that the result of this process is that workers' wages tend to reflect the (marginal) value of their contribution to the economy's output, that is, their economic productivity.

This is a concise explanation of the theory that most economists believe explains how labor incomes are determined in the American economy. Needless to say, numerous extensions, qualifications, and exceptions to this basic model have been developed in the academic literature, but after all is said and done, this remains the dominant explanation of why some earn a lot and others earn very little: Some people are more economically productive than others. It is notable that this is the consensus view among both politically liberal and politically conservative economists. One need only consult any mainstream labor economics textbook for confirmation of this (and to become acquainted with the empirical evidence supporting this theory).

Many people, and especially egalitarians, are reluctant to accept this theory because it seems at first glance to provide an aura of justification for vast inequalities in income. After all, the theory says that people receive an income equal to what they add to the economy's output. So if people are poor, they are poor because their economic contributions are small, and the rich are rich because they make large contributions to the nation's output. Isn't it fair that people get to take out of the economy what they contribute to it?

Not necessarily. To say that people's incomes *are* determined by their productive contributions is not the same as saying that this outcome is in all respects equitable, or fair. Those who are unfortunate to have severe mental or physical disabilities will often have low market productivities, and that *explains* why they have low earnings in a market economy, but it does not mean we have to judge this to be a *fair* outcome. Clearly, most people, including most nonegalitarians, would not wish to consign the disadvantaged to a life of misery or worse just because they are incapable of making more than a negligible contribution to economic output. The market does reward productive contribution, but there is more to fairness than that.

We will have more to say about fairness throughout this book, not only the fairness of the market but also the fairness of government welfare-state policies. But it must be stressed at the outset that *fairness* (or *justice*, or *equity*—I will use the terms interchangeably) is a multifaceted concept that defies any objective definition. People differ in what they consider just, and that is one reason why informed people differ over issues concerning the welfare state. Nonetheless, the egalitarian concept of *justice as equality* is one that, I will argue, has little merit.

Common views about how free markets determine incomes are widely at variance with the consensus among economists about this process in at least two respects. One is the belief that the size of the income pie—GDP or the combined incomes of everyone—is fixed and if one person or group receives more there is less for other people. But economics demonstrates that the rich do not get rich at the expense of the poor or anybody else; they get rich by adding greatly to the size of the economic pie. The determination of incomes is not a zero sum game like poker where some must lose when others gain. All can gain from the voluntary transactions that produce incomes in a free society.

A second common misperception is that capitalism *creates* or *depends on* or *perpetuates* income inequalities. Nothing could be further from the truth. As our discussion concluded, inequalities emerge when people's productive contributions differ. The reasons why productivities differ among people have little or nothing to do with whether the economic system is capitalistic or not. Put differently, if all workers were equal in their productivities, all would receive the same wage rates in a capitalistic system—the system would create no inequalities (except in the limited sense discussed in the next section). Capitalism is a very adaptable system for coordinating economic activities, and it will function efficiently when people are identical or very similar (producing little income inequality) *or* when people differ widely in relevant respects (more characteristic of the real world, and when income inequalities will be larger). Income inequalities arise because people have different abilities and make different choices not because capitalism produces these inequalities.

Before taking a closer look at the issue of the justice of market-determined incomes, let me briefly point out some of the ways capitalistic labor markets contribute to efficiency, that is, to high and rising levels of income for us all. First of all, pay in accordance with productivity encourages workers to use their skills where they are most valuable to other people. Most people can choose among many job options over their lifetimes, and other things equal, they will normally gravitate to the higher-paying ones. This is good for the economy only if the higher-paying jobs contribute more to economic output than lower-paying jobs—and that will be the case when pay reflects economic productivity. Economists would say that markets give workers the proper *incentive* to employ their skills in the way that adds the most to the output of the economy.

To see a tragic example of how labor markets can misperform when pay is not linked to productivity, consider public schools. As I mentioned, there are exceptions to the conclusions that wages are equal to economic productivity, and the prime source of exceptions is areas where government is involved. (The theory, after all, is developed to explain wage determination in private markets, and the theory need not apply when government dictates wages.) The question: Will people who are highly effective (productive) teachers be induced to enter the teaching profession? Or, to put it differently, do better teachers get paid more and worse teachers less? In today's public school systems, the short answer to these questions is no because teacher pay is not related to their productivity as teachers. Because of government's acquiescence in union pay contracts, wages are related to experience and credentials (degrees) and not to the quality of teaching. As a number of studies have shown, experience and credentials (especially degrees in education) are largely unrelated to teaching effectiveness.[9]

That is why public schools have difficulty attracting and retaining high-quality teachers—they don't pay them any more than the poor teachers. The problem is not that the average pay of teachers is too low, it is that the wages of poor teachers are too high and the wages of good teachers are too low. There is *too little inequality* in the incomes of public school teachers, and our children are paying the cost of this egalitarian pay scale.

Market-determined wage rates perform another important function: They provide incentive for workers to improve their skills to acquire higher-paying jobs, and this contributes to increasing total output when higher-paying jobs are also more productive jobs. Why do students go to college? In most cases, it is because they want to have higher-paying jobs than they could obtain with only high school diplomas. Again, this makes good economic sense only because the higher-paying jobs *actually* contribute more to society's output and therefore justify incurring costs to qualify for such jobs.

Competitive labor markets also promote the full utilization of the potential labor services available, that is, they tend to produce an outcome commonly described as one of "full employment." Wage rates adjust to a level where there is a balance between supply and demand, with jobs available for those who want to work at market-determined wage rates. That market forces operate to achieve full employment is greatly underappreciated, although it is important to understand that the process does not work without frictions and temporary setbacks (such as an OPEC oil price increase or a terrorist attack), and it does not adjust to changing circumstances instantaneously.

In the 57 years since 1950, the annual unemployment rate has never exceeded 10 percent, and has only exceeded 8 percent in three years. This means that in 54 of 57 years, at least 92 percent of those seeking jobs had employment. This accomplishment is even more impressive than it may at first seem because the minimum possible unemployment rate, given the way it is measured, is thought by economists to be in the 4 to 6 percent range; economists often refer to 5 percent measured unemployment as representing effective "full employment." Thus, we have really come within 3 percentage points (or less) of achieving full employment in 54 of the past 57 years. Government policies played some role in this achievement, but not as much as politicians would have you believe: It was primarily the result of labor markets adapting to constantly changing economic conditions.

In these and other ways, competitive labor markets (and competitive markets in general) tend to promote high and rising levels of output and income. Many egalitarians concede these points but emphasize that the resulting inequalities in incomes are not fair. Markets do promote efficiency, they might reluctantly concur, but fall far short on the criterion of justice. Let us consider in greater detail the reasons why incomes differ in a market economy to determine how much merit there is to this charge.

Just Inequalities

Judged by the attention they give to differences in income, egalitarians are convinced that these "inequalities" represent a major failing of capitalism to produce just outcomes. But people have different incomes for a wide variety of reasons, and when we examine why incomes vary, many of the differences will be seen to be perfectly consistent with what most people consider as justice or fairness.

To make the point most strongly, I ask you to imagine a society in which all people are equal in ability and opportunities, and luck plays no role. Markets are competitive, with incomes determined according to the principles outlined earlier. It might be thought that in such a utopian society incomes would be equal, but they would not be, for at least four important reasons.

First of all, people choose among jobs not based exclusively on pay; they care also about other characteristics, such as safety, security, location, flexibility of hours, and presence of congenial coworkers. When free markets operate under these circumstances, the monetary pay scales will differ among jobs. For example, suppose there are only two jobs—school teaching and long-distance truck driving—and workers think that teaching is a more attractive occupation. If pay were the same in the two jobs, workers would leave truck driving to become teachers, and this would lead to higher pay for truck drivers (fewer people competing for jobs as truck drivers leads to higher wages) and lower pay for teachers. This process would continue until the difference in pay was large enough that workers would no longer have incentive to change jobs. Monetary incomes would be higher for truck drivers, but *real* incomes—the overall compensations associated with the jobs, both pecuniary and nonpecuniary—would be equal. Economists call this difference in monetary pay an equalizing (or compensating) wage differential because the higher monetary remuneration for truck drivers compensates for the relative unattractiveness of that job. Here there is inequality in money incomes but that is in no sense unfair: This is a just inequality. A teacher might complain of low pay, but because he or she has the option to become a truck driver that complaint rings hollow.

A second reason why income inequalities can be just relates to the fact that some jobs require greater skills to perform, and it requires time, effort, and money for people to acquire these skills. Even though we are assuming that all people have equal abilities to acquire skills, that does not mean that they will be equally skilled at any point in time. Some would go to college and beyond, others would go to work after finishing high school. The college graduates would be paid more, however, because they would have to be compensated for the costs incurred in attending college, costs not borne by those going to work immediately after high school.

No one is surprised by the fact that college graduates earn more than high school graduates, and high school graduates earn more than high school dropouts. College graduates are more productive, and that is due to their having acquired more skills *and incurred costs to do so*. Fairness requires that they be paid more. Indeed, in our world-of-equals model, differential pay according to differences in acquired skills can be seen as a kind of equalizing wage differential, necessary to make the jobs equally attractive when all factors are accounted for. Of course, in the real world, higher pay for college graduates reflects *not only* compensation for costs borne *but also* their greater abilities, as discussed in the next section. I am not arguing that all of the higher pay received by more educated workers is necessarily fair, but clearly a substantial part of it is.

A third reason why some inequalities are fair arises from the fact that people have different preferences, or different likes and dislikes: Confronted with the same options, they will make different choices. We have assumed that people are identical in abilities, not in all respects. Differences in preferences lead people to make different choices, and many of these choices have an effect on their incomes. Let us consider a simple example: John and Justin are two young men who both have the opportunity to work at a job paying $10 per hour, and they are free to choose how many hours per week they work. John chooses to work 50 hours and Justin's choice is 25 hours, so John's earnings are $500 per week compared to $250 for Justin. There is substantial income inequality here but is there any unfairness? Most economists would say no, and I hope you would agree. Justin has half the income of John, but that is the result of his choice not to work as many hours—he had exactly the same options as John.

This is no small source of income inequality. There are many choices that people make that affect their present and future incomes. Choices of how much to study in school, as well as what courses to take and what to major in, all have consequences for future earnings. So do, importantly, decisions concerning how much to save since they influence how much income will be available in later years. It has often been speculated that people differ widely in the extent to which they weigh future consequences in their present decisions, and this affects their saving and other choices. People who have so-called short time horizons will make many types of decisions, including choices concerning education, which lead them to have lower incomes in later years. For example, consider the choice to smoke cigarettes, or to eat rapaciously and not exercise (leading to obesity): These choices may provide present benefits but future costs, including lower incomes (if for no other reasons than the health consequences). Another choice with repercussions for income inequality concerns whether a married couple will be a two-earner or one-earner family, which is related to the choice of whether to have children and how many. Different decisions in these matters contribute to large differences in family incomes.

Do people really make free choices that lead to substantial inequality? Let me pose a question for you. Suppose we compare the work effort of households whose incomes place them in the top 20 percent of the income distribution with the work effort of those in the bottom 20 percent. (Egalitarians often focus on the difference in incomes between these groups.) How much greater do you suppose the hours of work for the high-income group are than for the low-income group? (Only doctrinaire, and uninformed, egalitarians believe hours of work are greater for the low-income group.) I have been surveying students' opinions on this question for years, and the most common responses seem to be in the 25 to 50 percent range. But the correct answer is that the high-income group works around *700 percent more*, that is, nearly eight times as much as the low-income group! This is, in fact, one of the major reasons why the high-income group has much higher incomes than the low-income group. Isn't it just for people who work eight times longer hours per year to have a substantially higher income?

Before attaching too much importance to this fact, let me acknowledge that this was, in part, a trick question. These groups differ in many respects that make understandable why there would be wide differences in hours of work. The low-income group is composed of a higher percentage of retired and young households, as well as single-parent households and those on welfare, than the high-income group. In fact, the top group has more than twice as many people of working age (18–64) than the bottom group. (The groups do contain the same number of households, but the size and composition of households differ.) So to an extent, we are making an apples and oranges comparison here. But that is exactly what egalitarians do when they focus on income inequalities; they leave the impression that the high- and low-income groups are pretty much alike in all respects except that one just happens to have much higher income. If they really were alike in all relevant respects, it would indeed be unjust for there to be wide differences in income, but they are not.

Many other choices that people freely make lead to differing incomes without implying any injustice. Another example for a group of relatively homogenous people comes from the behavior of college students. The 2002 National Survey of Student Engagement found that about 20 percent of the students surveyed nationwide reported that they spent five hours or less per week preparing for class (studying), while at the other extreme, 14 percent said they spent 25 or more hours a week on class preparation.[10] (I have gotten quite similar results in surveys I have conducted in large classes at two different universities.) Of course, the harder-working students make better grades and will undoubtedly earn more once they graduate to the real world. Aren't the resulting inequalities in grades and incomes fair? After all, these students are similar in abilities and opportunities, and yet they are making vastly different choices, in effect, freely choosing different (unequal) incomes.

Choices freely made throughout our lifetimes create inequalities in income. One important choice as we get older is when to retire. In recent years, more than half of older workers have chosen to retire and receive Social Security benefits at age 62, even though that means their annual benefit is 25 percent lower than had they worked for three or four more years until they were eligible for full benefits. They chose to have a lower retirement income for the remainder of their lives, a choice that increases measured income inequality. How can there be any injustice when people, who can be presumed to know more about their circumstances, options, and needs than others, make a free choice about the best time to retire? But egalitarians see the resulting income differences as unfair.

As a final example of just inequalities in income, consider the influence of age on income. Typically, people's incomes vary systematically with age. Income generally starts out relatively low and then rises as a result of experience and hard work (which increases one's productivity) peaking sometime in late middle age, then declines as one approaches and enters retirement. When we look at the income distribution, as it is normally presented, we are comparing people at very different stages of their lives. It is not a coincidence that high-income earners are disproportionately middle-aged, while those at the bottom are disproportionately young or old. But does the fact that middle-aged people earn more than the young or the old, by itself, imply any unfairness? Clearly not. Suppose, for example, that everyone had exactly the same income at each age as everyone else, but incomes do vary with age. Everyone has the same lifetime experiences, but when we look at the income figures for one year—and that is what all conventional measures do—we observe substantial inequalities.

Income distribution figures, as normally presented, are a one-year snapshot of people at different points in their lifetimes. This invariably conveys the impression that inequality is greater than it really is. In 2005, for example, the median income of households aged 45 to 54 was two and a half times greater than that of households aged 15 to 24, and two times greater than that of households over 65. This means that even if everyone had the same income at each age, the one-year picture of the income distribution would show the top income category to have more than twice the income of the bottom category. Is it unfair for young households to have less than middle-aged households? In answering this, remember that the apparently wealthy current middle-aged households probably had even less than the current young when they were at that age. Fairness cannot be adequately judged by identifying income inequalities in a one-year snapshot, yet that is what most evaluations of inequality typically do.

I have tried to explain in this section some of the reasons why inequalities in annual (one-year) money incomes are often not only consistent with but required for fairness or justice. How much of actual inequalities in America is of the sort described here is far from clear, although some evidence pertaining to this issue is discussed in the next chapter. It should be clear, however, that these just inequalities are not trivial. One important implication of this is that government efforts to equalize incomes actually produce, to some degree, injustice, for they remove or reduce justified inequalities.

Now let us consider other sources of inequality in incomes to determine whether the egalitarians' charges of injustice can be sustained in these cases.

WHEN ARE INEQUALITIES UNJUST?

There are many possible causes of differences in incomes that most of us would agree are unjust. For example, when incomes result from fraud, corruption, or stealing; when exploitation, oppression, or discrimination enhance some people's incomes; when incomes result from monopoly pricing; when incomes arise largely due to luck (like winning the lottery)—in these, and probably other, cases we might agree that inequalities are unjust.

But these factors play an insignificant role in producing inequality in America. Recall that economists agree that people's incomes *are* closely related to their economic productivities, which implicitly denies that factors like those listed above play a major role.

What does play a major role in explaining income inequality is that people differ greatly in the abilities that are rewarded in markets. There are innate differences among people in strength and stamina, intelligence, musical talent, athletic talent, physical appearance, manual dexterity, ambition, and personality, and these differences lead to substantial differences in economic productivity and thus wages. While different jobs reward different abilities, I am going to focus on one type of ability, intelligence, which is arguably more important in modern technological societies than any of the others. My contention is that intelligence is an innate mental attribute that differs widely among people and that more intelligent people typically become more economically productive.

If you think that this is obvious and just common sense, then you should be aware that the conventional wisdom, as reflected in news media accounts, routinely denies this contention. So-called social problems, such as poverty, inequality, dropouts in schools, and people lacking health insurance, are seen as caused by "society" (generally meaning capitalism or bad government policies), implicitly denying that people's innate characteristics may be partly responsible. The last time you read an account of the school dropout problem, for example, were you informed that more than half of those with IQs below 75 drop out of high school, while less than 0.5 percent of those with IQs above 110 fail to complete high school? In such cases, rarely do you see an acknowledgment that intelligence plays a significant role in the creation of this and other so-called social problems. That is because egalitarians are inclined to interpret all inequalities as due to society and thereby correctable with the right welfare-state policies.

To many egalitarians, Herrnstein and Murray's *The Bell Curve,* published in 1994, was a heresy for providing evidence that IQ was linked to a wide variety of social problems.[11] The mainstream media's misrepresentation of the state of scientific knowledge in its savaging of this book led 52 experts in the field to sign a statement appearing in the *Wall Street Journal.* Their statement listed 25 propositions related to intelligence that they regarded as "mainstream among researchers on intelligence."[12] These mirrored almost exactly the substance of *The Bell Curve* that the media was intent on denying.

Three of these 25 propositions are directly related to the question of how IQ is related to earnings. Using the original numbering, the three propositions are:

2. Intelligence...can be measured, and intelligence tests measure it well. They are among the most accurate...of all psychological tests and assessments.
9. IQ is strongly related, probably more so than any other single measurable human trait, to many important educational, occupational, economic, and social outcomes.
14. Individuals differ in intelligence due to differences in both their environments and genetic heritage. Heritability estimates range from 0.4 to 0.8 (on a scale of 0 to 1), most thereby indicating that genetics plays a bigger role than does environment in creating IQ differences among individuals.

Lest it be thought that the 52 signatories of this document are an unrepresentative fringe group, in 1984 Mark Snyderman and Stanley Rothman surveyed 661 experts in the field of cognitive science. They found that "most experts continue to believe that intelligence can be measured, and that genetic endowment plays an important role in individual differences in IQ...and they believe that measured IQ is an important determinant of success in American society."[13]

Two of the conclusions cited in the *Wall Street Journal* piece are particularly relevant to our issue of the determinants of income inequality. One is the contention that IQ is a major cause of income differences, and the other concerns the issue of what determines IQ itself. Let's briefly consider each of these conclusions.

IQ is only one among many factors that influence one's earnings, so how can we be sure that its independent influence is significant? Statistical analyses provide evidence that IQ has substantial effects on earnings, but many of these studies are difficult to explain and interpret. But there is one study that provides convincing evidence of the influence of IQ that is easy to understand.

Consider why the earnings of siblings vary. To the extent that socioeconomic variables like schooling, housing, diet, parental attention, and so on influence children's earnings later in life, we would expect siblings to have similar earnings because they share the same background. On the other hand, to the extent that IQ affects earnings, we expect siblings with different IQs to have different earnings, despite their common upbringing. So by examining the earnings of siblings in relation to their IQs, we can get an idea of whether IQ or socioeconomic variables matter more in determining earnings.

Charles Murray investigated this issue with a sample of 2,148 siblings (1,074 sibling pairs) who were aged 27 to 35 in 1992 and for whom information on IQ and earnings was available.[14] They were carefully chosen so that one of the siblings in each pair had an IQ in the middle range (90–109) and the other lay outside that range. On average, siblings who are not identical twins have IQs that differ by 12 points, so it was possible to find some sibling pairs with substantially different IQs.

Murray found that earnings varied systematically with IQ among the siblings. Those with IQs of 125 or more had median earnings of $33,500, compared to $26,500 for those with IQs between 110 and 124, and $20,000 for those in the middle range. Note that these earnings difference arise *between siblings within the same families*—each of those in the high-earning group is matched by a (lower IQ) sibling in the middle-earning group. The correspondence between earnings and IQ continued among those with lower IQs. For those with IQs under 75, median earnings were only $7,500, while for those in the 75–89 IQ range, the median was $14,000. Thus, the high-IQ group was earning more than four times as much as the low-IQ group.

What this suggests is that differences in IQ by themselves are responsible for a large measure of inequality in earnings. Remember that these reported differences in earnings are not produced by different family backgrounds (the siblings came from the same families, after all). Looking at siblings is about as good a way as we have of controlling for other factors that influence earnings, and doing so suggests that IQ matters, and matters quite a lot.

That brings us to the question of what determines IQ itself. There are only two possibilities: genetic inheritance and everything else—commonly called the environment. The relative contributions made by genes vs. the environment, or in other words by nature vs. nurture, have been debated for centuries. And the battleground is not just over IQ but many other behavioral and personality traits that differ among individuals. In recent decades, the evidence has increasingly favored the nature side of the debate, and one part of this story is worth recounting.

It involves research using identical twins, twins that develop when a single egg fertilized by a single sperm divides and then develops as two embryos. These twins have the same genes and are in fact naturally occurring clones. Thus, if genes determine everything, identical twins will always have the same IQs (and other genetically transmitted characteristics). If environment determines everything, *and if the environments differ in relevant respects,* the twins will have different IQs. So to use identical twins to investigate the nature-nurture issue, they must have different environments. You can see the problem—most twins are raised in the same household and so share the same environment. Thus, when we find that the IQs of identical twins are *very* similar (which they are), we can't tell whether they are similar because they share the same genes or because they share the same environment, or both.

But some identical twins are separated at or soon after birth and adopted into different households, and this rare occurrence affords a unique opportunity to test the role of genes versus environment. These twins have the same genes but different environments, so to the extent that genes are controlling they will be alike, but if environment matters disproportionately they will be very different. Given how rare this situation is (a double rarity, actually, since identical twins occur in only 1 of 250 births, and few are separated), there are only a handful of studies, in a few countries, that have been conducted of identical twins raised apart.

The twin studies find that heritability of intelligence is about 0.78 on a scale of 0 to 1, with 1 meaning that intelligence is totally inherited.[15] This means that *both* genes and environment play a role in influencing IQ, but with genes playing a substantially larger role. Other approaches to estimating heritability come up with different estimates, varying from 0.4 to 0.8, as noted in the quotation from the *Wall Street Journal*, but the methodologically sounder studies tend to cluster toward the upper end of this range.

The evidence thus suggests strongly that nature, not nurture, is largely responsible for differences in IQ, and "Mother Nature is no egalitarian."[16]

However, all the evidence supports the view that the environment has some effect on IQ, but what exactly is it about the environment that influences IQ? What can be done to raise IQ? The heritability estimates do not tell us this because the environmental contribution is identified as everything left over after the genetic influence is removed; it is not directly estimated. Research has, however, suggested a number of ways in which the environment may influence IQ. David Armor, in his recent book enticingly titled

Maximizing Intelligence, presents evidence for eight environmental "risk factors" ("conditions or behaviors that have the greatest influence on a child's IQ").[17]

Some of these environmental conditions are not easily changed, and Armor narrows the list to four that suggest "the most promising and most consistent environmental effects for improving a child's IQ and academic achievement." They are:

1. Parenting behaviors that create a cognitively stimulating and emotionally supportive home environment.
2. Limiting the numbers of children to one or two, especially for single mothers whose education and financial resources are low.
3. Having both parents in the home to increase parenting resources and income.
4. Practicing breast-feeding for nutritional (and possibly nurturing) benefits.[18]

Armor's examination of the evidence leads him to conclude that "if *all* of these key risk factors could be at *optimal* levels, a child's IQ might be raised on the order of 10 points or so, perhaps somewhat less for math achievement" (italics mine).[19] This seems to be consistent with other evidence.

Several points are noteworthy. First, the maximum increases possible are large enough to be worth striving for but even if realized would not dramatically change the distribution of intelligence. Raising the IQs 10 points for those with scores of 80 is not going to produce potential college graduates (average IQ of 115) or even typical high school graduates (average IQ of 105). Second, these effective environmental conditions are largely under the control of the parents, and many parents, of course, are already creating these conditions. Notably absent from the list of risk factors are government policies, like Head Start or educational interventions. These are known to have little or no effect on IQ. Third, the emphasis on young children is significant. Much evidence suggests that efforts to increase IQ can only be successful at very young ages. Some scholars think that positive effects can be achieved up to age eight, while others put the critical age much lower, possibly three or four. Once children are in school, then, there is probably little that can be done to affect IQ.

What this means is that wide variations in IQ (and other abilities and behavioral characteristics, as well) will characterize our society for at least the near future.[20] As we have seen, economic outcomes are linked to IQ. Thus, in a free society there will be a substantial amount of economic inequality due to these factors. As stated earlier, capitalism does not create or depend on these inequalities—they arise because people bring different abilities into the world and later to the labor market.

That brings us back to our original question: When are income inequalities unjust? We see that they arise in part from differences in people's biological inheritances. Is it morally wrong for people to benefit from their God-given (or nature-given, or parent-given) talents? Egalitarians apparently believe it is, viewing this as a matter of chance or luck in a genetic lottery that benefits some more than others.

That is not an unreasonable position, but before concluding that this justifies our welfare-state policies, let's take a look at just how much inequality there is in America. Inequality in America is the subject of the next chapter.

Inequality

Each year, *Parade* magazine has a cover story entitled "What People Earn." In its most recent version, it displays photographs of 124 people together with their earnings, which vary from zero to many millions of dollars.[1] Twenty-five persons, one-fifth of the total, are shown with earnings of a million dollars or more. Is this an accurate picture of America today? If 124 people are selected to be representative of our society, how many would be millionaires? The correct answer is: none. Only 1 of about 500 Americans has earnings that high. It would perhaps make for less titillating reading to show only a handful of people (out of 124) with earnings in excess of $100,000, and no millionaires, but it would be more accurate.

Egalitarians like to produce stories that contrast the lifestyles of the rich and superrich with those of the middle class and poor, emphasizing the extent and unfairness of inequality. Partly as a result of this, it is no surprise that polls show that Americans greatly overstate the extent of inequality that does characterize our society. Yet if we are to have sensible policies to deal with this issue, it is clearly important to base them on an accurate account of how much inequality does exist. That is the major goal of this chapter.

THE OFFICIAL VIEW

Most discussions of income inequality rely on data collected by the U.S. Census Bureau. In March of each year it conducts a survey of about 60,000 American families (carefully selected to be representative of the whole population) and collects a wide array of information, including their incomes,

TABLE 2.1
Share of Aggregate Income Received by Each Fifth of Families

Year	Lowest Fifth (%)	Second Fifth (%)	Third Fifth (%)	Fourth Fifth (%)	Highest Fifth (%)	HiLo	Average Income ($)*
2005	4.0	9.6	15.3	22.9	48.1	12.0	73,304
2000	4.3	9.8	15.4	22.7	47.7	11.1	74,550
1990	4.6	10.8	16.6	23.8	44.3	9.6	61,773
1980	5.3	11.6	17.6	24.4	41.1	7.8	53,795
1970	5.4	12.2	17.6	23.8	40.9	7.6	48,353
1960	4.8	12.2	17.8	24.0	41.3	8.6	34,781
1950	4.5	12.0	17.4	23.4	42.7	9.5	N.A.

*Income figures are expressed in constant 2005 dollars.

concerning each family for the previous year. There are numerous ways to organize and present the data, and one of the most common is shown in table 2.1. Because this presentation is so widely used, both in academic studies and in the news media, it may be worthwhile to explain how it is constructed.

First, families are ranked in order of income from highest to lowest. Then they are separated into five equal-sized groups, each containing a fifth of all families. (These fifths are often referred to as *quintiles*.) The highest-income fifth contains the 20 percent of families who have the highest incomes, the second fifth contains families with incomes between the 60th and 80th percentiles, and so on. Then we add up the total income of the families within each fifth and express that sum as a percentage of the total income of all families (in all five groups together). The result is five percentages which give the *share of total income received by each fifth of families.* By construction, these shares add up to 100 percent. It's like a pie chart that breaks up the 100 percent total into five parts.

Table 2.1 shows the results for 2005, the most recent year available, and several selected earlier years. (We will concentrate on 2005 here and consider the changes over time in a later section.) Thus, we see that the lowest fifth (containing the 20 percent of families with the lowest incomes) received 4.0 percent of total income, while the highest fifth received 48.1 percent; the other fifths receiving shares falling between these. So, how much inequality is there, according to these numbers? Because I have always had trouble interpreting five income shares meaningfully, I am going to suggest that we focus on just one number to represent the extent of inequality.

That number is the ratio of average income in the top fifth to average income in the bottom fifth. This is, of course, just the ratio of the shares, or 48.1/4.0, which tells us that the average high-income family had in 2005 an income 12 times that of the average low-income family. I will refer to this ratio as the *HiLo* ratio and use it as a summary measure of inequality. It must be kept in mind that this number ignores the three middle fifths, and inequality is less apparent in the middle quintiles than when examining only the two extreme income classes. No single measure is perfect, but I have found that this one is easier for most people to relate to than some others, like the well-known but incomprehensible Gini coefficient.

A HiLo ratio of 12 suggests that there is a wide disparity in incomes separating the highest and lowest income classes. As we will see in the next section, however, this substantially overstates the degree of economic inequality that actually separates high- and low-income families in America. Before explaining why this is so, a couple of additional points should be made.

Because these data indicate only the shares of income, they tell us nothing about absolute levels of income. If all incomes double, the shares are unchanged even though everyone is better off. Thus, the shares are only indicative of *relative inequality,* how families stand relative to one another and not absolutely. Of course, the U.S. Census Bureau also provides information on absolute incomes, and I have provided in table 2.1 the average family income to provide an added perspective. In 2005, average family income was $73,304. Incidentally, armed with the overall average income and the shares, you can also easily calculate the average income within each of the five income classes (or simply look it up at the Census Bureau Web site if you wish).[2]

To complicate things a bit more, there is another set of income shares published by the Census Bureau for *households.* You might think that households and families are pretty much the same, and there is a lot of overlap: Most families are households, and most households are families. But according to the Census Bureau's definitions, there is one important difference: A household can be a single person living alone, whereas a family must be composed of at least two people. The family data that we have just been discussing do not contain single persons living on their own. As a consequence, the family data contain only 77 million families, while the household data contain 114 million households.

The income shares for *household* incomes were, in 2005: 3.4; 8.6; 14.6; 23.0; and 50.4. They display even more inequality than the family shares, a HiLo ratio of nearly 15 (50.4/3.4, or 14.8) compared to 12 for the family shares. It might be thought that the household distribution is a better indication of overall inequality because it does contain a larger share of the total U.S. population. Not so. It has one major defect, namely, that the number of persons per household varies widely among the five fifths. The number of households is the same in each fifth, but the number of persons is not. In fact, the top fifth of households contains 72 percent more people than the lowest fifth. Thus, income *per person* in the top fifth is only 8.6 times income per person in the bottom fifth. Egalitarians will often use the household income data without correcting for, or mentioning, the large differences in household size, which has the effect of exaggerating the amount of measured inequality.

There are also differences in the number of persons per family in the family income data, but they are a good deal smaller. For example, the top fifth of families contains 17 percent more people than the bottom fifth. That too calls for some adjustment if we are to get a truer picture of inequality, but the problem is not as great as for the household distribution. If we have to choose between these two distributions as they stand, the family income one is clearly preferable because family size varies less among the quintiles; high- and low-income families are more nearly comparable.

The data discussed here are beloved of egalitarians because they suggest that there are substantial differences separating high- and low-income Americans. Not that egalitarians like inequality, but they want to persuade the public that inequality is excessive and must be ameliorated by government redistribution of income. But the evidence shows that inequality is far less than these widely used numbers suggest.

LYING WITH STATISTICS

Most studies that deal with inequality rely on statistics that vastly overstate the extent of true economic inequality in America. As we will see, that is true of the widely used census data just described. This is not because the census estimates are inaccurate; they accurately measure what they say they measure. The problem is that what they measure is inadequate to judge the extent of inequality. This is what is measured: *One Year's Before-Tax Money Income of Families (or Households)*. Why do the resulting data overstate inequality? Let us count the ways.

First, the census figures are for before-tax incomes.[3] After-tax incomes are what counts in identifying economic inequalities. The after-tax distribution of income is more equal than the before-tax distribution because the relevant taxes fall more heavily on higher-income groups (that is, they are progressive, as I will explain in detail in chapter 9).

Second, much real income received by people is in nonmonetary form and so is not counted at all. Particularly important are government *in-kind* (noncash) transfers that add to people's incomes but are not counted as income. For example, food stamps, Medicaid, and housing assistance are not counted as income because they are in-kind, as distinct from cash, transfers. Even one important cash transfer, the Earned Income Tax Credit, is not counted, even though it contributed about $35 billion in income for low-income families in 2005. Counting these uncounted transfers as income produces a more equal income distribution because they are received mainly by low-income families.

Third, there are differences in the number of persons per family/household, as we have seen. Higher-income families/households have more persons to support, and not taking this into account leaves the impression that these families are better off than they actually are. One way to adjust for this is to measure not family income but income per person. On that measure, there is less inequality among the quintiles (fifths) than when just comparing family incomes.

Fourth, there are the great differences in the amount of work done among families, as noted in the last chapter. If one family is working twice as many hours as another and receives twice the income, we should not conclude that the first family is twice as well off. Indeed, in some cases we might reasonably conclude that the second family is as well off as the first. Although it is not obvious how best to adjust for the vast differences in work effort among the quintiles, any sensible approach would lead to a lower measure of inequality.

Fifth, it may be inappropriate to focus on income. People's standard of living is actually better evaluated by how much they consume. As we will see, consumption is more equally distributed than income.

Sixth, people move around in the income distribution from year to year. Looking at any one year's income can give a greatly distorted picture of longer-run economic well-being. Longer-run measures of income are more equally distributed than annual measures.

There are no studies that simultaneously correct the census data for all of these problems, but the available evidence shows that inequality is far less than suggested by the official view. Recall that the unadjusted data suggest that the wealthiest fifth of the population is 12 (for families) or 15 (for households) times better off than the poorest fifth. Let's see how these HiLo ratios look when corrected for some of the six defects noted above.

I will begin by describing an older study in which I was involved.[4] William R. Johnson and I started with the Census Bureau's household income data for 1976 and set out to correct it for the first four of the problems mentioned above. Specifically, we added in-kind transfers to household incomes, subtracted taxes, converted to a per capita income measure, and adjusted for differences in labor supply. The result was an income distribution where the wealthiest fifth had an adjusted income just *four times* that of the poorest fifth. A far cry from the 12 to 1 HiLo ratio (for 1976) in the official household income data. It's clear that adjusting for these four shortcomings in the official data has a dramatic effect on measured inequality.

We also extended the results to include public school spending since that should be considered as contributing to the real incomes of families with children in the public schools. That brought the final HiLo ratio down to 3.6 to 1. The equalizing effect of publicly provided schools is almost always ignored in studies that purport to measure inequality; none of the other studies I will be discussing addresses this issue.

The data in the Browning-Johnson study are now more than 30 years old, but fortunately there is a more recent study that adjusts census data for the same four issues. Robert Rector and Rea Hederman, Jr., used 2002 census household income data and then proceeded, as did Johnson and I, to subtract taxes, add in-kind income, and adjust for household size differences and differences in labor supply.[5] Their result? A HiLo ratio of 2.9 to 1! (The unadjusted census data show a ratio of 14 to 1 in 2002.)

Don't attach too much significance to the fact that Rector and Hederman found even less inequality for 2002 than Johnson and I did for 1976. This difference almost certainly reflected technical differences in the way the studies dealt with the data, especially differences in the way adjustments were made for labor supply and household size variation. Most scholars believe that inequality was greater in 2002 than in 1976, and I expect that is true. The important point is not the precise HiLo ratio, which we may never know or agree on, but that correcting for these defects in the official census income figures results in a spectacularly lower measure of inequality.

Now let's turn to the fifth issue on my list of problems with the census income data, concerning whether we should be using consumption or income to measure inequality. There are two reasons why one may favor consumption over income. First, if we are concerned with the economic well-being of people in a particular year, that is better indicated by how much they consume rather than by how much income they receive. Consumption is simply a better measure of current living standards than income.

A second reason for favoring consumption is, ironically, that it may actually be a better measure of long-term income than annual income itself. An individual's income often varies greatly from year to year, and if we look at just one year it may not be at all representative of longer-run economic status. Generally, people adjust their consumption in line with their expected longer-run income. For example, people consume less than their income as they save for retirement, and then consume more than their income in retirement (by drawing down their assets).

So how much economic inequality is there as measured by consumption? Much of our information concerning consumption comes from the Consumer Expenditure Survey conducted by the Census Bureau for the Bureau of Labor Statistics. It generates estimates of consumption (in total and with a detailed breakdown) and income for what it calls *consumer units*. A consumer unit is different from a household or family, as defined by the Census Bureau, but it is closest to the concept of household because a consumer unit can be a single person. So if we think of consumer units as comparable to households in our earlier discussion, we won't be too far off.

In 2005, according to the Bureau of Labor Statistics, the distribution of income among quintiles of consumer units featured a HiLo ratio of 15.3— slightly higher than the census household figures.[6] But in terms of consumer expenditures (not exactly the same as consumption, but close), the wealthiest class spent only 4.8 times as much as the lowest group, a HiLo ratio of about five to one for consumption. Consumer expenditures are far more equally distributed than is income. (The consumption shares for the fifths of consumer units are 8.2, 12.5, 16.9, 23.4, and 39.0.)

One finding in the Consumer Expenditure Survey is particularly striking: Low-income consumer units have substantially greater consumer expenditures than their incomes. In 2005 the poorest fifth in fact consumed *almost twice (1.98 times) as much as their before-tax incomes!* Exactly how this occurs is not entirely clear, although it probably relates to the fact that in-kind government transfers are not counted as income but do finance consumption. It might be suspected that this consumer spending is financed by the poor going ever deeper in debt, but if this were true we would expect to see the net worths of poorer households declining over time. That has not happened.[7]

Whatever the exact explanation for this phenomenon, it is important to recognize that low-income people in the United States consume on average much more than their current incomes. (Conversely, high-income people consume much less than their before-tax incomes.) We make a major mistake if we think that all low-income persons are living within their incomes. Yet that is a very common assumption, particularly evident in discussions of the poor—those with very low incomes.

The consumption data presented above are still far from a good measure of economic inequality. For example, it takes no account of the fact that there are fewer persons per consumer unit in the lowest quintile than in higher ones—just as we saw with the household income data. In the lowest consumption quintile, there are only 1.7 persons per consumer unit while there are 3.2 in the top quintile. The top quintile thus supports 88 percent more people with their consumer expenditures than does the lowest quintile. There are also three times as many earners in the top quintile, so differences in labor supply are also pronounced. Adjusting for these factors would produce an even more equal distribution.

Now let us turn to the sixth reason why the census data overstate inequality: Incomes in one year misrepresent longer-run economic status because people move around within the distribution from year to year. When people first encounter income data presented as income shares, they are often struck by how little the figures change over time (see table 2.1). Year-to-year changes are almost negligible, and even over a decade it is uncommon for any of the quintile shares to change by as much as 1 percentage point. The data seem to display a static, unchanging income distribution, suggesting that over time the rich stay rich and the poor stay poor.

Nothing could be further from the truth. Ours is a dynamic, constantly changing economy where people are frequently moving around within the distribution of income even though the aggregate shares don't change much. How this is possible, and its potential significance, is well illustrated by an analogy popular among economists: "Imagine a great hotel...with rooms of many different types and conditions—a presidential suite with gracious sitting rooms and huge baths, an executive floor of rooms with splendid views, many standard tourist rooms, a pauper's garret, an unheated attic, and a basement closet. If each room is occupied every night, then the distribution of rooms (read 'income') remains unchanged over time, regardless of who has which one. But how are the rooms assigned each night? If they are assigned at random, over time couldn't everyone be said to have had 'average' accommodations? In that case, the guests would be equal, even though the rooms were not."[8]

An unchanging income distribution can be the result *either* of people changing places over time (as in the hotel example) *or* of people remaining in exactly the same positions year after year. Which interpretation is more accurate matters a great deal. In the latter case, it would signify that we have a virtual class system, with people forever frozen in their place. In the former case, people have and utilize opportunities to better themselves over time, and no one is guaranteed to stay at the top, or in other words, people live in an open society.

Economists use the term *mobility* to refer to the extent of movement within the income distribution over time. There have been many studies of mobility, but I will report only a representative one completed by my colleagues Andrew Rettenmaier and Donald Deere.[9] In one part of their study, Rettenmaier and Deere examine how individual workers move around in the quintile distribution of *individual earnings* (not the family income classes, though other studies do examine this, with similar results). They use data from the National Longitudinal Survey of Youth to follow workers through periods of up to 15 years.

This database permits the authors to compare the wage quintiles workers are in during the first year of the sample with where they are in later years. For example, they find that of the workers in the lowest quintile in one year, 32 percent had moved to a higher quintile just one year later, with 1 percent jumping all the way to the top quintile. Among those in the top quintile, 25 percent had fallen to a lower quintile one year later with 2 percent falling to the lowest quintile.

Rettenmaier and Deere generate estimates not just for 2-year intervals, but also for 5-, 10-, and 15-year intervals. They find that the longer the time period studied, the greater is the mobility. For example, the findings for the 15-year interval are particularly dramatic. Of those in the lowest quintile in one year, fully two-thirds are in a higher quintile 15 years later. Twenty-four percent moved all the way from the bottom to one of the top two quintiles, with 10 percent reaching the highest quintile. At the other extreme, of those in the highest quintile in year one, 61 percent were in a lower quintile 15 years later. Eighteen percent had dropped into one of the bottom two quintiles, with 8 percent ending in the lowest quintile. People clearly do not stay in the same "hotel rooms" year after year.

Substantial mobility characterizes all aspects of economic life, and looking at only one year's data and noting that the overall distribution doesn't change from year to year yields a very misleading picture. We will see this again later in this volume when we examine poverty and unemployment, but another example is perhaps of interest here. In 2003, the Internal Revenue Service for the first time publicized the tax status of the 400 richest Americans. After our discussion above it will be no surprise to learn that the 400 people who occupy these exalted positions were not the same every year. In fact, over a nine-year period, 2,218 taxpayers were in the top 400 at least one year. Of these 2,218 taxpayers, three-fourths were among the top 400 for just one year, and fewer than 23 taxpayers were in the top 400 for all nine years.[10] Even at the very top of the income heap, being on top and staying there are very different things.

Recognizing the great mobility that characterizes the positions of people within the income distribution is significant for two somewhat different reasons. First, it shows that focusing on one year's data gives a misleading (and exaggerated) picture of economic inequality. That is relevant for a judgment concerning fairness. The second reason relates to another criterion widely used to evaluate the operation of our economy, equality of opportunity. As Verba and Orren put it: "Equal opportunity to make of oneself what one can has been the dominant norm in America."[11] These mobility studies certainly demonstrate that there is a great deal of opportunity, but whether it is exactly equal opportunity is a moot question.

In several instances, we have seen how looking at income in one year can misrepresent the economic well-being of a household. It would seem preferable to use a longer-run measure of income (or consumption), averaging the low- and high-income years to better indicate the absolute and relative standards of living. Indeed, many economists believe the ideal measure of economic well-being is *lifetime income,* roughly, the average income over one's entire life. As Don Fullerton and Diane Rogers make the point: "Many researchers who study income distributions have recognized that the distribution of lifetime income is a better index of differences in welfare than the differences in annual income."[12]

Whereas many agree with this in principle, there are great practical difficulties involved in estimating the distribution of lifetime incomes. I say "estimating" advisedly, for there are no data available that would permit us to directly measure lifetime incomes. Some of the ongoing longitudinal studies may in another 30 or 40 years have the data to construct actual measures of lifetime income, but in the meantime we have to rely on less exact approximations. There is, however, evidence that strongly suggests that the distribution of lifetime income is much less unequal than the distribution of annual income. That should come as no surprise after our discussion of mobility, for the clear implication of that evidence is that people at the bottom in any year have higher incomes (on average) over their lifetimes than in that one year, with the opposite being true for those at the top in any given year.

A major reason why the one-year snapshot of the income distribution misrepresents people's lifetime, or longer-term average, incomes is that it measures incomes at different stages of people's lives. As remarked earlier, the top quintile contains disproportionately middle-aged people at the peak of their life cycle of earnings, while the lowest quintile contains disproportionately the old and the young. This suggests a simple way to use the one-year snapshot data to construct a better measure of inequality: Compare households of the same age and family size.

Using the Browning-Johnson data described earlier, we can look at the distribution of income among all three-person households, and where the head of the household was in the 35 to 44 age bracket. After taxes and transfers, the lowest quintile of this group received a 9.2 percent share of total income, with the highest quintile receiving 36.3 percent,[13] a HiLo ratio of 4 to 1. Even this probably overstates inequality because it does not adjust for hours of work, and the highest fifth works twice as many hours as the lowest fifth. I interpret these figures as a clue to what a lifetime distribution might look like (by removing the normal variation in incomes over the life cycle), but they also serve as evidence of the importance of comparing like with like in making judgments about inequality.

The study by Fullerton and Rogers probably represents the most thorough and detailed study of lifetime income distribution yet undertaken. They use a sample from the Panel Study of Income Dynamics with 18 years' worth of data on individual incomes, and using a variety of other information they extrapolate the actual data so that it covers the entire lifetime. For each person in the sample they compute "average household lifetime income" (where average can be interpreted as an income-per-person measure for the household). Importantly, they take account of differences in labor supply by valuing differences in nonwork time (leisure) at each person's net-of-tax wage rate.

Following our earlier discussion, the results are perhaps not surprising. Fullerton and Rogers estimate quintile shares of net lifetime incomes of 10.3, 14.6, 19.0, 23.4, and 32.8, for a HiLo ratio of 3.2 to 1.[14] As they state: "We confirm the results of previous studies that find lifetime income distributions are *much more equal* [my emphasis] than the annual counterparts."[15]

It is easy to be overwhelmed by all the numbers reporting different measures of inequality, but don't lose sight of the one incontrovertible finding from this body of research: The Census Bureau's data on annual before-tax money incomes greatly exaggerate the amount of real economic inequality. Instead of the top income class receiving 12 or 15 times as much as the lowest class, based on the evidence presented here (and other similar studies), a better measure would be a HiLo ratio of 3 to 1 or 4 to 1. Yet egalitarians continue to use the highly flawed and misleading census data to argue that inequality is excessive.

There is another informative way to evaluate how much economic inequality exists; this method focuses on individual earnings rather than total family/household incomes.

ANOTHER PERSPECTIVE ON INEQUALITY

The labor market does not directly determine family incomes; instead, it determines wage rates and earnings of individual workers. To the extent that inequality is the result of our market economy, we should look directly at individual earnings to gauge its extent.

As explained in chapter 1, we expect more skilled (more economically productive) workers to have higher earnings in a free market economy. We cannot measure productivity directly, but we expect that productivity is related to the educational level achieved by workers. So it is no surprise that more educated workers have higher earnings. Taken from the Census Bureau database that produces the distributional data in table 2.1, here are the median earnings in 2005 for male workers aged 25 and over who worked full-time, year-round, as related to their educational attainments:[16]

9th to 12th Grade (No Diploma):	$27,189
High School Graduate (Includes Equivalency):	$36,302
Some College, No Degree:	$42,418
Bachelor's Degree:	$60,020
Master's Degree:	$75,025
Doctoral Degree:	$85,864

Ask yourself: Do these remuneration rates reflect great inequality and unfairness? Is it a serious social injustice that a college graduate receives 2.2 times as much as a high school dropout? Or that one with a master's degree receives 2.1 times as much as a high school graduate? Or that one with a PhD receives 3.2 times as much as a high school dropout and 2.4 times as much as a high school graduate? And keep in mind that these figures are earnings before payment of taxes and receipt of government transfers—the after-tax and after-transfer earnings differences would be even smaller.

Egalitarians often refer to the market-determined distribution of earnings as obscene, appalling, or unconscionable. Is that your reaction to these facts? If not, you are probably an ordinary American, who sensibly views inequality as no big deal.

But how do we square these facts with the much higher HiLo ratios reported in table 2.1 and beloved of egalitarians? After all, both are calculated from the same data collected by the Census Bureau. The answer, of course, is that high-income *families* typically have two well-educated earners, while low-income families typically have less than one poorly educated earner (on average, a third of an earner per household in the household distribution), who often works less than full-time. The market doesn't produce this outcome; it only determines individuals' pay. It is the diverse choices and circumstances of people that produce the apparently greater inequality among family incomes.

When confronted with the facts, even egalitarians often agree that differences in pay are not excessive. As evidence, I note a result from an interesting study by Harvard professors Sidney Verba and Gary Orren entitled *Equality in America*. This study reports the findings of a survey of 2,762 "leaders" in eight segments of American life, including academia, business, labor, feminists, and blacks—well to the left politically of most Americans. They were asked, among other things, to specify what they thought would be a "fair income" for an engineer and an elevator operator. Their average response was that it was fair for an engineer to receive 3.1 times the income of an elevator operator, a *larger* disparity than the actual ratio at that time (2.9)![17] They would have approved greater inequality than the market actually dispensed! I conjecture that the explanation of this apparent anomaly is that egalitarians believe inequality is much greater than it actually is, misled by numbers like those reported in table 2.1.

Before leaving the topic of the measurement of inequality, I should mention the most recent ploy of egalitarians: to focus on the incomes in the extreme upper tail of the income distribution, the incomes of the top 1 percent or even one-tenth of 1 percent, and contrasting these incomes with the rest of the population. (Consider the many articles on the alleged outrageous pay of CEOs.) Of course, it is not surprising that the incomes of the top 1 percent exceed the average by much more than when we contrast the top 20 percent with the average. Using the common one-year measure of income, the top 1 percent probably has incomes that are about 10 or 15 times the average income, but these incomes are already included in our top fifth and are not of much independent interest—except as a way to pander to envy. Moreover, these measures are all subject to the same six problems we identified earlier with the census data. To offer just one corrective, in the Fullerton and Rogers examination of lifetime incomes, they found that the lifetime income of the top 2 percent was only eight times the income of the *bottom 2 percent!*[18]

For those who are concerned about the incomes of the very rich, and the claim that incomes for the rest of us have stagnated or declined over the last 30 or so years (which is largely untrue), I can recommend recent books by Alan Reynolds and Gene Epstein,[19] who deal ably with these issues.

IS INEQUALITY INCREASING?

We have been examining the *extent* of inequality, with the intention of painting a more accurate picture of how much economic inequality there is now (or in a recent year). There is a separate, but related, issue of whether inequality has been increasing in recent years.

Most experts agree that a trend toward increasing inequality began sometime around the early 1970s and continued at least until the mid-1990s, and perhaps to the present day. We can see some of the evidence for this in the census figures back in table 2.1. (Although I have been critical of how people interpret the census data, there is little doubt that they accurately measure *annual before-tax money incomes*, unadjusted for family size or work effort. In each year, the data give a misleading picture, but whether they misrepresent the trend is a matter we will consider later.) Comparing 1970 and 2005, we see that the share of income received by the lowest quintile declined from 5.4 percent to 4.0 percent, while the share received by the highest quintile rose from 40.9 percent to 48.1 percent. Thus, the HiLo ratio increased from 7.6 in 1970 to 12 in 2001. These numbers appear to indicate a major upsurge in inequality.

This change in family incomes was driven primarily by changes in the distribution of wage rates and labor earnings. Highly skilled workers saw their wage rates rise sharply over this period, while low-skilled workers saw only a small increase, or perhaps a decline. The increased disparity in wage rates is clearly reflected in the earnings of college graduates compared to high school graduates. In 1970, college graduates earned about 50 percent more than high school graduates; by 2005, they were earning more than 70 percent more.

In interpreting the trend toward greater inequality, it is important to distinguish between *relative* and *absolute* changes in incomes. Low-skilled workers and families with low incomes did worse compared to others, but they did not suffer reductions in their standards of living. In fact, average real (adjusted for inflation) income for the lowest fifth in 2005 was 11 percent higher than in 1970. (On a per capita basis, the gain was about 15 percent because average family size declined over the period.) What happened was that incomes in the upper income classes rose faster than this, so relative inequality increased. The middle fifth, for example, saw its real income rise by 32 percent over that period, and the top fifth gained an impressive 78 percent.[20]

Because these estimates are based on the unadjusted money income data from the Census Bureau, it is probable that they understate the gains at the bottom and overstate them at the top. Remember that the census figures are before-tax and before-(most) transfers. Families at the top paid a large share of their (higher) incomes as taxes over this period, while those at the bottom received increased amounts of uncounted transfers. Real (adjusted for inflation) consumption expenditures for the poorest fifth of consumer units actually rose by 57 percent between 1972/1973 and 2002—far more than the reported 11 percent gain in income shown in the census figures.[21] So although relative inequality has increased somewhat, the real standards of living of those at the bottom (and everyone else) have improved significantly. It is clearly incorrect to view our recent experience as one in which the rich got richer and the poor got poorer. A more accurate statement would be: "The rich got richer, and the poor got richer but at a slower rate."

Although most agree that relative inequality has increased over this period, it has not increased as much as widely reported—because most studies rely on the flawed census income data. As one piece of evidence, Daniel Slesnick has estimated that the HiLo ratio based on consumption per person in the top and bottom quintiles stood at 5.1 in 1973 and only increased to 6.1 in 1995. By contrast, the HiLo ratio based on income (for consumer units) increased over this period from 10.4 to 13.7, nearly three times as large an increase.[22] Inequality did not increase as much as most conventional measures suggest.

But it did increase. At least this is true if we look only at the last quarter or so of the twentieth century. Taking a longer-run view reveals a different picture. Let's partition the twentieth century into three periods: 1900–1950, 1950–1975, and 1975–2000. The first half of the twentieth century was a period that saw a substantial reduction in economic inequality (in the relative sense of quintile shares; absolutely, of course, incomes across the board increased). Although we lack the hard data to document this concisely (the census started collecting information on incomes only in 1940), economic historians have pieced together a variety of evidence that makes this incontrovertible.[23]

For the 1950–1975 period there was a continuing reduction in inequality. (Recall that this period saw the massive increases in redistributive policies attendant upon Lyndon Johnson's Great Society programs.) We have better data for this period. Frank Levy has constructed a "corrected" family income distribution based on the census figures for 1949 and 1979 (exceeding our target period a bit). He adjusts for taxes, nonmonetary benefits (in-kind transfers), and family size differences. His "corrected" HiLo ratio for 1949 is 6.8, but this falls to 3.9 in 1979.[24] Over this period, the share of "corrected" income received by the lowest quintile rose from 5.8 to 8.7 percent, a substantial rise. Another study for the 1952 to 1972 period found an even greater increase in the share going to the bottom, an increase of almost 5 percentage points.[25]

Thus, the trend toward greater economic equality continued through the first three-quarters of the twentieth century. In the last quarter, there was a movement toward greater inequality. The question is: How much of the previous equalizing trend was undone in the last quarter century? The answer, I believe, is some, but not very much. We certainly had greater economic equality in 2000 than in 1900, and probably more equality in 2000 than in 1950.

One implication of this discussion is that the census income data not only overstate inequality in any given year but they have also overstated the increase in inequality over time. The reasons are to be found in the six shortcomings in the census data noted earlier: At least three of these have changed since 1950 in ways that mean the census data increasingly overstate inequality.[26]

Because it is widely agreed that there was an increase in relative inequality over recent decades, a natural question is why this has occurred. A common explanation—that it resulted from changes in government welfare and tax policies—turns out to be completely untrue: It is the before-tax and before-transfer distribution that has become more unequal. What we need to explain is why highly skilled workers earn more relative to lesser skilled workers today than in the past. What apparently happened in the late twentieth century is that technological advances (which contribute to economic growth) tended to favor those with greater skills. As one economist, summarizing the results of a conference devoted to inequality, put it: "In this symposium there was a clear consensus that a shift in labor demand away from the unskilled and disadvantaged, in favor of the skilled and socially adaptable, is the main reason for the rise in inequality. In other words, technology now favors brains rather than brawn."[27]

A homely example may clarify what this means. When I began my career, the production of research papers was a laborious process beginning with a handwritten version. A typist would produce a typewritten version, which I would proofread and return for a cleaner version to be typed. Back and forth it went through several versions before reaching a final product. Then came personal computers and word processing programs. Today, I never use a typist at all (does anyone?), and the whole process is faster, with less effort on my part, and the final result is far more attractive.

What I have described is a technological advance that makes researchers more productive and therefore leads to an increase in demand for their services (recalling that value productivity underlies the demand for labor). At the same time, this advance effectively makes typists less productive (in the value sense) and reduces demand for their services. The result is an increased gap in wages. This example, writ large to the economy as a whole, is how modern electronic and digital technology is thought to have widened the differences in wages between skilled and unskilled workers.

Of course, other factors may also have contributed to greater inequality, but they are generally thought to be of lesser importance than technological advances. For example, some economists believe globalization (increased foreign trade) may have played some role as increased imports produced by foreign unskilled workers displace products produced by domestic unskilled workers. Another factor that certainly played a role is immigration, which has swelled the ranks of unskilled workers in the United States. (We will discuss immigration in a later chapter.) But most experts believe the major culprit is technological advances.

We would not want to stop technological progress, even if we could. It is a benefit to the nation as a whole even though it does not benefit all groups equally and even though some may suffer, at least temporarily. In the recent past, technological progress has operated to increase the productive contributions of higher-skilled workers, and that is to their immediate benefit. In the longer run, it is also an *opportunity* for those with lesser skills who can now benefit more by improving their skills. It is no coincidence that as the so-called college premium has increased so too has college attendance.[28] Over time, more unskilled workers will upgrade their skill set and this may lead to reduced inequality. (When unskilled workers become more skilled, this means the supply of unskilled workers falls and the supply of skilled workers increases, which would tend to narrow the wage gap.) That process can take a long time, but it is already underway.

So should we be alarmed by the increase in inequality over the past quarter century? I don't think so. If inequality continues to increase, at some point it could constitute a serious problem, but we are far from reaching that point. Recall from the previous section that *even after* most or all of the recent trend toward inequality, the evidence suggests that economic inequality is represented by a HiLo ratio of only 3 to 1 or 4 to 1.

WHY NOT COMPLETE EQUALITY?

There is no disputing the fact that there are significant economic inequalities in America (and in every other society, for that matter). So what is the point of agonizing over exactly how much inequality there is? Why don't we opt for complete equality and dispense with these quibbles? I'm glad you asked.

One reason is that many inequalities are necessary if we are to have a fair distribution of income, as we saw in the last chapter in the section entitled "Just Inequalities." But here I will set that issue aside and focus on the consequences of complete equality for the productivity of the economy.

There is only one way to achieve complete equality, and that is for government to impose it on a society. Economists have a powerful objection to a policy that attempts to achieve complete economic equality, and that is that it would eliminate all incentives for people to be productive. What equality means is that those who work will have the same income (or consumption) as those who don't work, and those who work hard will have the same as those who slack off. It means that everyone's standard of living is unaffected by how much effort they make. So why work at all? And if no one (or few) works, there is zero (or little) income to divide equally. Remember that for a society, production equals income, and with no work there is no production of goods or services and hence no income. So complete equality seems to imply that everyone will have a zero income.

This is the bare bones case against complete equality—everyone is impoverished, if not exterminated, by it. But egalitarians have long held out hope that this dire result could be avoided, and I think it worthwhile to consider the issue a bit further. One possibility we can dispose of quickly—it is that people could be socialized into working for the common good even when there is no personal advantage to it. This, of course, was one of the tenets of communism and socialism—that human nature itself was pliable and could be changed by egalitarian policies. Few believe this today, not only because of the experience with communism in the last century, but also because recent research shows how powerfully human characteristics are influenced by genes and evolution.[29] People will almost always look out first and foremost for themselves and their families, and government policy can't do much to change that.

So the only way to get people to work in a world of equality is by requiring (forcing) them to work. Just require everyone to put in 40 hours a week, and those that don't work, don't eat. To some egalitarians, that may seem to solve the problem of providing productive incentives, but a little thought will show that the problems are just beginning.

Let's suppose that you can by edict induce people to work 40 hours a week. What are some of the issues still to be resolved? First of all, there is a vast difference between putting in 40 hours and being productive (or creative) for 40 hours. How do you get people to put forth their best efforts when they get no advantage from doing so? Perhaps even more important, what jobs will people be required to do? If I am going to have the same income regardless of what job I do (which is what equality means), I would like to be a restaurant reviewer or perhaps a movie critic. People obviously can't be free to choose what jobs they do—they will have to be assigned their jobs. How will the government decide who gets what jobs? For that matter, how will the government decide how many people are needed to perform each job?

It is no answer to say that people get the jobs they are trained for; it just raises the question of how to induce people to become trained at all when there is no gain to them. Will students continue to work in school when that holds no promise of enhancing their future incomes? Can we force people to learn in school or on the job? How many will put in the effort to become engineers, doctors, scientists, morticians, or accountants? And of course students can't be free to select their fields of study, for what would we do if they all chose English literature or ethnic studies or law?

In addition to issues related to work, there is the question of whether people can be free to spend their (equal) incomes as they wish. The basic problem here is that some people would like to choose to use their incomes in a way that will improve their lives in the future, say by saving or accumulating consumer durables. That can't be permitted, for it would allow inequalities to emerge in the future. Even consumption choices would have to be regulated to ensure that all stay at the same level.

The list of practical problems that come with a regime of complete equality could obviously be extended *ad infinitum*. The point, which I suspect is obvious by now, is that a policy of equality would require government to regulate and control virtually every aspect of our day-to-day lives. Getting people to work their 40 hours is just the beginning of our problems.

There are two consequences of a regime of complete equality that we can be fairly certain will occur. First, people would have no economic freedom to make the many choices that we now take for granted; all choices would have to be dictated by government. And, second, even if this policy were embarked upon, the productivity of society would plummet because government cannot run an economy with slave labor efficiently. It might be possible to achieve something close to (relative) material equality, but it would be at a much lower average income than that which emerges in a free and unequal capitalistic system.

Moreover, this is a best case scenario that assumes the government is benevolent and tries to promote the well-being of all its people. The power that government must have in this egalitarian world could be used for other ends and produce even worse results. It is worth recalling that communist regimes in the twentieth century are credited with killing 100 million of their own citizens not through wars but as a result of their domestic policies.[30]

Based on theoretical arguments like the above as well as the actual histories of allegedly egalitarian regimes, most thoughtful people have, I believe, rightly concluded that equality would not produce a utopian paradise but rather a dystopian nightmare. Modern egalitarians would probably concede these points but say that the entire argument is a red herring. No one, they would say, advocates *complete* equality, only *more* equality than we now have.

Yet this position raises the question of how we identify the proper degree of equalization. Unfortunately, there are few if any guidelines here. Most people who advocate more equality can't explain how we can determine when we have enough, and they disagree among themselves over the policies they would like implemented. Irving Kristol recounts an amusing episode from his tenure as editor of the influential journal, *The Public Interest*. After noting that some people ("mostly professors, of course") "are constantly insisting that a more equal distribution of income is a matter of considerable urgency," he invited several of them to write an article describing "a proper redistribution of American income" and giving "a picture of what a 'fair' distribution of income would look like." The response: "I have never been able to get that article, and I have come to the conclusion that I never shall get it. In two cases, I was promised such an analysis, but it was never written.... Despite all the talk 'about equality,' no one seems willing to commit himself to a precise definition."[31]

My own impression is that egalitarians will never be satisfied; no matter how little inequality there is, they will want government to redistribute still more. In any case, there is a clear risk in pursuing a goal that is so vague even in the minds of its proponents. How do we recognize when we have gone too far? As we will see in discussing actual egalitarian policies in later chapters, there is a good possibility that we already have.

Group Inequalities

When the word *inequality* appears in the news media, as likely as not it is in the context of recognizing disparities among groups: Blacks earn less than whites; Hispanics earn less than whites; women earn less than men, and so on. At first glance, it is surprising that so much attention is given to these inequalities among group averages because the differences are much smaller than those that separate, for example, the poor and the rich (irrespective of race or gender). Differences among groups do exist, however, and egalitarians harp on any differences that help to promote their redistributionist agenda.

The conventional wisdom holds that group differences are the result of discrimination in a racist/sexist society. This seems to contradict our conclusion (in chapter 1) that markets tend to generate "equal pay for equal work"—that all workers who are equally productive will receive the same wages regardless of race or gender. But our analysis there did not incorporate discrimination. In this chapter we will extend the basic model to include discrimination, with some surprising results—notably we will see that discrimination may exist and yet have no effect on the earnings of groups discriminated against. We will explain this analysis in the next section and then turn to a consideration of what other factors may contribute to differences among group outcomes.

First, however, let us consider some facts that cast doubt on the view that discrimination is the sole reason for differences among groups. From the decennial census of 1990 we learn that the median family income of African Americans was 66 percent of the overall median, while the median for Hispanics was 80 percent of the overall median. These figures, of course, are widely known and comport well with the discrimination story. But we also find that the incomes of Chinese families are 20 percent *above* the national median and that Asian Indian families have incomes 49 percent more than the national median. Further, Japanese families are 38 percent higher and Jewish families are also 38 percent higher.[1] If discrimination is the overriding determinant of differences in the economic fortunes of groups, how do we explain the higher incomes of these groups? Does society discriminate in favor of Japanese, Chinese, Indian, and Jewish families and against non-Jewish whites? Of course that is not true, but these facts should suggest that factors other than discrimination are capable of producing substantial differences among groups.

Discrimination in Labor Markets

Suppose that firm A wishes to discriminate against its black employees. *If* firm A is the only potential employer of these black workers, it will obviously have the ability to pay just about any wage it wants. If it pays lower wages to blacks, the workers have little recourse but to accept the reduced wage because it is better to work at a lower wage than not to work at all.

Now suppose more realistically that there are other firms that also employ workers with the same skills as those employed by firm A, and assume further that these firms do not discriminate in their employment practices. In this case, if firm A cuts the wages of its black workers, these workers have the option of seeking employment at other businesses. To be concrete, assume that the going market wage for workers with the same skills is $40,000 a year, and firm A will only pay its black workers $30,000. Then firm A's black workers have incentive to leave firm A and seek employment among the nondiscriminating firms where the going wage is still $40,000. And competition among the nondiscriminating firms for the displaced black workers will bid their wages back up to $40,000.[2]

What this simple example illustrates is crucial to thinking clearly about how labor markets work when *some* firms discriminate. Individual businesses do not determine market wage rates. Firm A may have wanted to pay black workers 25 percent less than white workers, but the result would be that its black workers went to work for a nondiscriminating employer. Firm A would end up having to pay the going market wage of $40,000 to get (white) replacements.

The model, if it can be so dignified, that seems to underlie most discussions of discrimination is one where firms can set wages anywhere they want without losing workers. The reasoning seems to be that if a business pays minorities less, it simply pockets the savings as profits. In that view, discrimination is profitable to the firm. But that view ignores competition among firms for the available workers. Firms don't have the power to pay workers less than they could get at other employers, at least not for long. If firms did have this power (to profit by reducing workers' wages), they wouldn't selectively apply it only to some workers; they would cut everyone's pay and realize enormous profits. Yet if that is our supposed theory, it does not explain even the most obvious characteristics of real world labor markets, such as why wage rates are far above subsistence levels and tend to rise over time.

To repeat, individual firms have little or no power to set wage rates; wage rates are determined by the interaction of all the actual and potential employers and workers. Then, *as long as there is a large enough nondiscriminating employment sector, discrimination by other employers has no effect on the wages of the discriminated-against group or other groups.* This conclusion does not say that discrimination can never affect wages, for an elaboration of the analysis will show that if discrimination is widespread enough (so the nondiscriminating sector is small or nonexistent), then it can have effects. Clearly, if *all* (actual and potential) firms were willing to hire black workers only at a lower wage than paid to equally skilled white workers, then black workers would be paid less as a result of discrimination. As this example may suggest, the sizes of the discriminating and nondiscriminating sectors relative to the size of the group being discriminated against is important in determining whether discrimination will affect wages.

As long as there are enough nondiscriminating employers, competitive labor markets operate to protect groups who are subject to discrimination in some sectors of the economy. Discriminated-against groups can end up with the same wages they would receive in a totally nondiscriminatory regime.

Obviously, the outcome depends on how prevalent discrimination really is. Unfortunately, this cannot be known with any certainty because discrimination relates to motivations that cannot be measured directly. There have been attempts to estimate the extent of discrimination, however, using a protocol known as an *audit study*. Typical of these studies are two undertaken by the Urban Institute in 1990. They used college students, carefully matched in pairs, one black and one white, who had as closely as possible identical qualifications. These matched pairs were sent out to apply for advertised jobs in Washington and Chicago. (A third study following this protocol was undertaken in Denver in 1991.) If the white college student was offered the job and the black wasn't, this would constitute evidence of discrimination.

Some observers believe that this sort of experiment is the best direct evidence of the extent of employer discrimination that we have. Others have criticized the technique, pointing out that the testers (the college students) were instructed about "the pervasive problem of discrimination in the United States," with the possibility that the students were inadvertently motivated to find what they were looking for.[3] In addition, the testers applied for jobs only at private businesses, ignoring the largest employer in the Washington, D.C., area (the federal government). For these and other reasons, it is not clear that this procedure is a fair test of employer discrimination.

Setting aside these issues, what were the findings of these studies? From among the 476 total pairs of job applications, in 82 percent of the cases either both the white and black student received job offers or neither did. So there was equal treatment 82 percent of the time. In 12 percent of the cases, the white student received an offer and the black did not, while in the remaining 6 percent of the cases the black student received an offer and the white did not.[4] On the surface, this seems to suggest that 12 percent of employers were discriminating against blacks, while 6 percent were discriminating against whites. Other interpretations are possible.

If we take these results at face value, however, they seem to show that employers who do not discriminate against blacks constitute about 88 percent of all employers (82 percent who treated them equally plus the 6 percent who favored the blacks), with discriminating employers accounting for 12 percent of employers. These findings are notable when we juxtapose them with our earlier discussion of how widespread discrimination must be to affect wage rates. With a nondiscriminating sector accounting for 88 percent of the jobs and blacks constituting about 11 percent of the total labor force, our analysis implies that black wages would not be affected at all. The nondiscriminating sector is more than large enough to absorb all of the blacks, so even if the 12 percent of discriminators don't hire any blacks at all, their wages would not suffer.

I do not mean to suggest that these figures (88 percent, 12 percent) are necessarily correct. The important point is that the best direct evidence we have of the extent of discrimination shows it is not widespread enough to produce lower wage rates for equally productive blacks. Too often people just assume that if there is *any* discrimination, that means the discriminated-against group's wages will suffer.

Another factor that limits the effects of discrimination is the profit motive. To the extent that a business tries to make as much money as possible, it will not discriminate in its employment practices. To be sure, it will try to hire the cheapest workers of a given quality that it can, but that is part of the process that ultimately leads to equal pay for equally qualified workers. Engaging in discrimination is actually costly to businesses: They sacrifice profits by discriminating. After all, by refusing to hire qualified minorities, businesses reduce their options and make it harder to find qualified workers from among the smaller set of nonminorities.

To see this point easily, let's suppose that on average blacks and women are equally qualified (equally productive) with whites and men but that they currently receive 20 percent lower wage rates. Now a firm that restricts its employment to white males is incurring labor costs that are 25 percent higher than necessary—it could replace its white male labor force with an all black and female (equally productive) labor force and lower its labor costs by 20 percent. That, of course, would greatly increase its profits. Indeed, any firm that hires a single white male is losing potential profits in this scenario, for it could have hired an equally qualified black or female for less. This does not mean that discrimination cannot occur, but it does emphasize that the discriminator must be willing to give up potential profits to engage in it.

And this sacrifice is substantial, at least if there is a 20 percent difference in wage rates for equally productive workers. Consider that of each dollar of sales revenue in the American economy, roughly 9 cents is (before-tax) profit and 70 cents goes to compensate workers. For a typical business, then, if it could cut its labor costs by, say, 15 percent by hiring the discriminated-against groups, the labor cost per dollar of sales revenue would fall to 59.5 cents *and the amount going into profits would more than double*. How many businesses would be willing to give up an opportunity to double their profits in order to have a white male labor force? Of course, to the extent that businesses try to realize this profit opportunity, they initiate a competitive process (more demand for minorities; less for nonminorities) that would tend to eliminate the disparity in wages.

It is this point that makes it difficult to believe that there is a *substantial* difference in wage rates among groups that are equally productive—there would have to be a pervasive willingness on the part of businesses to forgo the opportunity to greatly increase profits. Although one can imagine that some firms would be willing to do this, recall that it is not necessary for all firms to be nondiscriminators for the wage disparity to be eliminated. As we saw above, the nondiscriminating sector does not have to encompass all, or even most, of the firms to produce equality in wage rates.

Those who believe that discrimination is responsible for large differences in wages among groups have an easy way to benefit the discriminated-against group and themselves by investing according to their convictions. Let them put their life savings into starting a business and have the business employ only allegedly discriminated-against groups. If they are correct in their convictions, they could make enormous profits following this strategy, and at the same time benefit the discriminated-against groups. That we do not see this happening in the real world is very revealing.

The economic analysis of discrimination does not dispute that some people will engage in discrimination, but it does emphasize that there are economic forces that ameliorate or negate its harmful consequences. That understanding has led most economists to be skeptical of claims that discrimination is responsible for large differences in pay among groups. But if discrimination is not responsible for these differences, what is? That is the subject we will take up in the next two sections.

BLACKS AND WHITES

In 2005, we learn from the Census Bureau that African American families received incomes that were 60 percent of those received by white families.[5] That disparity is often cited as evidence of the unequal treatment of blacks in the American economy. Yet economists who investigate whether discrimination is responsible for economic differences rarely ever focus on comparisons of family incomes. The reason is that these comparisons can be exceedingly misleading, and that is known to be true for the black-white family income comparison.

Family incomes are influenced by a number of factors unrelated to pay differences. For example, how large the family is, whether it is a single-parent or two-parent family, whether both parents work or only one does, all play roles in determining family incomes. And there are pronounced differences in black and white family structures. Among white families, 80 percent were married-couple families in 2005; among black families only 46 percent were married-couple families. The flip side of these figures is that in 54 percent of black families, there is generally only one adult, whereas that is true in only 20 percent of white families. So when we compare the median family incomes of these groups, we are in effect comparing a white married-couple family with a black single-parent (generally female-headed) family. Because single-parent families understandably have lower incomes, this comparison may tell us more about the importance of family structure than it does about inequalities in wages.

If we are going to compare family incomes, it is thus important to compare similarly structured families. When we do this, a very different picture emerges. For example, among married-couple families, median black income was 84 percent of median white income in 2005. Among married-couple families where both spouses work full-time, the ratio was 89 percent.[6] It is clear that comparing similarly structured families reveals much less inequality than suggested by the overall ratio of 60 percent.

So an important reason for the differences in family incomes is the difference in family structures. Labor markets presumably do not determine family structure, so to examine how markets influence black-white differences economists generally emphasize individual earnings or wage rates. Markets do determine wage rates, and there are significant differences between blacks and whites. In 2005, among men who worked full-time year-round, black median earnings were 77 percent of white median earnings.[7] Among women, the ratio was 90 percent. So black men typically receive about 23 percent less than white men, and black women about 10 percent less than white women. It is these differences that we want to examine.

There are two major potential explanations for these differences in wages. One is that they reflect differences in economic productivities. As we saw earlier, economics suggests that wage rates tend to reflect economic productivity, and so when there are differences in wages it is natural (for an economist!) to consider first that this is due to a difference in productivities. The second possibility is that discrimination is responsible for the differences. Of course, these competing explanations are not mutually exclusive; it may well be that both play a role in producing the 23 percent difference between black and white male earnings.

Because discrimination cannot be measured directly, what we would like to do is determine how closely black and white wages reflect their productivities. Unfortunately, the economic productivities of individual workers also cannot be measured directly or with any great accuracy, at least with data available in large nationally representative samples. So we have to use proxies to suggest how productive a worker is. An example will illustrate how this is done.

Consider men's (NBA) professional basketball: Are black and white players paid based on their productivities? Ultimately, the economic productivity of a professional basketball player reflects how many people will attend games (or watch on television) based on his contribution to the team because spectators' interest in a team is what brings in the money. But an athlete's contribution is difficult to determine. We might suppose that an athlete's contribution is related to how good an athlete he is, and his contribution can be measured with rough accuracy with statistics like field goal percentages (field goal percentage being a proxy for productivity). So the question becomes, do white and black athletes with the same skills (stats) receive the same pay? In this case, "Productivity being equal (number of seasons played, games played per season, career points, field goal percentage, rebounds, assists, and so forth)," writes one research team, "black professional basketball players on average earn about the same as white players." And in other sports the story is similar: "The empirical evidence indicates that wage differences between white and black players in football and baseball are negligible once salaries are adjusted for productivity differences."[8] "Productivity" is not, of course, measured directly but with stand-in proxies of the sort described. Based on this kind of evidence, we could conclude that discrimination has little or no effect on the pay of professional athletes because productivity differences account fully for pay differentials.

These studies suggest how economists approach the issue of comparative pay: Use proxies that are related to productivity, and compare and contrast the pay rate of groups who have similar characteristics. Unfortunately, finding proxies for productivity for workers in general is not as easy as it is when we restrict attention to professional sports.

From what we know about the determinants of wages (productivity) in general, there are several measurable factors that may be relevant. For example, education is one. Both theory and evidence support the position that more-educated persons tend to be more productive. Note that for this factor to be relevant in explaining black-white differences, blacks and whites must differ in the amounts of education achieved; there is no need to control for a factor where there is no difference between the groups. In this case, there is a difference. In 2000, for example, 26 percent of whites had a bachelor's degree (or more), compared with 17 percent for blacks. And 15 percent of whites lacked a high school diploma, while this was true for 22 percent of blacks.[9] Thus, considering this factor alone, we expect whites to be more productive on average because they have more education on average, suggesting that some of the overall disparity in wages is due to this factor.

Another factor related to productivity is age, especially as it is relates to job experience. As pointed out in chapter 1, earnings tend to vary with age, starting relatively low and rising to a peak generally in the 40s or 50s. The reason for this, economists believe, is that as workers gain more experience (or even formal on-the-job training), they become more productive and more valuable employees. So it is not surprising and does not reflect age discrimination that middle-aged workers earn more than young workers. This is relevant in comparing blacks and whites because there is a significant difference in the age structures. The median age of whites in 2000 was 38, but for blacks the median was only 30. Black workers are, on average, younger than white workers, so some of their lower earnings may be due to their relative lack of experience.

We should also take account of where people live because there is some regional variation in earnings (and costs of living). Fifty-five percent of blacks in the United States live in the South, compared to 34 percent of whites. Earnings of both blacks and whites are lower in the South, but the larger share of blacks in that region has a disproportionate effect on national averages of earnings for blacks.

There is also some evidence that blacks work shorter hours than whites with similar education. William Johnson and Derek Neal find that among young males, blacks with less than a high school diploma work 25 percent fewer hours per year than whites. For those with a high school diploma (and no more), blacks worked 13 percent fewer hours, while for those with college degrees the difference was negligible.[10] This directly contributes to lower annual earnings for blacks.

One other significant difference between blacks and whites is in marriage patterns. As suggested by our discussion of family structure, blacks are far less likely to be married than whites. For example, among men aged 25 to 29, 42 percent of whites are married (with wife present), whereas only 25 percent of blacks are. The difference is even greater for the 45 to 54 age range; here, 72 percent of white males are married but only 50 percent of black males.[11]

Perhaps surprisingly, marital status of men is related to their individual earnings: "Wage studies consistently find that married men earn higher wages than do men who are not currently married [regardless of race]."[12] Why this is true is not entirely clear. One hypothesis is that "marriage makes men more productive by allowing them to specialize in non-household production [i.e., their jobs]."[13] Recent evidence supports this hypothesis, implying that marriage directly leads to higher earnings for men. If this is correct, then the differences in marital status between black and white men contribute to the lower relative earnings of black men. (Married men also tend to work longer hours than unmarried men, and perhaps this is part of the explanation for the differences in work effort cited above.)

So there are a number of systematic ways blacks and whites differ on average that are likely to be related to earnings. What is the *combined effect* of these differences on the earnings of blacks and whites? (It is not sufficient to look at each factor, like education, separately because even among equally educated blacks and whites there are still other relevant differences.) Many studies have been undertaken to investigate this issue, often using elaborate statistical procedures, which, fortunately, we do not have to explain. After surveying the extant studies in 1985, Ronald Ehrenberg and Robert Smith summarized the range of results in this way: "From 50 to 80 percent of the difference in average earnings can be explained by differences in productive characteristics [of blacks and whites]."[14]

What exactly does this conclusion mean? Suppose we conclude from these studies that the best estimate (in the 50–80 percent range) is two-thirds. Recall that in 2005, black males earned 23 percent less than white males. Then these studies tell us that two-thirds of this actual difference in wages is accounted for, or due to, differences in productivity (or productivity proxies). Put differently, this says that if we compare blacks and whites who are identical in terms of these factors, the difference in wages will not be 23 percent but only 7.6 percent. So if the factors examined in the studies are good proxies for productivity, the implication is that the economic productivity of whites on average is greater than that of blacks, and this difference in economic productivity is responsible for a large part of the difference in wages.

How do we interpret the remaining 7.6 percent difference in wages? This is the residual or the part of the actual 23 percent difference that is not accounted for or due to the productivity proxies used in the studies. This residual is often interpreted as the part of the overall wage gap that is due to discrimination. This may or may not be true. Literally, the residual is only the still-unexplained difference that remains after adjusting for productivity-related factors, and only if the proxies are used accurately to completely mirror productivity could we claim that equally productive blacks are paid 7.6 percent less than whites. Nonetheless, the residual certainly may be due to discrimination, and it is commonly interpreted in this way.

The studies reporting that 50 to 80 percent of the overall wage gap is due to productivity-related factors were conducted before 1985. More recent studies have emphasized a defect in most of these early studies, namely, that they measure educational achievement in the wrong way. Education is often measured just by years of schooling completed (or credentials obtained), but that is not a very good measure of how education affects economic productivity. What matters is the cognitive skills acquired in school, and that is very imperfectly indicated by how long one has spent in a classroom. Instead, most recent studies have emphasized direct measures of cognitive skills in the form of standardized test scores.

This is relevant to the black-white wage gap because blacks score lower on a variety of standardized tests than whites. For example, in 2003 the mean combined score of blacks on the Scholastic Assessment Test (SAT, formerly called the Scholastic Aptitude Test) was 857, while the corresponding figure for whites was 1060. On the Armed Forces Qualification Test (AFQT), an achievement test of verbal and mathematical skills, according to June O'Neill, "among high school graduates ages 18 to 22 in 1980 the black median AFQT score was 65 percent of the white median."[15]

Other tests display similar differences between whites and blacks. The National Assessment of Educational Progress (NAEP) regularly tests nationally representative samples of school students in grades 4, 8, and 12. In recent NAEP tests (1998–2001), Abigail and Stephan Thernstrom report that "blacks nearing the end of their high school education perform a little worse than white eighth-graders in both reading and U.S. history, and a lot worse in math and geography. In math and geography, indeed, they know no more than whites in the seventh grade."[16]

Among adults who have completed school we find a similar pattern. In 1992, the National Adult Literacy Survey administered tests of *prose literacy* and *quantitative literacy* to a large representative sample of adults. According to the Thernstroms: "The lowest level of 'prose literacy' was defined as being unable to 'make low-level inferences based on what they read and to compare or contrast information that can easily be found in [a] text.' By that definition, two out of five black adults—two and a half times the figure for whites—were either functionally illiterate or close to it. In 'quantitative literacy' almost half of African Americans were on the bottom level, compared to about one-seventh of whites." Further, "The average black college graduate...is no more adept at reading than the typical white who attended college only briefly, leaving before receiving even a two-year degree. Even worse,...the quantitative skills of the average black with a bachelor's degree are no stronger than those of whites who only graduated from high school and did not attend college—a four year gap."[17]

These and other tests document that blacks and whites with equal schooling do not have equal academic skills. That means that using academic credentials or years of schooling is an inadequate proxy for the productivities of workers. Recent studies have incorporated some measure of test scores as a productivity proxy instead of, or in addition to, the more traditional measures of education. With this change, these studies can explain an even larger part of the overall wage gap between blacks and whites. For example, June O'Neill reports how the black-white gap is affected by incorporating different variables: "The black-white hourly earnings ratio is 82.9 percent [for young males in 1987] before adjusting for any characteristics.... after adjusting for region, schooling and potential work experience—which are the standard variables...the ratio rises to 87.7 percent. The addition of AFQT [test scores] raises the ratio to 95.5 percent, at which point close to three-quarters of the gap is explained. Adding actual work experience virtually closes the gap....the adjustment for AFQT differences for the college group raises the black-white ratio to over 100 percent."[18]

In another important study, Neal and Johnson find that controlling *only* for AFQT test scores reduces the male black-white wage gap by three-fourths and reverses it for black females who are found to earn more than white females with the same test scores. Studies of this sort have led economist (and Nobel laureate) James Heckman to conclude: "A careful reading of the entire body of available evidence confirms that most of the disparity in earnings between blacks and whites in the labor market of the 1990s is due to the differences in skills they bring to the market, and not to discrimination within the labor market."[19] The Thernstroms' conclusion is similar: "A number of sophisticated studies demonstrate clearly that whites and blacks who are truly equally educated are equal earners."[20]

I believe the evidence, together with the presumption suggested by economic theory in the last section, supports the conclusion that blacks and whites who are equally skilled receive the same wages, with discrimination being responsible for virtually none of the overall wage gap. Not everyone agrees that discrimination has no effect at all on earnings differences, but it is fair to say that all competent researchers in this area concur that most of the differences in earnings between blacks and whites are due to productivity differences, with discrimination playing at most a relatively minor role.

Whatever was true a generation or two ago, it is not discrimination that today keeps black earnings below white earnings; it is a relative lack of skills. In view of this, it is natural to look to the public school system for a solution. After all, that is where most children acquire the mental skills that many of these tests measure, and if blacks are underperforming whites, then the schools must be to blame. But that is, at best, a partial truth. For many of these mental disparities arise even before children set foot in a school. Several studies have confirmed this. For example, the Thernstroms report a study from the National Center for Education Statistics that examined "a representative sample of 22,000 pupils enrolled in kindergarten in the 1998–1999 school year. Since the children were tested shortly after they first arrived, the racial disparities found in the study clearly predated school....From a third to half of black...pupils entered kindergarten already testing in the bottom quarter of students in reading, math, and general knowledge. Only a sixth of whites scored that low."[21] As Heckman and Wax similarly observe: "Young black children lag significantly in school readiness before traditional school programs and expectations of discrimination could have much effect."[22]

Recent research has increasingly emphasized the importance of early childhood environments in influencing later success in school. Once children start school it may already be too late to effect meaningful improvements: "Like it or not, the most important mental and behavioral patterns, once established, are difficult to change once children enter school."[23]

There are pronounced differences in the early childhood environments of black and white children that may be the primary cause of test score differences recorded much later in (and after leaving) school. And these differences are not due significantly to the lower incomes and higher rates of poverty among blacks: "Young black children are exposed to much lower levels of cognitive and emotional stimulation than white children, even in families with comparable income, education, and IQ. They watch more TV, read fewer books, and converse and go on educational outings with their families less often. They are more likely to be raised in homes without fathers, family mealtimes or fixed routines. These disparities lead to big gaps by age three or four (the earliest age at which they can be measured reliably)."[24]

Or consider the implications of the greater prevalence of single-parent families among blacks. In combination with the tendency for blacks to have somewhat larger numbers of children, "These two facts together mean that the ratio of children to parents is uniquely high for African Americans: *roughly three children per parent, as compared with one child per parent for whites* [my emphasis]. And, in turn, that means black children necessarily receive less individual parental attention."[25]

The good news here is that these factors can be changed, and it is within the power of African Americans themselves to effect these changes—governmental interventions or social reorganizations are not required. The bad news is that there are few signs that blacks—or whites, for that matter—recognize that these factors may be ultimately responsible for most if not all of the earnings (and other) disparities between blacks and whites, preferring to blame racism, discrimination, or the "system" instead.

WOMEN AND MEN

In 2005, among full-time year-round workers, the median earnings of women were 77 percent of those of men, a 23 percent disparity. Many of the usual suspects that we identified in evaluating black-white differences do not work to explain this disparity. For example, there are only small differences between men and women regarding age, region of residence, marital status, or educational levels. Moreover, standardized test scores display only small differences on average for men and women.

Although the differences in test scores probably play little or no role in explaining differences in average (or median) pay, they may be relevant in certain circumstances. There are two notable differences in test outcomes. First, although the average scores are similar, male scores are more spread out around the average (the variance is higher). This means that males will be overrepresented in the tails of the distributions. For example, men are one and a half times more likely to have intellectual disabilities than women, considering the left tail of the distribution. In the right tail, "among a large sample of talented seventh and eighth graders who took the Scholastic Aptitude Test between 1972 and 1991, there were thirteen boys for every girl who scored above 700."[26]

A second difference is that "girls tend to perform better on verbal and language tests, and boys tend to perform slightly better on math reasoning and science tests."[27] Whether these differences are innate or the result of socialization (environment) is not clear, but they are of long standing. However, differences in the extreme tails of the IQ/ability distribution have little relevance for the vast bulk of men and women, who fall between the extremes.

There are two easily measurable factors that account for a large part of the overall earnings gap between women and men. One is that women work shorter hours than men. This is true even among full-time workers (those who work at least 35 hours per week): "According to the Department of Labor statistics, women's full time average hours of work, including time taken for maternity leave, were 92 percent of men's in 1999."[28] This means that the hourly pay of women is about 84 percent that of men, a 16 percent discrepancy rather than the 23 percent gap in annual earnings.

The second important factor is that job experience differs among men and women of the same age. If we compare working men and women at age 50, for example, men will have worked more years than women: "By the late 1980s, the typical woman worked only about 71 percent of her potential years of labor market experience. In contrast, the typical man worked about 93 percent of his potential years of labor market experience."[29] This means that over their lifetimes men work about 25 percent more years than women, at least as of the late 1980s. (This difference has diminished over time and probably will continue to do so.)

This is of obvious importance to productivity, as job skills will atrophy with time spent out of the labor market. In some rapidly changing occupations, even a year or two away from work may result in obsolescence of hard-won skills. In other jobs, it probably plays a smaller role. Indeed, there is some evidence that women enter occupations (like teaching or nursing) where a year or two away from work will not greatly affect their employability. But in general, "a worker who drops out of the labor force for five years earns one-third less than an identical worker who has been employed continuously,"[30] so this may be a major factor contributing to male-female earnings differences.

It is easy to document the importance of the experience factor. Suppose we compare the earnings of workers early in their careers when experience differences could not be great. For example, among those with a bachelor's degree working full-time in 2005 and aged 18–24, women earned 91 percent as much as men. (The remaining difference is likely due in part to different choices of college majors.) Yet by age 45–54, when there is a significant difference in experience, women with bachelor's degrees are earning only 62 percent as much as men. Similarly, among those with doctoral degrees aged 25–34, women earned 96 percent as much as men, but by age 45–54, women with doctorates were earning 64 percent as much as men.[31]

In every education category, the pattern is the same: Younger women earn more relative to men than do older women. This is consistent with the theory that experience is an important productivity proxy because the difference in experience is greater among older workers. Of course, one could also explain these facts with a discrimination story, but it would have to hold that employers discriminate much more against older women than against younger women. That seems implausible, especially because older women are less likely to quit or cut back on work to have a child than are younger women.

These two factors—differences in hours worked and experience—explain a large part of the overall earnings gap between men and women. But there is probably a single reason that is even more fundamental in explaining the difference in earnings: Women have babies and men do not. That fact, and the implications that flow from it, is probably the basic reason for differences in earnings among men and women. It is not *just* the fact that women have babies that matters, but the choices made pursuant to (and in anticipation of) that event also affect earnings.

Consider that in 1999, 38 percent of married women with children under the age of six did not work (outside the home), and of those who did work, fewer than half worked full-time. Among women with children over the age of six, 23 percent did not work.[32] Of course, caring for children is the main reason why women work shorter hours and have less experience on average, but having and raising children often leads to other more subtle effects on earnings. For instance, during pregnancy "fatigue is even more common-place [than other side effects], affecting about three-quarters of all pregnant women." And after birth, "postpartum fatigue is equally normal....Two different studies have found that at six months postpartum more than 75 percent of mothers have not achieved full functional status."[33] That has obvious implications for the desire to be employed as well as how effectively jobs are performed.

In addition to giving birth, women shoulder a large share of the responsibilities that come with having and raising children. Whether we like it or not, there is a very definite trade-off between being an effective parent and devoting oneself wholeheartedly to making money. This leads many women—and some men, too—to cut back on hours of work, refuse overtime, or strive less diligently for a promotion, or to look for a job with flexible hours or a short commute. In these and other ways, women who do work must balance parenting and their jobs, but often the choices made lead them to have lower earnings than they would have achieved if they had no children.

How do we know that having children produces large consequences for women's earnings? "Women without children and with similar levels of education and experience earn as much as their male counterparts. Data from the National Longitudinal Survey of Youth...show that among people ages twenty-seven to thirty-three who have never had a child, women's earnings are close to 98 percent of men's. In another study using the same data set comparing mothers and childless women with similarly educated men, mothers with the same education earned 75 percent of the men's earnings while childless women earned 95 percent. The divergence can be attributed to differences in choices of hours and occupations."[34] Other studies show that marriage per se does not lead to lower wages for women but having children does. And, not surprisingly, other factors being equal, the more children a woman has, the lower her earnings.[35]

Ardent feminists sometimes acknowledge facts like these, but argue that men and women would have equal earnings and representations in all occupations if familial responsibilities were fairly divided. That they are not is interpreted as the result of social constructs imposed by a patriarchal society instead of simply being consonant with the inherent natures of men and women. Whatever merit this position has, it has become increasingly apparent in recent years that men and women are biologically and innately different. For instance, "The brains of men differ visibly from the brains of women in several ways. Men have larger brains with more neurons (even correcting for body size), though women have a higher percentage of gray matter. (Since men and women are equally intelligent overall, the significance of these differences is unknown.)"[36] Further, "Positron emission tomography (PET) scans show that women seem to use more neurons for almost every activity tested. The typical woman's brain seems to be 'networked,' the typical man's compartmentalized. The woman's way seems to be better for many verbal tasks and for recovery from strokes, the man's for spatial tasks."[37]

It is not entirely clear what these differences really mean, but males and females are different at an age too early to be influenced by so-called societal pressures: "Compared with one-day-old male infants, one-day-old females respond more strongly to the sound of a human in distress. One-week-old baby girls can distinguish an infant's cry from other noise; boys usually cannot. Three-day-old girls maintain eye contact with a silent adult for twice as long as boys. Girls will look even longer if the adult talks; it makes no difference to boys. Four-month-old girls can distinguish photographs of those they know from people they do not; boys the same age generally cannot. On the other hand, five-month-old boys are more interested than girls in three-dimensional geometric forms and in blinking lights."[38]

Whether or not these innate differences are related to the differences observed in males and females later in life is not proven but that many differences do exist is demonstrable. "Mothers are more attached to their children, on average, than are fathers. This is true in societies all over the world and probably has been true of our lineage since the first mammals evolved some two hundred million years ago.... Not only are women the sex who nurse, but women are more attentive to their babies' well-being and, in surveys, place a higher value on spending time with their children."[39] Perhaps the division of labor in families for child-rearing responsibilities is more than just a social construct; perhaps it reflects our innate nature.

Men and women also differ in ways that may be related to their career and occupational choices: "Men say they are more keen to work longer hours and to sacrifice other parts of their lives—to live in a less attractive city, or to leave friends and family when they relocate—in order to climb the corporate ladder or achieve notoriety in their fields. Men, on average, are also more willing to undergo physical discomfort and danger, and thus are more likely to be found in grungy but relatively lucrative jobs such as repairing factory equipment, working on oil rigs, and jack-hammering sludge from the inside of oil tanks. Women, on average, are more likely to choose administrative support jobs that offer lower pay in air-conditioned offices. Men are greater risk takers, and that is reflected in their career paths when qualifications are held constant."[40] It is probably no coincidence that 92 percent of workplace deaths are male,[41] as males are disproportionately represented in high-risk occupations. And high-risk occupations are more highly paid, an equalizing wage differential as we saw in chapter 1.

We may never know exactly how many of the differences between men and women are hardwired into our natures, or how many are the result of social norms or traditions, or a combination of these factors. But whatever the causes, men and women are different in ways that relate to career choices, preferences about hours of work, and general lifestyle decisions. These differences, in turn, can be expected to result in different earnings in labor markets, even if there are no differences in innate abilities.

So is any of the observable difference in earnings between men and women the result of discrimination in labor markets? As in the black-white case, it is difficult to say with complete certainty. However, the economists most familiar with the evidence believe discrimination plays a very minor role. In 1996 a survey was conducted of 65 prominent labor economists (the specialists whose field encompasses discrimination in labor markets). The survey requested responders to estimate "the percentage of the male-female wage gap attributable to employer discrimination." The median response was 17.5 percent.[42] Note that this does *not* mean that discrimination causes a 17.5 percent gap but that 17.5 percent of the overall gap is due to discrimination. It is not clear whether the labor economists interpreted this question as applying to the annual earnings gap (23 percent) or the gap in hourly earnings (16 percent). In the former case, the responses imply a disparity of 4 percent due to discrimination; in the latter case, a disparity of less than 3 percent. Either way, it's clear that these experts in the relevant field believed discrimination had only a modest effect on the earnings of women in 1996. Today, I suspect such a survey would suggest an even smaller role for discrimination.

THE DISCRIMINATION MYTHS

There are two myths that are prevalent concerning discrimination in American society today. One is that discrimination against minorities and women is widespread and an integral part of our economic system. The other is that discrimination is responsible for the differences in economic outcomes among groups.

Like many myths, these contain an element of truth. That some people are prejudiced and make economic decisions based on that prejudice is without doubt true, but they are certainly in the small minority today. (Recall the audit studies.) It is also possible that some of the wage gaps that exist may be due to discrimination, but as we have seen, this is at most true for a tiny part of the existing differences. Moreover, it is certainly correct that both these beliefs contained a great deal more truth in the not-so-distant past.

Few would deny that discrimination was widespread and that it likely affected economic outcomes in the first half of the twentieth century. But at least for the last 20 or 30 years, these beliefs deserve to be called myths.

Yet they continue to be promulgated as if they are facts. For example, President Bill Clinton in a speech in 2000 asserted that women "get paid only 75 percent for the same kind of work....It's as if [women] were only picking up three paychecks, instead of four, in four pay periods. The average woman has to work, therefore, an extra 17 weeks a year to earn what a similarly qualified man in the same kind of job makes."[43] The refrain was repeated by Senator Hillary Clinton in her campaign for the Democratic presidential nomination in 2007: "But here we are at the beginning of the twenty-first century, and women still earn significantly less money than men for doing the same job. Women who work full-time year-round earn just 77 cents for every dollar that a man makes."[44] (I must somehow have missed the news that Hillary's Senate salary is lower than that of male senators.)

Statements of this sort that assert the pay differences are for the "same job" are, of course, untrue: The data cited simply compare the average or median pay for all male and female workers. Of course, it is not unknown for politicians to utter untruths, but this one, especially when it is repeated (as it often is) with respect to racial disparities, is particularly pernicious in its consequences.

One consequence is that it perpetuates a fundamental misunderstanding of our capitalistic economic system. That employers will not reward people fairly (according to economic merit) without government forcing them to do so is a clear implication of the Clintons' statements. If we are to continue to enjoy our freedoms and our prosperity, it is important for people to understand what private unregulated markets accomplish. Markets don't always work perfectly, but they do tend to reward people according to their productive contributions, and by implication, markets achieve equal pay for equal work.

Another consequence of accepting these myths is that they are divisive. Believing them, it is easy to conclude that the "system" is a thinly veiled conspiracy structured to benefit white males and to hold all others down. Baseless claims of this sort are common, and there is little doubt that they serve to inflame racial (and gender) relations. They are poisonous to society and to democracy, however many votes politicians can acquire by repeating these falsehoods.

Unfortunately, there is an entire industry composed of people whose livelihoods depend on perpetuating these myths, so they are not likely to disappear in the near future.

Incomes around the World

A news item you did not see in today's news coverage: "More than 20,000 people perished yesterday of extreme poverty." It was unreported not because it didn't happen—it did—but because the event does not qualify as news since it occurs on average every day.[1] Additionally, virtually none of these deaths occur in the United States; almost all occur in third world (i.e., poor) countries, and Americans typically display little interest in what happens in other countries.

Even though the focus of this book is the United States, we can learn a good deal that is relevant to us by examining, albeit briefly, conditions around the world. Inequality and poverty are by no means unique to the United States, and a consideration of the experiences of other countries puts our own problems in a much-needed broader perspective.

INCOMES AT HOME AND ABROAD

The United States is the wealthiest country in the world. Everyone knows that, at least in an abstract way, but few appreciate the magnitude of the gulf that separates living standards of Americans from those prevailing in much of the remainder of the world. To measure living standards for a country, we will use recent (2003) World Bank estimates of average income per capita. More precisely, we will be using gross national income (similar to gross domestic product) per person, a very broad measure of average income.[2]

According to the World Bank, average income in the United States in 2003 was $37,500 per person. For the rest of the world, comprising more than 95 percent of the world's population, average income was $6,760. The average American thus enjoys a standard of living that is *more than five times as great* as that realized (on average) by the 19 out of 20 people on earth who live in other countries. Put succinctly, most of the world is extremely poor by American standards.

Of course, these averages conceal a great deal of variation that exists both among and within individual countries. The United States is not the only wealthy country; there are several others (such as Germany, Japan, the United Kingdom, and France) where incomes stand at roughly three-fourths the level in the United States, and one (Norway) with an average income nearly equal to the United States. If we define *high income* as any country with an average income of at least half the U.S. level, then there are 23 countries that meet this standard. All together, they contain 13 percent of the world's population. Thus, seven-eighths of the people on earth live in countries where the average income is less than half that in the United States.

At the other extreme, there are many countries with incomes much lower than half our level. Among the poorest countries on earth are Ethiopia (average annual income of $710 per person), Malawi ($600), Sierra Leone ($530), and Tanzania ($610). As these examples may suggest, sub-Saharan Africa is the poorest region in the world, with an average income of $1,770 for the 48 countries comprising the region. Thus, the average American has an income that is *more than 20 times greater* than the average African.

The two most populous nations on earth, China and India, are also quite poor, despite rapid improvements (especially in China) in recent years. China's 1.3 billion people have an average income of $4,990. While nearly three times as high as Africa's, China's average income is only about one-seventh of that in the United States. India's 1.1 billion people are poorer still, with an average income of $2,880.

In addition to the great differences (inequalities) that separate the average incomes of nations, there is also substantial inequality of income within each country. When examining inequality within the United States in chapter 2, we used shares of income for quintiles (fifths) of the population, and the associated HiLo ratios, as our preferred measures of inequality. The World Bank also provides estimates of quintile shares of income for most of the world's nations, and we will rely on its estimates here. For the United States, the World Bank gives 5.4 and 45.8 for the lowest and highest quintile shares, implying a HiLo ratio of 8.5. (Recall that the HiLo ratio is the ratio of the top quintile's income to that of the bottom quintile.) Note that this implies less inequality than the unadjusted Census Bureau figures discussed in chapter 2 (where we saw the HiLo ratio to be about 12). There are two technical differences in the ways the World Bank and the Census calculate these ratios that account for the Bank's estimate of less inequality. The differences need not detain us;[3] what matters here is that the World Bank utilizes the same measurement procedure for all countries so the comparisons are meaningful. (However, these quintile estimates are subject to most of the criticisms leveled at the Census estimates in chapter 2, and so these estimates probably overstate economic inequality, though probably to varying degrees for different countries.)

Substantial inequality of incomes characterizes every country in the world, according to the World Bank's figures. There are only two countries in the world (of the more than 130 listed by the Bank) where the share of income received by the lowest fifth of households exceeds 10 percent. They are Japan (10.6%) and the Czech Republic (10.3%). In all other countries the average household in the poorest quintile has an income less than half the national average. At the top of the scale, only one country in the world is reported to have an income share for the top quintile that is under 35 percent: the Slovak Republic with 34.8 percent.

The variation in inequality within most countries is, however, surprisingly great. Let's use the HiLo ratios to get a feeling for the diversity among countries. By this measure, several of the most unequal countries in the world are in Latin America. For example, the highest quintile in Brazil receives *32 times* the income of the lowest quintile (recall that for the United States the ratio is 8.5): The quintile shares are 2.0 and 64.4. Chile, Argentina, and Mexico are not far behind, with HiLo ratios of 18.9, 18.2, and 19.0. But the most unequal country on earth is to be found in Africa. Namibia, where the top quintile receives 78.7 percent of total income and the bottom quintile a miniscule 1.4 percent, has the astounding HiLo ratio of 56.2.

Two other notably unequal societies are Russia and China. Communist China has a HiLo ratio of 10.6, and formerly communist Russia is nearly the same at 10.5, both displaying greater inequality than the United States.

The most equal countries tend to have HiLo ratios around four. Japan, with a HiLo ratio of 3.4, is the most equal society in the world by this measure. Following close behind are some of the welfare states of western Europe and Scandinavia. Norway, Sweden, and Denmark sport HiLo ratios of 3.9, 4.0, and 4.3, respectively. Germany, France, Italy, and the United Kingdom come in at 4.3, 5.6, 6.5, and 7.2.

These examples may suggest as a generalization that the wealthier countries tend not only to have higher incomes but also more equally distributed incomes than poorer countries. As a rough generalization, this may be correct, but there are some notable exceptions. Low-income India has a HiLo ratio of 4.7, while (lower-income) Ethiopia and Rwanda do even better at 4.3 and 4.0.

How does the United States look in comparison to the other countries of the world? Is inequality here noticeably greater? Based on the World Bank data, it appears that the United States stands pretty much in the middle of all countries, with about half the countries displaying higher HiLo ratios and half lower.[4] However, critics of inequality in America tend to emphasize comparisons only with the other high-income countries of the world, especially the European welfare states. From the available evidence, it is true that inequality is greater in the United States than in most of these countries, as the numbers cited above suggest. Do not forget, however, the many defects in this type of data as measures of economic inequality that were spelled out in chapter 2. Inequality in the United States is certainly less than these World Bank quintile shares suggest, but of course that may also be true for the other countries as well. I suspect that more accurate measures of inequality would continue to favor the European welfare states, but the differences would probably not be as great as implied by the differences in HiLo ratios reported here.

In this connection, an important point to keep in mind is that these quintile shares only measure *relative* inequality within a society, and using them in comparisons across societies with differing average incomes can often be misleading. Consider France. According to the World Bank, the poorest quintile in France receives a 7.2 percent share, while the corresponding quintile in the United States receives only 5.4 percent. Nonetheless, because of the higher average income in the United States, Americans in the lowest quintile actually have higher *absolute* incomes than the French who are in their lowest quintile. A smaller share of a bigger pie can imply a higher absolute standard of living.

Indeed, one of the most striking implications of these international comparisons is how well off in an absolute sense even low-income Americans are compared to most of the people in the world. Consider India, a very egalitarian society (HiLo ratio of 4.7), but one with low average income ($2,880). Households in the lowest quintile in the United States actually have incomes that are nearly twice as high as the households in the *highest* quintile in India. That our poor are rich by standards prevailing in most of the low-income countries of the world is not adequately appreciated.

If any further evidence is needed to show how rich Americans (and those in a handful of other high-income countries) are relative to most people in the world, it is provided by the World Bank's tabulation of world poverty. The World Bank uses two income thresholds to estimate the number of world poor. People with income of less than $1 per day are said to be in extreme poverty, while those between $1 and $2 per day are in moderate poverty. (These are *not* the poverty thresholds used to measure poverty in the United States.) Based on these definitions, the World Bank estimated that in 2001, 1.1 billion persons were in extreme poverty and another 1.6 billion were moderately poor. Nearly 45 percent of the people in the world are poor by this very stringent standard!

And it is a very stringent standard, even if we adjust for the fact that it is based on prices prevailing in 1985. The $2 threshold is about $3 per day in 2003 prices.[5] Adjusted for the change in prices, the threshold for poverty is equivalent to an annual income per person of $1,095. For a family of four, this translates to an annual income of about $4,400. To put this in perspective, the poverty threshold for a family of four used by the U.S. government in 2003 was about $18,000. Needless to say, few if any of the persons counted as poor in the United States using our poverty thresholds are poor by the World Bank standard. Yet 2.7 billion people in other countries are.

When next you hear someone agonizing over the plight of hardworking low-income Americans or the struggling middle class, reserve a little sympathy for the majority of people on earth who are so much poorer.

WHY ARE SOME SO RICH?

The vast differences in income levels among the countries of the world cry out for an explanation. Often the question is posed as: Why are some countries so desperately poor? But that is not really the most instructive way to approach the issue. Poverty has characterized most of humanity throughout its history and continues to do so in most countries today; it requires no explanation. The anomaly to be explained is the small number of countries that have in recent generations escaped this fate and become relatively rich. We need to understand how they have done this if the poor countries are ever to escape their present impoverishment.

In approaching this issue, a key insight is provided by the tautology (discussed in chapter 1) that a nation's output (production) *is* the income of its people. They are two sides of the same coin. Rich nations are rich because their citizens produce a lot of goods and services; poor nations are poor because they produce little. Ethiopia is not poor because other nations have appropriated its resources or exploited it; it is poor because Ethiopians produce very little.

What factors, then, are responsible for high output (income) per person in a country? Innumerable factors can plausibly play some role, but economists believe the most important of these can be classified into four categories.

First is the amount of capital per person (or worker). Capital here refers to the productive resources that are employed in conjunction with labor effort to produce goods and services. Capital includes things like buildings, equipment, power lines, computers, roads, and vehicles, all of which obviously contribute to an economy's output. In general, the more capital there is per worker, the higher will be output per worker, and thus the higher incomes will be. The entire stock of capital in the United States is valued at roughly $33 *trillion* (in 2002), so the typical worker's productivity is enhanced because he or she is able to utilize $240,000 worth of capital in their jobs.

The present capital stock of the United States represents the cumulative effects of past investment and saving decisions. Clearly, since the capital stock is nearly three times the total annual output of the economy, and only a small part of that output is capital goods, the accumulation of a large capital stock is a gradual and often slow process. Countries cannot become rich quickly.

Capital and labor cooperate to produce output, so it is natural to look to labor as another factor influencing income levels. Here, what is important is the level of productive skills possessed by workers because more skilled workers are capable of producing more. (Economists sometimes refer to the skills of workers as their *human capital* because, by analogy with physical capital goods, human beings can contribute to production over a period of years.)

Workers' skills are often measured by years of formal schooling completed, but this is admittedly a very imperfect measure because many important skills are acquired on the job. Nonetheless, it is true that rich countries tend to have highly educated workers. The United States, for example, ranks second (Canada is first) in the world in the percentage of the adult population who have completed college, and first in the percentage who have completed high school.[6] While 86.5 percent of U.S. adults have completed high school, only 20.5 percent of Mexicans have, and that is surely one of the reasons for higher incomes in the United States.

A provocative recent contribution to this subject is the book by Richard Lynn and Tatu Vanhanen entitled *IQ and the Wealth of Nations*.[7] As suggested by the title, they propose that IQ plays a role in determining income levels in various countries. Since we have seen that the IQs of individuals within a country influence their productivity and earnings, it would make sense that if nations differ in their average IQs this would affect the average incomes they produce. And Lynn and Vanhanen document substantial differences in the average IQs among nations. While they estimate that the world average IQ is 90, countries of northeast Asia, like Hong Kong (107), South Korea (106), and Japan (105), have substantially higher IQs, in fact, the highest IQs in the world. Next come western European countries (98–102) and the United States (98), with Latin American countries averaging around 85. The countries of Africa have the lowest IQs, averaging around 70. (China's average is given as 100 and India's as 81.)

Lynn and Vanhanen show that the estimated average IQs of nations correlate highly with income levels and the rates of growth in incomes (the correlation coefficient is about 0.7). Garrett Jones and W. Joel Schneider have used the IQ data from Lynn and Vanhanen combined with other variables in the more sophisticated statistical approaches favored by economists.[8] They conclude that "IQ easily outperforms the best-performing measure of human capital [based on schooling, from a widely used dataset]" and that "overall our results indicate that IQ is associated with an economically large and statistically significant increase in growth rates [of average income]."

Needless to say, this work has been largely ignored because it challenges the prevailing egalitarian view that all societies (if not all individuals) have equal potential. It is certainly premature to claim (and I do not) that this work establishes IQ as an important reason why some countries are rich and some are poor. But the preliminary evidence is too compelling to be dismissed, and if we base our expectations and our policies on the possibly mistaken assumption that all human populations are equal, we may be in for some disappointing results.

Ask most Americans why living standards here are so much better than a hundred years ago and you will almost always get some variation of a one-word answer: "Technology." Our so-called high-tech society certainly displays much tangible evidence of the influence of modern technology in our daily lives. Indeed, about three-fourths of the goods and services that Americans consume today did not even exist in 1900. And most of the remaining goods and services (like food) that did exist in 1900 are today produced using vastly improved and more productive techniques that were unknown in 1900.

That technology plays a role in influencing productivity and living standards is palpable. This, then, is our third factor affecting income levels in countries. But the exact way technology may help to enrich a country requires some further consideration. The essence of the contribution technology makes is not its material trappings (the computers and cell phones) but the creation of the knowledge that can be used to produce these life-enhancing things. What matters is the creation of the know-how; the know-how is what technological progress is really all about.

It is important to distinguish the knowledge that makes modern things possible from the corporeal items that embody this knowledge. Although computers benefit only those who possess them and will deteriorate over time, the knowledge of how to build a computer can be utilized by everyone, and the potential value does not decline over time. Technology, in the sense of technological knowledge, is what economists call a public good, capable of benefiting many people simultaneously and where one person's (or country's) use of this knowledge does not deprive another of benefiting from it. (The term *public good* does not mean that the government produces it but refers to the nature of the good itself.)

Thus, the essence of technology's contribution to prosperity is the creation of useful knowledge. It is foremost the creation of this knowledge, and secondarily its subsequent use, that has contributed to (and continues to contribute to) improving our lives. Note that this means that technology does not explain why some countries are rich and some are poor for they all have access to the same body of knowledge. Poor countries are not poor because they lack technology, but (in part) because they have not effectively utilized the existing technology.

Our fourth factor influencing income levels helps to explain why some countries more effectively utilize existing technology. It is a somewhat amorphously defined factor that I will refer to as *policies and institutions*. In large part, policies and institutions refers to the way governments affect income levels through taxation and spending, regulations, and laws. Some government policies help to increase living standards and some tend to reduce them.

Given the enormous variation in government policies, it is not easy to identify precisely what policies are favorable and which are unfavorable. But the evidence is clear that the institutions and policies we associate with capitalism (free markets with limited government interference in the economic actions of people) make a positive contribution to prosperity. No country has ever become rich that did not rely heavily on private markets, and there are numerous examples of countries that have become (or remained) poor following a different approach.

To provide a bit of evidence for this, let us consider the Economic Freedom index constructed by the Fraser Institute of Canada.[9] This index assesses the extent to which the economies of the world are free based on a scale of 1 to 10, with 10 being most free. Generally the more capitalistic an economy is the higher will be its score on the freedom index.

For 2003, an economic freedom index was calculated for 127 countries. Nations in the top quintile in terms of economic freedom have average incomes that are 10 times the levels of countries in the bottom quintile. From the top down, each successively lower quintile on the freedom scale has a lower per capita income. From this it is apparent that capitalistic institutions are associated with high incomes around the world; the correlation is high throughout the ranking. This does not prove causation, of course, but economic theory does explain why a causal connection is expected. Capitalism provides incentives that encourage people to utilize resources effectively and to engage in activities that augment output and incomes.

The United States ranks third in the world on the economic freedom index (with a score of 8.2, tied with Switzerland and New Zealand), slightly behind Hong Kong (8.7) and Singapore (8.5). Relative to other countries in the world, Americans continue to enjoy a wide measure of freedom and of course the tangible benefits (high incomes) it helps to produce.

Another indication of the importance of policies and institutions is provided by the Ease of Doing Business index constructed by the World Bank for 155 countries.[10] This index ranks countries in terms of how favorable a climate they provide for private businesses to operate, based on things like the difficulty of getting licenses and enforcing contracts, and the ease of hiring and firing workers. According to this index, the top 14 (easiest to do business) countries are among the two dozen wealthiest nations, while all 14 at the bottom are among the poorest nations of the world. The United States ranks third in this ranking, behind New Zealand and Singapore. Twelve of the 14 at the bottom of the ranking are in Africa.

Some of the differences in the business climates of countries are striking. In the United States we find that it takes 5 days to start a business (to comply with the laws and regulations); in Venezuela 116 days; and in Mozambique 153 days. (The average for all low-income countries is 65.8 days.) Registering property takes 12 days in the United States, but it takes 74 days in Mexico, 274 days in Nigeria, and 354 in Rwanda. (The average for all low-income countries is 99.6 days.)[11] Because businesses are the institutions that actually produce most of the income, at least in high-income societies, it seems likely that impediments such as these that governments place on businesses in poor countries contribute to their remaining poor.

Among the four factors that influence income levels among countries, some economists believe that this last one, policies and institutions, is the most important of all. For if a country has a well-functioning capitalistic economy, it does not have to take active steps to augment the other three factors (capital per person, skills per person, and technology). Capitalism provides incentives for people to accumulate capital, augment their skills, and use the best available technologies (as well as develop new technology). This is not to say that government can never play a positive role in these other areas but only to suggest that the contributions it can make are likely to be of a second order of importance.

ECONOMIC GROWTH

Ask economists why some countries are richer than others and you will often get a more succinct answer than that given in the last section: They will tell you that the rich countries have experienced a rate of economic growth that is higher and/or sustained over a longer period of time. Focusing on economic growth provides, in fact, a very helpful perspective on the present differences in living standards among countries. *Economic growth,* as we will use the term here, refers to increases in real (adjusted for inflation) income per capita over time because this is the measure of growth that best corresponds to improvements in the material conditions of life.

Most of us have come to take economic growth for granted and find nothing remarkable about the fact that we live so much better than our parents or grandparents. From a historical perspective, however, growth is a comparatively recent phenomenon. Over most of human history, living conditions did not improve from generation to generation. Up to about 1700, as Nobel laureate Robert Lucas pithily summarizes world history, "Living conditions in all economies in the world 300 years ago were more or less equal to one another and more or less constant over time."[12]

All countries were "more or less" equally poor in 1700. Things began to change initially in the United Kingdom, as incomes there commenced for the first time in history a steady and substantial rise, an event emulated soon after in a few other countries. By 1820, some countries were noticeably richer than others. The United Kingdom, the richest country, had average incomes at that time about four times greater than the poorest countries.

Since 1820, most countries in the world have experienced economic growth, but at very different rates. Over the next 180 years per capita incomes in the United States rose at an average annual rate of 1.8 percent. This may seem like a pitifully slow pace of development, but because of the miracle of compound interest it was sufficient to increase incomes in the United States by a factor of 25, making it the wealthiest nation on earth. To put this transformation in perspective, it is interesting to note that Americans in 1820 had lower incomes than Africans do today (and the United States was thought to be a relatively prosperous country at the time).

African nations have also grown since 1820, but the average growth rate has been only 0.7 percent per year. As a result, African incomes are today more than triple the level of 1820, but that, as we have seen, leaves them at the lowest levels in the world now. In 1820, U.S. incomes were less than three times as great as African incomes, but 180 years of slightly faster growth widened the gap to more than 20 to 1. Seemingly insignificant differences in annual growth rates produce stunningly different outcomes over long periods of time.

The transformations effected by economic growth are often dramatic even over shorter periods of time. Consider Taiwan and the Central African Republic. In 1960, the Central African Republic had an income that was nearly 50 percent greater than Taiwan—roughly, $2,500 compared to $1,700 (in 2003 dollars). In 2003, incomes in Taiwan averaged $23,400, more than 20 times the average of $1,080 for the Central African Republic. Taiwan had become much richer over this 43-year period, while incomes in the Central African Republic actually declined by nearly 60 percent. In terms of growth rates, Taiwan's incomes grew at an annual rate exceeding 6 percent a year, while in the Central African Republic incomes declined at a rate of more than 1 percent a year.

A slightly less striking transformation is provided by a comparison of Mexico and Japan. In 1960 these countries had similar incomes—about $5,300 for Japan and $4,700 for Mexico. In 2003, by contrast, incomes in Japan ($28,620) were more than triple the level in Mexico ($8,950). An average rate of growth of 4 percent a year in Japan resulted in incomes there increasing more than fivefold, while Mexico's rate of 1.5 percent a year failed to double its incomes.

Most countries of the world have experienced positive economic growth over the past half century or so (although at different rates), noticeably improving the quality of life for their residents. Tragically, as suggested by the example of the Central African Republic, there are exceptions. Indeed, taking the countries of sub-Saharan Africa as a whole, incomes are now about 11 percent lower than they were in 1974.[13] Nor are examples of negative growth restricted to Africa. Venezuela, for instance, was in 1960 one of the wealthiest countries in the world, with an average income of nearly $9,200 (almost double that of Mexico, and nearly two-thirds that of the United States). Today, thanks to negative economic growth, Venezuelan incomes average $4,740 and stand at half the level of Mexico and an eighth the level of the United States.[14]

There have also been some amazing success stories in the past half century. The so-called Asian Tigers (Hong Kong, Singapore, Taiwan, and South Korea) have metamorphosed from poverty stricken to prosperous during this period. They achieved this miracle by experiencing economic growth at a rate of about 6 percent for 30 or more years. A small number of other countries, such as Japan and China, have also achieved growth rates of this magnitude for several decades.

Such outcomes do, without a doubt, deserve to be called miraculous. At a 6 percent rate of growth a country's average income increases *sixfold* in the course of a single generation (31 years to be precise). That is a larger increase than the United States experienced over the entire twentieth century. At a rate of growth of 1.5 percent, similar to that experienced in the last 30 years by Europe, it takes 120 years for incomes to increase by a factor of six.

As these examples suggest, it is thus possible to explain why some countries today are rich and some are poor in terms of their economic growth rates. Today's rich nations have grown at faster rates, or over longer periods of time, than have the world's poor nations. Thanks to compound interest, even apparently modest differences in growth rates produce vastly different outcomes when they persist for a generation or longer. Appreciation of these points lends credence to a statement allegedly made by economist Robert Lucas: "Once you start thinking about economic growth, it's hard to think about anything else."[15]

All of which brings us to the fundamental questions: Why do some countries grow faster than others? And similarly, what can be done to increase the rate of economic growth of a country? Although complete answers to these questions remain elusive, we have already suggested the broad outlines of what economists know about this matter. In the previous section, I discussed four factors that influence the level of income in a country: capital per person, skill level of the labor force, technology, and policies and institutions. These same four factors, when evaluated as changes over time, are largely responsible for a country's growth rate.

For example, a high ratio of physical capital per person contributes to a high income per person, while a growing ratio of capital per person over time contributes to a growing income. In the same way, increases in the skill level of the labor force over time would be expected, other things equal, to lead to growth in incomes. Technological progress is obviously relevant, and changes in policies and institutions are probably particularly important.

The relative importance of the contributions these four factors make to economic growth is likely to vary from country to country. To see a particularly important implication of this, let us contrast U.S. growth to the rapid advances achieved by the Asian Tigers. Over the last half of the twentieth century, incomes in the United States grew at an average rate of around 2.2 percent per year, producing a tripling of income over this period. In contrast, the Asian Tigers experienced growth rates of close to 6 percent for much of this period, and average income in these countries grew by at least a factor of 10, dwarfing the U.S. achievement.

There is an important lesson in this juxtaposition, and it is *not* that the U.S. economic performance was poor—quite the contrary. U.S. economic growth was quite good *in comparison to other high-income countries of the time*. What made high growth rates possible for the Asian Tigers was that they had much lower incomes than the leading economies at the beginning of the period. Poor countries have an advantage when it comes to growth rates in comparison to the rich countries: They can play catch up.

The key to understanding this is the role played by technology. Rich countries are already using the best available technologies (otherwise they would not be rich), and they must wait for (and possibly produce) future technological progress to benefit further from this source of growth. Judging from the historical record, it is probably impossible for any advanced economy to have economic growth much exceeding 2 percent per year for an extended period because technological progress is not generally that robust. (Of course, economies can grow due to improvements in the other three factors, too, but their contribution is also apparently limited.)

Poor countries, on the other hand, are not now effectively utilizing the technologies already available. They have a backlog of a century or more of technological advances from which to choose; all they need to do is adapt those best suited to their circumstances. That is the reason why poor countries can potentially grow much faster than wealthy countries. Once their incomes approach those in the wealthy nations, their growth rates invariably decline, as the growth rates have with the Asian Tigers.

The Asian Tigers and a handful of other countries have demonstrated that poor countries have the potential to experience much higher growth rates than wealthy countries, and therefore improve the living conditions for their citizens relatively quickly. That is good news for the bulk of the world's population that is still poor today.

POLICIES AND INSTITUTIONS

That government economic policies (policies and institutions) can have a pronounced impact on the material well-being of people is apparent from the experiences of different countries in the twentieth century. Perhaps the most striking evidence is provided by the tragedy of communism.

Communism was ushered onto the world stage by the Russian Revolution of 1917, which led to the formation of the Soviet Union. In the ebbing years of the twentieth century, as many as a third of the world's inhabitants were living under one form or another of communist regime before the collapse of the Soviet Union in 1989–1991.

It may be difficult, and certainly should be embarrassing, to recall the appeal that communism held for many in the noncommunist world a half century ago. Communism made two broad claims, that it would promote greater material prosperity (higher average incomes) than capitalism, and that these incomes would be equally shared by its people. Many in the West approved of these goals and believed the Soviet Union was well on the way to achieving them by the 1960s.

When Nikita Khrushchev pounded the podium with his shoe at the United Nations in 1961 and proclaimed, "We will bury you," he was not threatening nuclear war, rather he was predicting that the Soviet economic model would triumph over Western-style capitalism. At that time, it was widely reported that the Soviet Union was experiencing an extraordinarily high growth rate, often claimed to be as high as 10 percent, that exceeded anything accomplished in the West. At that rate, it was breathlessly reported by many in the media that Soviet incomes would exceed American incomes by the mid-1970s and pull further ahead in the years to follow.

Even as recently as the mid- to late-1980s, when the Soviet Union was on the eve of self-destruction, many respected analysts were proclaiming the economic virtues of Soviet-style central planning. In the 1985 edition of his textbook, economist (and Nobel laureate) Paul Samuelson wrote: "What counts is results, and there can be no doubt that the Soviet planning system has been a powerful engine for economic growth....The Soviet model has surely demonstrated that a command economy is capable of mobilizing resources for rapid growth."

Not to be outdone, economist Lester Thurow wrote in 1989: "Can economic command significantly accelerate the growth process? The remarkable performance of the Soviet Union suggests that it can....Today the Soviet Union is a country whose economic achievements bear comparison with those of the United States."[16]

We now know that the Soviet Union's allegedly strong economic performance was largely a mirage, fueled by overreliance on data provided by the communists themselves. When the Soviet Union finished collapsing in 1991, Russian incomes were between a fourth and a third of those of Americans. By 2003, average income in Russia was less than one-fourth of the American average and was about equal to that in Mexico—testimony to the difficulty of recovering from the consequences of 75 years of bad economic policies.

A single comparison, the United States to Russia, is not sufficient to conclude that capitalism outperforms communism/socialism because the countries differed in other respects than just their economic systems, and these differences may have contributed to the final outcome. But other examples support the same conclusion.

In 1955, incomes in Spain and Poland were roughly similar, with Poland's being about a third higher. Both countries were largely Catholic and had populations of the same size, but Poland had recently come under the control of the Soviet Union. By the time Poland became independent of the Soviet Union in 1989, the average income of its citizens no longer exceeded Spain's but had declined to one-half the level of Spain's.[17] This transformation was produced by communism in just over a single generation.

Perhaps the strongest evidence, however, is provided by the instances where a single nation was fractured by World War II and the Cold War into two parts, one communist and one which embraced capitalism. In this category we have North and South Korea, China and Taiwan, and East and West Germany. In every instance the market-oriented system proved superior, sometimes amazingly so.

At the time of reunification, West Germans had incomes that were about 50 percent greater than East Germans. The East German performance under communism, poor as it was, was apparently the best achieved by any communist regime. North Korea is still communist and estimates place incomes there at about *one-tenth* the incomes in South Korea. In capitalist Taiwan, incomes are about five times greater than in communist China as of 2004, and that is after 20 years in which China has been growing rapidly as a result of adopting some market-oriented reforms. (In 1988, incomes in Taiwan were 10 times greater than in China,[18] a fairer comparison of capitalism and communism.)

Familiar with these examples and other evidence, even some diehard socialists have had to grudgingly admit that capitalism is superior in its economic consequences to communism/socialism. As early as 1989, socialist economist Robert Heilbroner acknowledged: "Less than seventy-five years after it officially began, the contest between capitalism and socialism is over: capitalism has won. The Soviet Union, China, and Eastern Europe have given us the clearest possible proof that capitalism organizes the material affairs of humankind more satisfactorily than socialism: that however inequitably or irresponsibly the marketplace may distribute goods, it does so better than the queues of a planned economy."[19]

What exactly do we learn from this great and tragic "contest" between capitalism and communism/socialism? One hopes that we learn more than just to avoid politicians or ideologies that go by the labels of communist or socialist. Instead, it seems to me that the main lesson, at least in terms of economic effects, is that economic policies and institutions can have momentous consequences for people's material quality of life. Policies matter, and matter a lot, even if citizens may not be cognizant of exactly how these policies affect their lives. Fifty years ago, who would have thought that a "planned economy," dedicated to promoting economic growth, could impoverish a nation in a single generation?

It should be clear that even powerful totalitarian governments cannot significantly increase a country's growth rate, but they certainly can reduce it greatly. There is no doubt that the Soviet Union, and its satellites, used their great power in an attempt to promote faster economic growth and ended up producing slower growth. To look to government to plan or run an economy, rather than relying on the plans and actions of individuals and businesses as coordinated by markets, is a fatal mistake.

Another lesson concerns the dangers of egalitarianism. According to historian Richard Pipes, the "principal objective" of communism was to "enforce equality."[20] There is little doubt that it is the egalitarianism of socialism and communism that attracted many to these ideologies. Today, the major criticism of capitalism is not that it fails to deliver the goods (since the great contest resolved that issue in capitalism's favor), but that it doesn't produce so-called social justice because it distributes its largesse "inequitably or irresponsibly" (to use Heilbroner's phrase). Whatever the merits of this charge, we need to be aware that empowering a government to aggressively promote equality, as presumably communist regimes did and do, can at best lead to equal suffering by rich and poor alike. Egalitarianism is itself an ideology, and potentially as harmful as communism, especially if pushed too far.

While the contest between communism/socialism and capitalism may be over, there continues today a struggle within the wealthy capitalist economies over how far egalitarian policies may be extended without decimating the benefits produced by capitalism. This, the second great contest of the twentieth century, is exemplified by the contrast between the United States and the countries of old Europe. All these countries, including the United States, have welfare states carrying out substantial redistributions of income, but those in Europe are more extensive in scope. Total government spending (most of which is on social insurance or welfare, the components of the welfare state) in many European economies approaches or exceeds 50 percent of their GDPs (with correspondingly high tax rates), whereas in the United States the ratio is significantly lower at about a third.

These differences did not always exist. In fact, the emergence of extensive welfare-state activities is a comparatively recent phenomenon. It was during the period between (roughly) 1960 and 1980 that most wealthy economies vastly expanded their welfare states, producing the differences that persist to this day. In 1960, government spending in the United States, at 27.0 percent of GDP, was quite similar to that in the other high-income countries: The average for 17 high-income countries at that time was 27.6 percent.[21] That was soon to change.

By 1980, government spending in these 17 countries had increased to an average of 43.1 percent, a stunning and unprecedented (except in wartime) 56 percent increase in the share of national income spent by governments in a period of just two decades. In some countries, like Sweden and Belgium, the government share nearly doubled, reaching 60.1 percent in Sweden and 57.8 percent in Belgium. The United States experienced the smallest increase of any of these countries, with its government share rising only from 27.0 to 31.4 percent, leaving it in 1980 with the lowest government expenditure ratio among all these countries. This modest overall increase, however, conceals the expansion of the U.S. welfare state because it coincided with a substantial reduction in spending on national defense. Excluding defense, government spending in the United States rose by 44 percent in this period, from 18.2 to 26.2 percent of GDP. But in the end, the United States did emerge with one of the smallest welfare states (perhaps the smallest) among the wealthy countries, a condition that continues today.

Exactly why all these countries simultaneously chose to greatly expand their welfare states at this particular time is a mystery, but whatever the reasons we now need to evaluate the consequences. The contrast between the United States and western Europe provides the focus for the evaluation.

Between 1980 and 2004, the United States experienced a growth rate (in inflation-adjusted per capita terms, of course) averaging 2.0 percent.[22] France, Italy, and Germany achieved rates of 1.7, 1.6, and 1.6 percent, respectively. Sweden, the poster child for many egalitarians, also experienced a growth rate of 1.7 percent over this period. It is apparent that even expansive welfare states have not forestalled positive economic growth, but we should remember that small differences of these magnitudes can compound over time to substantial differences in the levels of incomes.

To see what these differential growth rates mean for income levels, in 1982 per capita income in France was 84.9 percent of that in the United States; by 2004, the ratio had declined to 74.3 percent. The corresponding relative decline in Italy was from 78.7 percent of the American level to 69.4 percent, and in Germany from 87.9 percent to 71.9 percent.[23] Sweden saw its average income fall from 84.5 percent of America's to 76.4 percent over the period.

As these comparisons suggest, if the apparently small differences in growth rates persist for another generation, families in Europe will have incomes of around half of their American counterparts.

Therefore, it is clear that following the greater expansion of the European welfare states, European incomes have fallen relative to American incomes. Is the decline attributable to the higher expenditures, taxes, and more extensive labor market regulations in Europe? I believe the evidence supports that interpretation, but the differences are perhaps not large enough to support the slam dunk conclusion possible in the comparison between communism and capitalism.

Many advocates of European-style welfare-state policies for the United States argue that the benefits of more expansive policies offset the costs of lower incomes and lower growth. After all, people get greater security, a more leisurely life, and lower (relative, at least) inequality. Whether this trade-off is worthwhile is a decision each person must make for himself, but there is a bit of evidence that suggests many people are less than happy with the consequences of the European welfare states.

In 2004/2005 the Harris polling organization conducted a poll of Americans and Europeans. Among the questions asked was this: "On the whole, are you very satisfied, fairly satisfied, not very satisfied, or not at all satisfied with the life you lead?" That would seem to be the ultimate question about different social systems, at least if we believe people can accurately assess their own lives. Among Americans, 58 percent answered that they were "very satisfied" with their lives. In sharp contrast, only 18 percent of the French answered this way, joined by 21 percent of the Germans and 16 percent of the Italians. (Forty-four percent of Swedes gave this positive response, and the average for the European Union as a whole was 31%.) It is remarkable that Europeans feel this way after decades in which their elites have pontificated about the superiority of their systems over the selfish so-called cowboy capitalism imposed on the unfortunate Americans.

Any comparison between the United States and Europe is handicapped somewhat due to the fact that all the countries have welfare states. It is possible that the United States would have done even better had it not expanded its redistributive policies so greatly over the 1960–1980 period. Much of the remainder of this book investigates the consequence of that expansion in more detail.

But what about the poor countries of the world? What is the solution to their poverty? As I hope is clear, there is no quick fix, but achievement of reasonable and sustained growth rates is evidently the best long-run solution. As we have seen, it is possible for poor countries to grow at rates of 6 percent for at least a generation, as the experience of the Asian Tigers and others have shown. At that rate, income per person doubles in just 12 years, and quadruples in 24 years. Moreover, the historical evidence shows that when average incomes rise due to economic growth, the benefits are generally shared across all income classes. As William Easterly summarizes the findings of a paper by his World Bank colleagues: "A 1 percent increase in average income of the society translates one for one into a 1 percent increase in the incomes of the poorest 20 percent of the population."[24] The poor within any society have as much to gain from economic growth as the wealthy.

Can the richer nations of the world help the poor nations to grow faster? That has actually been the focus of much of the foreign aid dispensed in the last 50 years, and the results don't bode well for the effectiveness of this type of redistribution. Easterly's survey of World Bank efforts to spur growth in poor countries is replete with examples of failure after failure. Between 1950 and 1995, Western countries gave about $1.5 trillion[25] to poor countries in aid, with about one-third of this total going to Africa. Yet, as we have seen, Africans are poorer today than they were in 1974.

We have to face the possibility that the rich nations are rather limited in their ability to help the poor nations to grow faster. Part of the reason is that aid often has to be channeled through the governments of the poor nations, and these governments are often incompetent and corrupt, more interested in solidifying their political power and enriching themselves than developing a vibrant economy. But experience shows that even when the recipient government is well intentioned, we do not know enough to design foreign aid policies that will reliably promote economic growth.

We do know what it takes for a poor country to grow rapidly, if not in detail at least in broad outline. Here is how Michael Mandelbaum summarizes the requirements: "There was, at the end of the twentieth century, a consensus among economists on what is required for economic growth everywhere: a liberal, market-enhancing state that protects property rights and encourages investment; freedom for firms to enter and compete in markets; openness to trade with and investment from the rest of the world; sound monetary and fiscal policies with modest deficits and low inflation."[26] While one may quibble over details, Mandelbaum is certainly correct that capitalism provides the model for a country that wishes to grow.

It is precisely here that the West bears some responsibility for the poverty in the world today: It has not unambiguously and vigorously proclaimed the benefits of free markets and limited government to the world. Indeed, for much of the twentieth century elite opinion in the West was highly critical of capitalism and promoted some version of socialism. Many of the leaders in third world countries today received their educations at Western institutions in which anticapitalist doctrines were routinely taught. It is no surprise that when they returned home and implemented what they had learned their economies suffered.

In this regard, the situation is somewhat better today. Nonetheless, the prevalence of the anticapitalist rants that reverberate through our academic and media institutions continue to send a message to the poor nations of the world that is decidedly counterproductive. Countries that are already rich (thanks to their capitalistic past) can afford a degree of anticapitalism; poor countries do not have that luxury. Fixating on the evils of capitalism, and in particular its defects on distributional grounds, is not likely to lead poor countries to adopt policies and institutions conducive to economic growth.

I cannot do better than conclude this chapter with further wisdom from Nobel laureate Robert Lucas: "Of the tendencies that are harmful to sound economics, the most seductive, and in my opinion the most poisonous, is to focus on questions of distribution. . . . But of the vast increase in the well-being of hundreds of millions of people that has occurred in the 200-year course of the industrial revolution to date, virtually none of it can be attributed to the direct redistribution of resources from rich to poor. The potential for improving the lives of poor people by finding different ways of distributing current production is *nothing* compared to the apparently limitless potential of increasing production."[27]

Poverty

President Lyndon B. Johnson announced the "War on Poverty" in his 1964 State of the Union address. Today we are still fighting that war, and egalitarians for once do not insist that a war must have an exit strategy. This chapter evaluates how we are doing in this apparently never-ending war.

POVERTY: THE OFFICIAL VERSION

Every year the government reports how many Americans are poor. How does the government identify who is poor? The government's official definition of poverty had its origins in a 1965 paper by an analyst at the Social Security Administration, Mollie Orshansky.[1] Orshansky developed a set of "poverty thresholds" based on levels of income below which people were deemed to be poor. These thresholds, or poverty lines, (after some minor adjustments) became the official determinants of poverty status as a result of a Bureau of the Budget directive in 1969. They are still the basis for our measurement of poverty today.

Poverty was conceived by Orshansky to be a level of income too low to purchase the basic material necessities for a decent standard of living. The central ingredient in determining the cutoff income level was the cost of obtaining a nutritionally adequate diet, which was estimated at $1,000 a year for a family of four in the mid-1960s (based on the "economy food plan" developed by the Department of Agriculture). Of course, there are other necessities in addition to food, but no objective way was found (and still doesn't exist today) to identify minimally adequate housing, clothing, transportation, medical care, and other needs. But some allowance clearly had to be made for nonfood items. The expedient that was used relied on actual consumption patterns of American families. In a 1955 survey for the Department of Agriculture, it was found that families devoted approximately a third of their budgets to food. Based on this, the $1,000 poverty level food budget was multiplied by three to obtain a poverty-level total budget of around $3,000. The reasoning seemed to be that if a family had an income of $3,000, they would be spending $1,000 on food, achieving the minimally adequate diet and by assumption, achieving minimal adequacy in terms of other goods and services.

Thus, the original poverty lines were based on two things: the cost of an adequate diet and a so-called food multiplier (the inverse of the share spent on food) to make allowance for other things. Of course, this procedure had to be done for families of different size and structure, so there were a number of different poverty thresholds. (Today there are 48.) The only major change since the 1960s is to adjust for rising prices. The government does not price out the economy food plan today and multiply by three. Instead, starting in 1969, it has simply adjusted the poverty lines upward with changes in the overall price level, using the consumer price index (which, of course, depends on food and other prices). So the poverty line for a family of four[2] (sometimes misleadingly referred to as "the" poverty line) in 2005 was $19,971. Ideally, it represents the same purchasing power as did the $3,223 poverty line for a family of four in 1965.

The arithmetical calculation of the original poverty standards is easy to understand, but does it make sense to define poverty in this way? Trying to identify an income level at which people get enough will always involve making some subjective judgments, but anchoring the poverty threshold to nutritive adequacy, which is more or less (but not fully) objective and scientific, seems reasonable. Having no such standards for nonfood items, however, we should take a hard look at the use of the food multiplier method that was used to adjust the food budget to a total poverty threshold. And it is here that the government analysts appear to have made a major error, an error pointed out by Rose Friedman soon after the first poverty definitions were formulated.[3] There is a logical way to calculate poverty lines from household budget data and a specified food budget, she explained, but the government didn't use it.

Recall that the Agriculture Department's survey found that families devoted one-third of their budgets to food. That was an *average* figure for *all* families in 1955. If *every* family spent exactly one-third of its income on food, then we would know that a family with $3,000 would be consuming $1,000 in food—roughly the amount required for nutritive adequacy. And those with less than $3,000 would not be getting the minimally adequate diet; they would be poor by the objective food standard. However, not all families devote exactly one-third of their budgets to food; the fraction is higher for low-income families and lower for high-income families. So where should the poverty line be set? It should be set at the level of income at which families actually consume the diet costing $1,000. The presumption is that if their income is adequate to place them at the poverty threshold in terms of food, then it is by inference adequate for other goods as well. (There is, in fact, a basis in economic theory for this judgment.[4])

Using the same data that were used to formulate the official poverty lines, Friedman found that families (of four) with incomes of about $2,200 actually achieved the requisite spending on food required by the economy food plan. They were spending nearly half of their income on food at this point, not one-third. She argued, persuasively in my opinion, that if we accept the food standard as the basis for defining a poverty level of income, the poverty threshold should have been $2,200, at which nutritive adequacy is attained, not the roughly $3,000 level established by multiplying the food budget by three. So by setting the poverty line at about $3,000, the government overstated the amount of income required to attain nutritive adequacy by more than 35 percent. Friedman also found that the number of people counted as poor with a $2,200 poverty threshold was only half the number found when using the government's $3,000 threshold.

I don't intend these remarks to demonstrate that the government's original poverty thresholds were too high. Any poverty standard is going to reflect some subjective and more or less arbitrary judgments, and $3,000 (in mid-1960s dollars) seems to me a not-unreasonable standard. Rather, the point I think should be emphasized is that there is no logic to using the *average* proportion of budgets devoted to food as the basis for a multiplier to determine poverty thresholds. One repeatedly encounters people today asserting that if we constructed the poverty thresholds anew today, they would be much higher because Americans now devote about one-sixth of their budgets to food.[5] Multiplying the economy food budget by six yields a poverty threshold of around $40,000, nearly 75 percent of median family income. In a decade or two, when expenditures on food will be an even smaller proportion of budgets, it is likely that following this procedure would yield a poverty threshold greater than median family income.

Understanding the error committed by analysts constructing the original thresholds is important so we don't make the same error again, should we decide to compute a new poverty standard. The *average* proportion of budgets devoted to food tells us nothing concerning the incomes people require to achieve nutritive adequacy.

In the end, any objective standard for measuring poverty is certain to be somewhat arbitrary; recall that the World Bank bases its poverty estimates on poverty thresholds that are much lower than those the U.S. government uses. Whether we think our poverty thresholds are too high or too low, most of the information we have concerning poverty in America is based on these thresholds, so we have little alternative but to use them if poverty is to be discussed.

So how many Americans are poor by this standard? Each year the Census Bureau releases estimates for the previous year, and these represent the official accounting. In 2005, 12.6 percent of Americans had incomes below their respective poverty thresholds. That was 37 million people. And the total poverty numbers can be broken down in many different ways. For example, 12.9 million of the 37 million poor were children (under 18 years of age). The ethnic breakdown among these 37 million poor was: 16.2 million whites, 9.2 million blacks, 9.4 million Hispanics, and 1.4 million Asians.

All these people have incomes below their respective poverty thresholds, but of course some have incomes quite close to the thresholds and others lie far below. Some of the poor are poorer than others, and it is important to keep this in mind. There are, in fact, a surprisingly large number of people with very low incomes. The Census Bureau estimates that 43 percent of the poor have incomes of *less than half* their poverty lines. This is 15.9 million persons, or 5.4 percent of the population. Even if we used poverty thresholds that were half their current values, there would still be 5.4 percent of the population counted as poor.

These few facts give a concise overview of the official portrait of poverty in America. Later, we will want to consider *why* so many are poor, and also how the picture has changed over time. But first, it is important to consider whether these Census estimates are accurate. Are one in eight Americans really poor, and exactly how poor are they?

POVERTY: AMERICA'S WORST STATISTICAL INDICATOR?

For the title of this section, I have appropriated part of the title of a short piece by Nicholas Eberstadt because it seems particularly appropriate for the material discussed here.[6] The central point is that poverty is overstated by the Census Bureau data cited in the last section. There are several reasons for this; most of them are familiar from our discussion of income inequality statistics in chapter 2. We saw there that the conventional data overstate inequality, in part because they understate the standards of living of those with low incomes. Because low income defines poverty status, the points made there are directly applicable to evaluating data on poverty.

Consider first the issue of mobility. Just as there is a lot of turnover among income classes, there is also turnover in the poverty population. Many people who are poor this year will not be next year. A study by Mary Jo Bane and David Ellwood, for example, found that among the nonelderly poor in a given year, 45 percent are not poor a year later.[7] They found that 70 percent leave poverty within three years. (The poverty rate doesn't go down because these people are replaced by others who temporarily have low incomes.)

There are many reasons for short-term poverty, including divorce, having a child, unemployment for whatever reason, and attending school. Most people can cope with a temporary loss of income, so the more serious problems are associated with those who remain poor year after year.

The official poverty rate makes no distinction between short-term and long-term poverty as it is based on income in a single year. Several studies have, however, developed estimates of longer-term poverty rates. Greg Duncan found that only 2.6 percent of the population was poor in 8 of 10 years between 1969 and 1978. Richard Coe defined persistent poverty to occur when a family's income was below the poverty line in every year in the nine-year period from 1967 to 1975, and he found that only 12 percent of the official poverty population satisfied this definition (so the persistent poverty rate would be about 1.5 percent of the total population). More recently, Rebecca Blank used data spanning the period from 1979 to 1991 and found that only 1.5 percent of the population was poor in all 13 years. However, 4.9 percent were poor in at least 10 of these 13 years.[8]

So the number of people who are poor for extended periods of time is much lower than the number counted as poor in each year. The one-year snapshot of poverty, just as of inequality, presents a distorted picture. Yet even within the one-year time frame of most poverty data, there are a number of shortcomings in the way poverty is measured, to which we now turn.

As we have seen, the original conceptualization of poverty was in terms of what people actually consume (the economy food basket plus allowance for other goods). Yet when poverty is actually measured, the poverty thresholds are compared with household incomes, not consumption. Presumably, the reasons for this are that consumption data were generally unavailable in the 1960s, and "the substitution of income for consumption was rationalized by the assumption that the two must be the same for the poverty population."[9] Yet we now know that the low-income population has consumed more than twice its annual income in recent years, as explained in chapter 2. So if the poverty thresholds are compared to actual consumption levels, as they arguably should be, we would expect poverty rates to be lower.

Daniel Slesnick has provided the most detailed estimates of poverty rates based on consumption data. He found that 7 percent of the population would be counted as poor in 1995 if their consumer expenditures (rather than their incomes) were compared to the poverty thresholds.[10] In 1995, the official poverty rate (based on income) stood at 13.8 percent, suggesting that a consumption-based measure cuts the poverty rate in half.

Slesnick further points out that there is underreporting of consumption levels in the household surveys. It has long been known that people underreport their incomes and consumption in these surveys, partly because people are asked in March about their finances over the entire previous calendar year and it is difficult to recall all the pertinent facts with accuracy. Slesnick makes an adjustment for underreporting and finds that the poverty rate (for 1995) using the adjusted estimates of consumption stood at only 1.4 percent—one-tenth the official poverty rate![11]

Is it really true that the official poverty rate overstates poverty to this extent? To evaluate this possibility, let us return to a consideration of defects in the official income-based measure of poverty. The Census Bureau itself recognizes several shortcomings in the official measure of poverty and provides alternative estimates of poverty rates after correcting for them. The two most significant defects in the official poverty count turn out to be not counting many welfare benefits and overstatement of inflation.

Many welfare benefits that the poor receive are not counted as income and therefore do not reduce measured poverty at all. In most cases, this results from the fact that the official definition of the poverty thresholds is in terms of cash income.[12] When welfare benefits like food stamps, housing subsidies, and Medicaid (these are *in-kind* transfers) are received by the poor, they are not considered as income because they are not received as cash. Of course, it is widely recognized that these welfare benefits should be counted: It makes no sense to say that a poor person's income goes up when he is given cash and purchases food, housing, and medical care with it, but that if you give the goods directly to him his income does not go up at all.[13] It turns out that *more than four-fifths* of all government welfare spending is in forms that are simply not counted as income in the official measure of poverty! Counting these benefits as income would increase the measured incomes of the poor and reduce the poverty rate.

The second problem has to do with the way inflation affects the poverty rate. As mentioned earlier, the poverty thresholds are adjusted upward as prices rise; the intention is that they represent unchanged real standards of living. In making this adjustment, it is obviously important that price increases be accurately measured, and the problem is that we know that price increases have been overstated by the inflation measure (the consumer price index, or CPI) the government uses to adjust the poverty thresholds. When the CPI overstates inflation, this also leads to a too large increase in the poverty thresholds. With the poverty lines rising faster than inflation correctly measured, they produce a rising real poverty standard over time instead of an unchanged one. An overstated poverty threshold means, in turn, that too many people are counted as poor.

So on these two counts the official poverty rate is likely to be overstated. As mentioned, the Census Bureau does develop estimates of the poverty rate that attempt to correct for these two (and several other smaller) problems. In 2005, when the official poverty rate was 12.6 percent, the corrected poverty rate was estimated to be 8.2 percent.[14] (In most years, as in 2005, these corrections reduce the estimated poverty rate by about one-third.) This is certainly a more accurate estimate of poverty than the official rate, but as we will see it still overstates poverty significantly.

On the rare occasions that you see anyone cite these Census-adjusted poverty figures, it is implied that these estimates fully correct for the underlying problems. But that is not true. Let's first look at the correction for in-kind transfers, uncounted in the official poverty measures but supposedly accounted for in the adjusted 8.2 percent figure. Several years ago I couldn't believe how little difference this adjustment made to the poverty estimates, so I acquired the underlying data from the Census Bureau. The year was 1989;

in that year the government spent about $136 billion on in-kind programs. What I found was that the Census Bureau counted only $29.5 billion as incomes received from these programs—only 22 percent of spending was counted as income![15]

This enormous undercount of in-kind benefits is due to two factors. First is that many in-kind government transfers (there are dozens of them) are not counted at all—only the easily estimated are evaluated. (In recent years, apparently all medical assistance, like Medicaid, is not counted at all, and Medicaid is the largest welfare program of all.[16]) But a further reason is that the census doesn't count the market value of the in-kind benefit as income; it uses something it calls "recipient value," which is supposed to measure how much the housing, food, or other items are valued by the recipient. If, for example, the government provides a $700-a-month apartment to a poor family, it is not counted as $700 in monthly income but only perhaps $400. I think a good case can be made that the $700 figure should be used, especially because the Census Bureau cannot possibly know how much the family values the housing.[17]

A second reason why the 8.2 percent poverty rate still exaggerates poverty relates to the measurement of inflation. As mentioned above, the Census does make an adjustment for the overstatement of inflation by the official CPI in calculating its 8.2 percent poverty rate. However, the adjustment it makes falls far short of correcting the overstatement of inflation independent economists have found the CPI to involve.

Michael Cox and Richard Alm cite 14 studies by economists that unanimously conclude the CPI overstates inflation.[18] The extent of overstatement estimated ranges from a low of 0.4 percentage points per year to a high of 1.7 percentage points, for an average figure of 1.1 percentage points. This has a significant impact on the measurement of poverty because the poverty thresholds are linked to the CPI, as already discussed. Even though the overstatement may appear very small in a single year, the effects add up over time. For example, if the overstatement is 1.1 percentage points per year over the past 30 years, this implies that today's poverty thresholds are nearly 35 percent higher in real purchasing power than they were 30 years ago. Yet the Census Bureau correction for overstatement of inflation is far smaller than this, so their estimates continue to overstate the number of poor persons if inflation were correctly measured.

A third (and final) reason why the 8.2 percent poverty rate of the Census Bureau overstates true poverty is that the census does not take any account of underreporting of income. That income by low-income families (and other families, as well) is underreported in the census surveys is well established. Bruce Meyer and James Sullivan cite several studies supporting this conclusion. Based on their own research, "We present strong evidence that income is under-reported with substantial error, especially for those with few resources....[Other comparisons] show that government transfers and other income components are severely under-reported and the degree of under-reporting has changed [increased] over time."[19] We do not know, of course, exactly how much this affects the poverty rate.

We cannot be sure what the poverty rate would be if it were corrected for these three issues; to determine the real poverty rate with any accuracy would require a major research effort that probably only the Census Bureau has the resources to undertake. But it should be apparent from the above discussion that the Census-adjusted poverty rate of 8.2 percent is a substantial overstatement of the amount of real poverty.

My own conjecture (based on some indirect evidence)[20] is that if the census figures were corrected for the three problems discussed here, the final poverty rate would be in the range of 1 to 3 percent. Thus, to answer the question posed earlier (whether the true poverty rate could really be as low as 1.4 percent), that appears to me to be eminently plausible. Moreover, recall that the adjustments discussed here relate to the one-year income-based measure of poverty. Using consumption instead of income, or basing the poverty rate on persistent long-term poverty, would produce an even lower poverty rate.

It should be clear by now that the official poverty rate bears no resemblance to reality, presenting a vastly exaggerated view of the number of people with very low standards of living. In short, I concur with Nicholas Eberstadt's judgment that the official poverty rate may be "America's Worst Statistical Indicator" (though the "income shares" approach to measuring inequality is perhaps as bad). In arriving at this conclusion, let me emphasize that I am conceiving poverty as the absolute (real) standard that was the basis of the government's original definition of poverty. If one thinks that norm was too low then, or is too low by today's standards, then one may well conclude that a good deal of poverty exists in America today. No one denies that the 12.6 percent of the population the government identifies as poor have standards of living well below that of the typical American family. But before we redefine poverty, we should acknowledge that poverty as conceived when Johnson declared the War on Poverty has been largely eradicated.

It is interesting that neither the political left nor political right is particularly interested in publicizing this accomplishment. On the left, I suspect that the motivation involves a fear that the American public would be less sympathetic to increased spending on welfare (which the left wants) if it knew the truth. On the right, the motivation may be they do not wish to suggest that some government welfare programs may have actually worked.

How Poor Are the Poor?

Many readers, I suspect, will not find these arithmetical manipulations particularly convincing. They obviously do not convey what the living conditions experienced by the poor are really like. How poor are the 12.6 percent of the population the government classifies as living in poverty? Some indications are provided by the following facts, all based on government studies of those officially defined as living in poverty:[21]

- Forty-six percent of those classified as living in poverty own their own homes. (Sixty-five percent of all Americans are homeowners.) The average home owned by the poor is a three-bedroom, one-and-a-half-bath home with a garage. The median value of homes owned by the poor was $86,000 in 2001 (70% of the median value of all homes in America).
- More than two-thirds of the poor occupy housing with more than two rooms per person. Only 5.7 percent of the poor live in overcrowded conditions, defined as having more than one person per room.
- Seventy-six percent of the poor have air conditioning. (Thirty years ago, only 36% of all Americans had air conditioning.)
- Nearly three-fourths of the poor own a car or truck. Thirty percent of poor households own two or more vehicles.
- Ninety-seven percent of the poor have a color television. (Twenty-five percent have a large-screen TV.) More than half the poor have two or more color TVs.
- Seventy-three percent of the poor own a microwave oven.

These facts suggest that serious material deprivation is not widespread among those counted as poor.

There is also a good deal of information available concerning the food consumption and nutrition of the poor. Because the original poverty standard was based on nutritive adequacy, it is worthwhile considering food and nutrition. According to Robert Rector and Kirk Johnson, "the average consumption of protein, vitamins, and minerals is virtually the same for poor and middle-class children and, in most cases, is well above recommended norms. Poor children actually consume more meat than do higher-income children and have average protein intakes that are 100 percent above recommended levels." Rector and Johnson go on to report a survey of the poor that found "89 percent of poor households reported they had 'enough food to eat' during the entire year, although not always the kinds of food they would prefer. Around 9 percent stated they 'sometimes' did not have enough to eat because of a lack of money to buy food. Another 2 percent of the poor stated that they 'often' did not have enough to eat due to a lack of funds."

If we interpret these self-reported beliefs by the poor that they have enough food to eat as implying nutritional adequacy (which, of course, they may not), we can use the finding that 11 percent of the poor sometimes or often don't have enough to eat to calculate the percentage of the population that doesn't get a nutritionally adequate diet all the time. Remember that this is 11 percent of the poor, and because the poor are 12.6 percent of the population, this means that 1.4 percent of the total population sometimes or often have an inadequate diet. If we use the stricter standard based on those who often don't have enough food to eat, we would calculate a poverty rate of one-fourth of 1 percent (2% of 12.6%).

Actually, an overabundance of food seems to be a more common problem for the poor. As Douglas Besharov observes, "about 65 percent of all Americans are overweight, and nearly half of those are obese. The best estimates place the rates for the poor at 5 to 10 percentage points higher. Adolescents from needy families are twice as likely to be overweight." He goes on: "Although there is still some real hunger in America, it is found predominantly among people with behavioral or emotional problems, such as drug addicts and the dysfunctional homeless."[22] It is not due, in other words, to a lack of financial resources.

These findings certainly suggest that inadequate nutrition is extremely rare in America, buttressing our conclusion that material poverty has been largely eradicated.

THE CAUSES OF POVERTY

Having just argued that true poverty is very rare, it may seem almost superfluous to try to identify its causes. But in this section, I will be discussing the reasons why the *official* poverty population (12.6% of the population in 2005) have the low incomes that they do. Whether one views this figure as an overstatement of real poverty, it is undeniable that these 37 million people have incomes well below those of typical Americans. It is also arguable that they are the poorest 12.6 percent of the population, so why they have this status is worth investigating.

As explained in chapter 1, for most Americans, earnings is the largest source of income, and (apart from government transfers) this is particularly true for the poor. So we begin by considering the earnings and earnings opportunities for those with limited skills. In this context, it is often argued that the minimum wage is inadequate to support a family above the poverty line. At $5.15 in 2005, a minimum-wage job will yield a full-time worker (2,000 hours per year, or fifty 40-hour weeks) an income of $10,300. This is above the poverty line for a single person ($9,973), but it is significantly below the poverty line for a three- ($15,577) or four-person ($19,971) family. From this, many conclude that unskilled workers earn so little that they cannot support their families with an income above the poverty threshold.

Despite its plausibility, this line of argument is largely specious. And I don't mean just because it ignores the fact that a minimum-wage worker, if he or she has two children, can receive about $2,700 in food stamps and $4,300 in cash via the Earned Income Tax Credit (which would result in an income above the poverty line for a family of three, although neither of these transfers is counted in determining official poverty). The important point is that the minimum wage is not the relevant wage for most of the poor. Most of those who receive the minimum wage are not poor, and most of the poor who work receive more than the minimum wage, as we will document in chapter 8.

So how can we evaluate the jobs and job opportunities available for poor workers supporting families? I suggest that the best indicator is the median annual earnings of male high school dropouts over the age of 25 who work full-time. That figure for 2005 was $27,189. This is 36 percent above the poverty line for a family of four, and indeed is above the poverty line for a family of six ($26,683). For a married couple, both high school dropouts and each earning at the median level (the median for women is $20,125), the combined earnings would be $47,314, nearly 85 percent as much as median family income, and 2.4 times the poverty threshold for a family of four.

That the American economy provides these job opportunities for such unskilled workers is amazing. And high school dropouts are very unskilled. They have IQs averaging around 85,[23] and most are functionally illiterate.[24] Yet in America they can earn above most of the poverty thresholds.

High school dropouts can earn above most of the poverty thresholds, if they work full-time. And that brings us to the most fundamental cause of poverty: Most of the poor do not work full-time and, indeed, do not work at all. In 2005, among poor adults (aged 18–64), 56 percent did not work at all during the year, 30 percent worked part-time, and only 14 percent worked full-time.[25] With only one in seven of the poor working full-time, the very concept of the "working poor" is nearly an oxymoron. "The Nonworking Poor in America," to use the subtitle of Lawrence Mead's book,[26] is a more apt description of poor adults today, and the lack of work explains why so many Americans have incomes below the poverty thresholds.

Why do so many of the poor work so little, or not at all? There can be, and are, many legitimate and understandable reasons. But some common explanations favored by egalitarians don't work. Mead describes these fallacious explanations as: "The first theory proposes that the poor earn such low wages that there is little point in their working...; the second, that they are barred from work by a lack of jobs...; the third, that jobs exist but there are other 'barriers' to employment such as racial bias or a lack of child care."[27] Mead devotes an entire chapter to each of these hypotheses and presents convincing evidence that they are largely untrue. Our own discussion will be much briefer, though the reader is referred to Mead's book for a fuller treatment.

That high school dropouts have such (relative to poverty thresholds) high *actual* earnings disposes of the first theory above, and our discussion of discrimination in chapter 3 disposes of part of the third theory (see Mead on the child care issue). That leaves the "lack of jobs" theory. To an economist, this is simply nonsense. Labor markets work, as we explained in chapter 1, to produce jobs for all those seeking employment at wages commensurate with their skills. We actually have direct evidence bearing on this from the poor themselves. Each year the Census surveys poor nonworkers for the main reason why they didn't work. In 2005, among nonworking poor adults, only 6.2 percent gave "could not find work" as a reason for nonwork.[28] Thus, it is not a "lack of jobs" that explains nonwork among the poor.

Other reasons for nonwork given by the poor are "ill or disabled" (32.8%), "retired" (9.2%—recall that this is among those under age 65), "home or family reasons" (31.1%), and "school or other" (21%). Whether these reasons justify nonwork by the poor is moot (surely illness or disability can), but the main point is that freely chosen nonwork (or working only part-time) is a major cause of poverty. To underscore the importance of work in alleviating poverty, Isabel Sawhill presents the following scenario: "First take every family where there is at least one adult who is not too old or sick to work. Next assume that that adult is employed full-time at a wage commensurate with his or her education and experience. Under this assumption, almost half of those who are currently below the government's official poverty line would not be poor."[29]

In addition to work behavior, several other factors contribute to the likelihood that a family will be poor. Lack of education, or, more precisely, lack of skills that we think education should provide, is an important cause of low incomes and hence poverty, as we discussed in chapter 1. The poverty rate for those without a high school diploma (and over 25 years of age) was 23.8 percent, more than double the rate for those who completed high school (10.8%).[30] (Of course, this means that more than three out of four high school dropouts are not poor, which is related to the earnings figures cited above.)

Family structure is perhaps an even more important factor related to poverty. Among families with children who are poor (21.6 million persons in 2005, about three-fifths of the total number in poverty), more than 60 percent are in single-parent households, most of which are female-headed households. More than half of all poor persons in families with children are in female-headed households, and the poverty rate among female-headed households was 38 percent in 2005—about five times the rate for married-couple families (7.4%).

Within the category of female-headed families, it is important to distinguish between divorced and never-married mothers. Poverty is far more prevalent among never-married mothers. Nearly half (47%) of the children in families with a never-married mother are poor, roughly double the rate (25%) for children in families with a divorced mother.[31] Not only are never-married female-headed households more likely to be poor, they also stay poor longer; persistent poverty is higher among never-married households, whereas divorced mothers escape poverty more quickly.

In addition to the structure of the family, the size of the family is also relevant. Families with large numbers of children are more likely to be poor. Indeed, among the 21.6 million people in poor families with children, more than 10 million are in families with three or more children, and more than one in five are in families with four or more children.[32]

Data of the sort reported here have convinced many that most (but certainly not all) poverty is the result of the behavioral choices made by people. Do certain things, and you are likely to be poor; do other things, and you are unlikely to be poor. Here is the way Senator Joe Lieberman put it during his campaign for the Democratic presidential nomination in 2004: "Experts tell us that you need only do three things in this country to avoid poverty: finish high school, marry before having a child, and marry after the age of 20. Seventy-nine percent of people who fail to do this are poor."[33]

The 20 members of the Working Seminar on Family and American Welfare Policy express the same conclusion as: "The probabilities of remaining involuntarily in poverty are remarkably low for those who: complete high school; once an adult, get married and stay married (even if not on the first try); stay employed, even at a wage and under conditions below their ultimate aims. Those who do these three traditional things may experience periods in poverty but are quite unlikely to stay involuntarily poor."[34] But I think the most concise and trenchant formulation of the same idea is probably by Sawhill: "Those who graduate from high school, wait until marriage to have children, limit the size of their families, and work full-time will not be poor." She goes on to point out that "the poverty rate for those households where the primary wage-earner had finished high school, was married, had no more than two children, and worked full-time . . . was trivially small—1 percent."[35]

In pointing out that much poverty results from behavioral choices concerning schooling, work, family, and children, I run the risk of committing the heresy that has come to be known as "blaming the victim."[36] Although *blame* is not the term I would use, I do believe that bad choices made by people do cause a large portion of measured poverty. (But certainly not all poverty—recall, for example, that 33 percent of the nonworking poor [that's 3.8 million people] say that illness or disability is the reason for not working.) Egalitarians prefer to believe that poverty itself causes these self-destructive behaviors. As Sawhill points out, "most of the academic community has coalesced around the view that bad behaviors are a consequence, rather than a cause, of poverty."[37]

Given the diversity of the human condition, it may certainly be true that poverty sometimes contributes to counterproductive behavioral decisions. But to believe that this is the whole story is something that only the "deep thinkers" in academe could conjure up. It takes a vivid imagination to believe that poverty causes people to drop out of school, have children out of wedlock, and not work, rather than believing that these behaviors cause poverty. As we saw in the last two sections, poverty as originally conceived (lack of material resources) has been largely eliminated in America, yet these dysfunctional behaviors have in most instances actually increased.

POVERTY, RISING OR FALLING?

Our examination of poverty to this point has been based on recent data, trying to get an understanding of poverty as it exists today. Here, the focus changes to a consideration of the trends in poverty over time. Once again, we will begin by considering the official poverty rate and then look at how the picture differs when a corrected measure is used.

Although the official estimates of poverty begin with 1959, we do have retrospective estimates that go back further in time. Thus, in 1939 it is estimated that fully two-thirds of all Americans had incomes below the thresholds established in the 1960s.[38] By 1950, the poverty rate had declined to 30 percent and then further to 22.3 percent in 1960 and 12.6 percent in 1970. Over these 30 years, poverty declined steadily and substantially by the official measure, but that was soon to change. Since 1970, there has been no significant change in the poverty rate at all. In 1980 the rate stood at 13.0 percent, and then at 13.5 percent in 1990, 11.3 percent in 2000, and finally at 12.6 percent in 2005. There were some minor ups and downs from year to year in this period, but it is reasonably accurate to say that the official poverty rate has not changed *significantly* since 1970 (or even 1968, when it was 12.8%).

Anyone familiar with the downward trend in poverty in the early years would have confidently predicted, when Johnson declared the War on Poverty in 1964, that poverty would be eliminated by the mid-1970s. That obviously didn't happen, and the question is why. Specifically, why did poverty decline sharply in the 1939–1970 period and then stop declining altogether?

The progress in the earlier period is easily explained: It was due to economic growth. Economic growth means increases in *real* income per capita and with a fixed real poverty standard more and more people realized incomes above the thresholds. Rising real wage rates were the tangible embodiment of this growth; people earned more and escaped poverty. It is notable that government welfare spending played little or no role in the reduction in poverty in this period. Welfare spending as a percentage of GDP was under 1 percent throughout the 1950s and until the mid-1960s; it was not growing and so could not have contributed (directly, at least) to declining poverty.[39] The whole story for this period is economic growth.

What happened, then, after the late 1960s to bring this progress to a halt? This is not so easy to explain. Economic growth has continued, albeit at a slower rate. Even so, today's real income per capita in the United States is more than double the level of 1970. In addition, welfare spending has increased dramatically. Today it is about 5 percent of GDP, compared to under 1 percent in the earlier period. And spending on Social Security and Medicare (not counted as welfare programs) has also expanded greatly. In view of these changes, it is hard to see why poverty did not continue to fall after 1970.

But some things have changed that, taken by themselves, have acted to increase poverty rates and offset (apparently completely) the positive effects noted above (economic growth and increased government spending). I will mention four factors that, taken together, provide a pretty good explanation of why the poverty rate is no lower today than 40 years ago.

First, as we discussed in more detail in chapter 2, the economic growth that has occurred since 1970 has not increased the real wages of all workers in the same proportion. Specifically, the real wages of unskilled workers have lagged, either increasing modestly or perhaps not at all (depending on the specific time period and which inflation measure is used to convert nominal to real wages). That means that the type of economic growth we have had has not been as effective in improving living standards at the bottom as was economic growth in the earlier period.

Second, there has been a major change in the demographic composition of society. Most important is the growth in female-headed households. In 1960, only 9 percent of children were in families with a single parent. By 2003, 27.6 percent of children were in single-parent families, and 83 percent of those were in female-headed families. Because female-headed families have a poverty rate that is nearly five times that for two-parent families, when you have fewer two-parent families and more female-headed families, the overall poverty rate tends to rise (unless offset by other changes, of course). The reason for this demographic change is, of course, the increases in divorce and illegitimacy that have occurred.

Third, there has been a decline in work by members of lower-income households. Among households in the lowest quintile in 1960, two-thirds of the household heads were working (not all full-time). By 2005, the proportion who worked had fallen by nearly half, to 36 percent; only 14 percent worked full-time, year-round.[40] Obviously, economic growth (increasing real wages) does not increase the earnings of those who do not work.

Finally, the surge in immigration in recent decades has put upward pressure on the poverty rate. It does so in two ways. It does so directly by increasing the number of unskilled persons in the labor force whose earnings are not enough to raise them above the poverty thresholds. (Today, roughly 20 percent of the poor are in immigrant households.[41]) Immigration indirectly increases the poverty rate by reducing wage rates for native American workers and thereby lowering their earnings.

These four factors together, in my judgment, explain why the poverty rate has not declined despite economic growth and increased welfare (and Social Security) spending. What requires further consideration is whether some of these factors may themselves be the result of the increase in welfare spending, a matter we take up in the next chapter.

But, as we have seen, the official poverty rate overstates the true poverty rate by a large margin. Indeed, by my estimates, in recent years a corrected poverty rate would be extremely low, perhaps 1 to 3 percent. What would the trend in such a corrected poverty rate look like? We don't really know, but we can make a pretty good guess by considering how the three main defects in the official rate (uncounted transfers, inflation adjustment of the thresholds, and underreporting) would have distorted the official poverty rate in the mid-1960s. At that time spending on uncounted transfers was very small (the major in-kind programs didn't even exist), so that source of bias is minor. Similarly, no inflation adjustment is required for the first year (1963) because it is only rising prices over time that are at issue. That leaves only underreporting to bias the early poverty measures, and that problem was less severe then than now because the largest underreporting is in transfers, which were small at the time.

Consequently, the official poverty rate probably overstated true poverty to a very small degree in the early years. (That is also true for the retrospective estimates before the 1960s.) So the official poverty rate has become increasingly unreliable over time, measuring fairly accurately in the 1960s but greatly exaggerating poverty today. The true poverty rate has certainly declined over the period since 1970, and this is in large part due to the increased welfare and Social Security spending that has occurred.

Has the War on Poverty been won? In terms of eliminating material hardships as identified in the original poverty thresholds, I have argued that it largely has. But this success has been achieved by making a large portion of low-income families heavily dependent on government for their material needs. I estimate that about 75 percent of the total income of the lowest quintile of households comes from government (when in-kind transfers are counted). Without those transfers most of these households would be poor. Is this dependence on government to be counted as a victory in the War on Poverty?

The Census Bureau publishes yet another (unofficial) estimate of the poverty rate that is of interest here. This is the rate that counts only the market incomes (earnings and capital income) and identifies how many are poor (relative to the official thresholds) based on their own resources. That rate was 21 percent in 1965; it is still virtually unchanged at 18.9 percent in 2005.[42] By the standard of how many people earn enough to be nonpoor, we have made virtually no progress since 1965.

This suggests a fundamental question: What do we wish to achieve with government antipoverty policy? If our goal is only to make sure everyone has material goods and services in adequate amounts (as poverty is officially conceived), then our policies have succeeded. But if our goal is for people to be self-supporting and independent through their own efforts, then there has been little progress made at all. Indeed, as we will see, government welfare-state policies may well be responsible for the lack of progress in reducing poverty in this sense.

Our Trillion Dollar Welfare System

In this and the following chapters, our focus shifts to an examination of the government policies that transfer resources from some people to others. Of course, we have touched on some implications of these policies in earlier chapters, especially regarding how they affect measures of poverty and inequality. But now we want to consider more carefully how the policies operate, what consequences they have, and whether alternative policies might produce better results.

This chapter deals with the U.S. welfare system. To many people, *welfare* means a single program, Temporary Assistance for Needy Families (TANF, formerly known as Aid to Families with Dependent Children, or AFDC). Actually, that program is not the only, and is far from being the largest, welfare program in the United States The authoritative *2004 Green Book* identifies 85 separate programs that "provide cash and noncash aid that is directed primarily to persons with limited income."[1] These programs, together with Social Security, Medicare, and public schools, constitute the welfare system in the United States.

We begin by examining how much is transferred to low-income persons through these programs.

How Generous (or Stingy) Are We?

Egalitarians continually complain that Americans don't do enough to help those with low incomes. Are they correct? Let's look at the facts.

In 2005, total (federal, state, and local government combined) expenditures on the 85 welfare programs listed in the *2004 Green Book* were $620 billion.[2] (Of this total, about 70% was financed by the federal government.) Is this a miserly sum? On the one hand, it is only 5 percent of our nation's total income (GDP); on the other hand, it is larger than total spending on national defense ($495 billion) or on public schools ($472 billion).

Perhaps a more appropriate sort of comparison is to relate the $620 billion expenditure to the size of the problem it is intended to deal with: poverty. In 2005, the official poverty count was 37 million persons. Expenditure per poor person thus turns out to be $16,750. For a poor family of three persons (the average poor family has 3.4 persons), welfare expenditures are over $50,000, more than triple the poverty line for a family of three in 2005 ($15,577). Apparently, we are spending more than enough to completely eliminate poverty, even if the poor have zero earnings or other sources of income on their own.

This raises an obvious question: How can we be spending so much and still have 37 million poor persons? One answer, beloved of conservatives, is that the welfare bureaucracy siphons off most of these funds and they never reach the intended beneficiaries. Administrative costs are included in the $620 billion figure, and it is true that the resources available to help the poor are therefore less than suggested by the total outlays. However, administrative costs are not as large as many believe. The largest program of all, Medicaid, has administrative costs of only 4 percent of outlays. Overall, I estimate that administrative costs are no more than 10 percent of total outlays on these programs.

There are two other reasons that, together with administrative costs, explain the coexistence of these huge outlays (in relation to the number of poor) and continued poverty. One is that many of these programs provide benefits to people whose incomes, while low, are above the poverty thresholds. The other reason is perhaps more important, and we have already discussed it in the previous chapter. It is that most of these programs provide benefits to recipients that are not counted as income when the government counts the poor. In fact, only about 15 percent of this $620 billion is in the form of cash assistance that gets counted as income when the official poverty rate is estimated.

So it turns out not to be paradoxical that we have large welfare spending (relative to the number of poor persons) and still have many counted as poor. Of course, a proper count, as we explained in the previous chapter, would find very few truly poor persons.

This $620 billion figure actually understates the resources transferred to the low-income population because it considers only those expenditure programs that meet the definition of welfare. A welfare program is one that provides benefits *only* to those with low incomes. They are sometimes referred to as means-tested programs, implying that you must have limited means to qualify for benefits. But the poor also receive benefits from other policies that are not means-tested. Prominent among these programs are public schools, Social Security, and Medicare. Low-income households receive benefits (at taxpayer expense) from these programs, but they are not considered welfare programs because benefits do not go only to those with low incomes.

What share of the benefits from these three programs goes to those with low incomes is not so straightforward to determine, but I give my rough estimates below. For Social Security, Medicare, and public schools, these figures are the benefits received by the lowest-income quintile, *not* total spending on these programs.[3] I also include two other sources of benefits accruing to low-income persons, namely, private charity and uncompensated medical care for the uninsured. Here are the figures for 2005:

Social Security	$100 billion
Medicare	$115 billion
Public schools	$105 billion
Private charity	$78 billion
Uncompensated medical care	$40 billion

These programs therefore contribute in total some $438 billion a year in benefits to those with low incomes. Combined with the welfare programs discussed earlier, the grand total is just over $1 *trillion*. To be conservative, let's say that each year Americans transfer roughly a trillion dollars in resources to those in need. This, then, is our trillion dollar welfare system.

If this sum were divided equally among the 20 percent of the population (60 million persons, larger than the lowest quintile) with the lowest incomes, each person would receive about $17,500. Coincidentally, a trillion dollars equals the total before-tax money income of *middle-income households* (the aggregate income of the middle quintile of households, according to the Census Bureau)! It is difficult to see how transferring this amount to the low-income population could be characterized as inadequate, but that's how egalitarians view it.

A different perspective is afforded by considering the size of the cost for those who pay for this transfer. Most of this cost is borne by those in the upper half of the income distribution who pay most of the taxes (as we will see in chapter 9). A $1 trillion cost shared among the 57 million households in the upper half of the income distribution amounts to a cost of $17,500 per household. A trillion dollars is also slightly larger than the total revenue collected by the federal income tax, which was $927 billion in 2005. So if you think of your cost as roughly equal to your total federal income tax liability, on average you would be correct.

The commitment of resources to provide benefits to those with low incomes at taxpayer expense is sizeable by any reasonable standard. What results do we get from this expenditure? We will discuss Social Security and Medicare in the next chapter, but the remainder of this chapter is devoted to an examination of the narrowly defined welfare programs that provide benefits only to those with low incomes.

How Welfare Programs Work

No one understands fully how the welfare system operates; it is just too complicated. There are six major programs and scores of smaller programs. Knowing how these individually work is difficult enough, but when we recognize that many welfare recipients receive benefits from several policies simultaneously and that interactions among the program rules must be evaluated, the impossibility of a complete or succinct description is apparent.

There is a way, however, of getting a reasonable overview of this system that helps us identify the major issues and consequences. It is based on the fact that almost all welfare programs share one common characteristic: Most welfare programs give larger benefits to those with fewer resources of their own (i.e., lower earnings). For example, a family with $10,000 in earnings might receive $5,000 in welfare assistance, but a poorer family with only $2,000 in earnings would be given more, say $10,000. Most people regard giving more assistance to those who are poorer as required for fairness, which is probably why so much of our welfare system operates like this.

Understanding the implications of this sort of arrangement takes us a long way toward fathoming what sorts of consequences are produced by our welfare system. The key thing to appreciate is the significance of the rate at which welfare benefits are reduced when a family's own earnings is increased. Suppose that when the family's own earnings increases by $1,000, the welfare benefit it receives is reduced by $400. That means that the reward for the family increasing its effort to earn an additional $1,000 is only an increase of $600 in its disposable income. Clearly, this is going to have an impact on whether the family feels it is worthwhile to make the effort to earn the extra $1,000; its incentive to work harder or longer will be guided by the net addition to its income ($600) rather than by how much its paycheck rises.

Economists refer to the rate at which welfare benefits are reduced when earnings rise as the *marginal tax rate* of the welfare program. Of course, the welfare program is not a tax, but the rate of benefit reduction has similar consequences to the marginal tax rates contained in the federal income tax. In the above example, for instance, the net effect of earning an additional $1,000 is the same whether the welfare benefit is reduced by $400 or the extra earnings are taxed at 40 percent and the welfare benefit unchanged; either way, net income rises by $600.

As this example may suggest, a critical feature of welfare programs is how fast benefits are reduced as earnings rise, that is, how high the implicit marginal tax rate is. For instance, if the marginal tax rate is 80 percent, then earning an extra $1,000 only increases disposable income by $200. That clearly would give the family less incentive to increase its own earnings than in the case when the marginal tax rate is 40 percent.

With this background, let's look at how the actual U.S. welfare system operates. To do this, it is important to consider all the transfers received as well as taxes paid because many low-income families receive benefits from multiple welfare programs and also pay taxes on any earnings. I will focus on one example constructed by economist Aaron Yelowitz,[4] which is itself based on an example provided by the government's authoritative *Green Book*. The example is constructed to reflect how the welfare (and tax) system affects a mother with two children living in Philadelphia, Pennsylvania, in 1996. (Unfortunately, the *Green Book* stopped updating this example after the 1996 welfare reform, so the example is based on 1996 data. However, the situation today is not greatly different since the welfare reform affected primarily only one welfare program, Aid to Families with Dependent Children.)

This Pennsylvania family is eligible for assistance from five of the six largest (in terms of total expenditures) welfare programs: Medicaid, food stamps, housing assistance, Aid to Families with Dependent Children (now called Temporary Assistance for Needy Families, or TANF, after the 1996 welfare reform), and the Earned Income Tax Credit (EITC). It might, of course, also be eligible for benefits from some of the fourscore smaller programs, but they are ignored in this example. If this family had no income of its own, it would receive a combined total of $19,217 (evaluating the benefits at their market value). Note that although this is comfortably above the $12,516 poverty line for a family of three in 1996, this family would be counted among the official poor because only one of the welfare benefits it receives is counted as income. These welfare programs effectively place a floor of $19,217 under incomes, and for that reason the $19,217 figure is sometimes referred to as a guaranteed income.

Now suppose the mother earns $5,000 (about half-time work at the minimum wage). She would receive *larger* benefits under the EITC,[5] but the family would then lose benefits under AFDC, food stamps, and housing assistance (Medicaid benefits are unchanged). The mother would also have to pay Social Security payroll taxes on her earnings and incur some work expenses. The net effect would be that her disposable income rises from $19,217 to $20,730, or only by about $1,500 when she earns $5,000. Her *effective* marginal tax rate (combining the rates in the individual programs) over this range is thus around 70 percent.

Now let us assume this working mother increases her earnings from $5,000 to $10,000 (roughly, a full-time job at the minimum wage). She will gain a larger benefit from the EITC but lose some of her food stamp and housing benefits and all of her AFDC and Medicaid benefits (she is now above the cutoff point for these programs, sometimes called the break-even income levels), plus pay additional taxes and incur additional work expenses. The net effect: she now has disposable income of $18,253, less than she had when she earned only $5,000 and even less than when she didn't work at all! Her effective marginal tax rate over the $5,000–$10,000 range is over 100 percent. If a minimum-wage job is the best she can do, she has little (or no) incentive to work.

If she can increase her earnings from $10,000 to $15,000, she loses food stamp benefits and receives lower EITC and housing benefits as well as paying more in taxes. The net effect: disposable income rises from $18,253 to $18,436. She has gained less than $200 by increasing her earnings by $5,000. Her effective marginal tax rate is close to 100 percent.

If she can make the jump from $15,000 to $25,000, she loses most of her remaining EITC benefits and all of her housing benefits, plus now pays federal and state income taxes in addition to the Social Security payroll tax. The net effect: disposable income is now $16,929, lower than when her earnings were $15,000, and also lower than when earnings were zero. Her effective marginal tax rate over this range is well over 100 percent.

If she increases her earnings from $25,000 to $30,000, she loses the small remaining EITC benefit. At this point, she is receiving no welfare benefits at all, just paying taxes. Her disposable income rises from $16,929 to $19,837, a gain of almost $3,000 from earning an extra $5,000 (an effective marginal tax rate of 40 percent, primarily due to taxes not welfare programs). However, her disposable income at $19,837 is not much more than the welfare package of $19,217 she received when she didn't work at all!

This example graphically illustrates how a combination of welfare programs and taxes can remove virtually all financial incentive for low-income families to work. And, although hypothetical, it is representative of how the current system affects many low-income families. In particular, it is common for low-income families to confront effective marginal tax rates that are significantly higher than those applying to other Americans, even the rich.

When people first learn of this characteristic (high marginal tax rates on the low-income population) of our welfare system, their immediate reaction is often that government should simply reduce those rates. Thinking about how this could be done helps us see why welfare is so hard to reform.

There are only two ways to reform the welfare system so low-income families confront lower marginal tax rates. First, we could maintain the amount given to those with zero earnings at about $20,000, as in the above example, and then more slowly reduce the benefits at higher levels of earnings. Suppose we decide to use a 50 percent rate; then it follows arithmetically that the level of income at which benefits become zero will be $40,000.[6] This reform has some notable downsides: It extends welfare for the first time to families earning between $30,000 and $40,000, confronting this group with a 50 percentage point *higher* overall marginal tax rate; it increases the benefits received at every income level above zero and so increases the cost of the system; and it thus requires higher marginal tax rates on the taxpayers who fund the programs. Conservatives, in particular, don't find this reform too attractive.

The other way to lower marginal tax rates for low-income families is to reduce the guaranteed income received by those with zero earnings. If that was reduced from $20,000 to $15,000, for example, we could use a 50 percent marginal tax rate and benefits would be paid only to those earning up to $30,000. This would reduce the welfare benefits received by all those earning under $30,000. You can see that this method of reducing marginal tax rates would be opposed by egalitarians.

It is easy to be critical of the high marginal tax rates in the welfare system, but it is not so easy to suggest a reform that would be supported by the political left and right.

Before turning to an examination of the consequences of our welfare system, let me emphasize that the numerical example described above is not representative of how the system affects *all* low-income families. In our system, single-parent families with children are often in situations like the example, but other family types generally receive assistance from fewer programs and confront lower effective marginal tax rates. For example, a married-couple family with earnings of $20,000 might receive benefits only from food stamps and the EITC. Their effective marginal tax rate would be in the 50 to 60 percent range, still very high but not as high as that of our illustrative single-parent family.

CONSEQUENCES

Transfer programs can have a bewildering variety of consequences, and here I will focus on three general effects of welfare programs that I think most people believe are important. They are: how the welfare system affects work effort (labor supply) of recipients; how it affects family structure and size; and how it affects the material resources, or consumption, of the recipients. Another important set of consequences is those for the taxpayers who fund the programs, and these consequences will be discussed in chapter 9.

WORK

Most people understand that the provision of welfare reduces the incentive of recipients to work and support themselves. Actually, economists argue that a welfare program affects work in two conceptually different ways. One of these we have already discussed—by utilizing a marginal tax rate to reduce transfers at higher levels of earnings, the net wage rate of recipients is reduced, reducing the payoff from working. Note that this effect depends on the marginal tax rate alone, not on the size of the transfer; the higher the rate, the lower the net remuneration received and the greater the work disincentive. The other way a transfer program can affect work is, however, dependent on the size of the transfer: the bigger the transfer, the less the need to provide your own support, and so the greater the work disincentive. This effect is conceptually distinct from, and in addition to, that produced by the marginal tax rate in the program.

With the welfare system we have, both of these effects operate to reduce incentives to work.[7] Transfers are provided, reducing the need to work, and a marginal tax rate is used, reducing the payoff from work. So, according to standard economic theory, a welfare system of the sort we have would be expected to reduce work effort by recipient households. And so it does, but exactly how much is an empirical issue that is not easy to resolve.

A clue to how large an effect the welfare system may have on the labor effort of low-income Americans is provided by the trend in work effort over time. In 1960 nearly two-thirds of households in the lowest-income quintile were headed by someone who worked (at least part-time). At that time, welfare expenditures were under 1 percent of GDP. In 2005, when welfare expenditures had increased to about 5 percent of GDP, the proportion of workers in the lowest-income quintile had fallen by half. And among those who do work, hours of work have fallen among low-wage workers over the past half century, at the same time that higher-wage workers were working longer hours. While many things have changed over this period in addition to the expansion of the welfare system, there is little doubt that the welfare system has played a major role in decreasing the labor supply of low-income households.

More sophisticated statistical studies support this conclusion. Summarizing three major reviews of studies dealing with how AFDC affected work by female family heads, Robert Moffitt concludes: "The studies as a whole confirm that AFDC reduces labor supply, and the estimates of its effect range from 10 to 50 percent of non-AFDC levels."[8]

Of course, AFDC has morphed into TANF as a result of the 1996 welfare reform, so it is not clear whether such estimates are applicable today. Moreover, one of the difficulties in interpreting such studies is that they generally focus on one or a small set of programs, but what we would really like to know is how the whole system affects work effort. As explained earlier, the cumulative effect of several taxes and transfers can produce amazingly high marginal tax rates even if each of the individual policies applies modest rates. Some studies have tried to investigate the interaction among several programs. For example, Barbara Schone considers the combined effect of AFDC, food stamps, and public housing, and she estimates that together they reduce the labor supply of female-headed households by 42 percent.[9] But because these families are also affected by other policies (notably Medicaid, the EITC, and payroll taxes), the overall effect is likely larger than she estimated.

It is clear, then, as three prominent economists have recently put it, that "Overall, our system is very generous to those at the bottom of the income ladder. But the price of that generosity is an incentive structure that strongly discourages those with the lowest skills from participating in the labor market."[10]

But why do we care if people work less when given welfare benefits? Perhaps it is unnecessary, but I believe it is worthwhile to enumerate four reasons for concern.

First, when recipients work less, they receive larger transfers from the welfare programs that characterize our system. That means that the cost to taxpayers is greater.

Second, reduced work effort suggests to economists that the welfare program is inefficient, that it distorts private decisions regarding labor supply.[11] The culprit here is the marginal tax rate that discourages work. The upshot of inefficiency is that the benefit to the recipient is lower than the amount of transfer received because the transfer comes with strings attached—the marginal tax rate, and possibly others—that make the transfer less valuable.

Third, reductions in work mean that the welfare policy does not increase the recipients' consumption as much as it could. If, for example, a person is given $100 but responds by earning $40 less, then his consumption only increases by $60 at a cost of $100 to taxpayers. I will discuss this further below.

Finally, if we take it as the goal of welfare to improve the lives of the more disadvantaged among us, we should think of what makes for a satisfying and fulfilling life. If it is only material resources, then we are already doing a good job because we are transferring around 8 percent of GDP downward. But many people, including me, believe that people must be independent and self-supporting to the degree possible if they are to have a satisfying life. If welfare encourages them to become dependent on government, rather than on their own efforts, they cannot be truly happy with their lives.

To many egalitarians, this last argument sounds like just an excuse to cut back welfare, and in truth it supports that position. That makes it no less true, but of course it is only one consideration in evaluating the welfare system.

FAMILY EFFECTS

In our earlier discussion of how our welfare system operates, I mentioned that it was especially generous to single-parent families. That has profound implications for the consequences of the system, as Moffitt points out in his survey: "The conventional perception of the U.S. welfare system as largely favoring single-parent families over two-parent families and childless couples and individuals is essentially correct. This favored treatment affects incentives to marry as well as incentives to have children."[12]

A predictable consequence of these financial incentives is the formation of more single-parent families, by increasing both divorce and illegitimacy. Some people find it hard to believe that base financial considerations could influence decisions concerning love, marriage, and children, but one doesn't have to believe that money is the only motivating factor to believe it plays some role. Indeed, the most well-established relationship in economics implies that a welfare system like ours will lead to increased childbearing, illegitimacy, and divorce. That relationship is called the law of demand, and it holds that when the cost of something people normally consume goes down (other things unchanged), they will consume more of it. The welfare system does reduce the cost to an unmarried woman of having a child by providing financial and in-kind assistance to single-parent families, so we should expect more of this type of behavior. It similarly reduces the cost of divorce and childbearing, but I will emphasize the issue of illegitimacy here.

Illegitimacy has risen enormously in America over the past half century. In 1950, 3.9 percent of all births were to unmarried women, but that figure had risen almost tenfold to 36.8 percent in 2005. That is the single most important reason for the growth in single-parent families (the second most important is, of course, divorce). Could welfare be responsible for some or all of this growth? Few familiar with the evidence believe that welfare is the only factor involved here, but it has become increasingly clear that it has played a significant role.

The timing of the increase in illegitimacy is certainly consistent with a connection to welfare. Consider the fact that prior to 1965 total welfare expenditures were under 1 percent of GDP in every year (except for several years during the Great Depression). Illegitimacy was also low throughout this period though it was increasing slowly: It stood at 3.0 percent in 1920, 3.9 percent in 1950, and 5.3 percent in 1960. Welfare expenditures increased rapidly after 1965, rising from 1 percent to 3.9 percent of GDP by 1980. The percentage of children born to unmarried mothers jumped from 5.3 percent in 1960 to 18.4 percent in 1980. Since 1980, welfare expenditures have risen further to 5.0 percent of GDP in 2005, and the illegitimacy ratio then stood at 36.8 percent.

For black families, the rise has been even greater, though it started from a higher level. In 1940, 14 percent of black children were born to unmarried women; this increased to 22 percent in 1960. But that growth was nothing compared to what was to follow. By 1980 more than half of all black children (55%) were illegitimate, and the fraction stood at a staggering 69.5 percent in 2005. (For white women, the ratio was 3.0% in 1950 and 25.4% in 2005.)

As we know, correlation does not prove causation, and indeed the correlation is not as close as the above data may suggest. Specifically, between 1975 and around 1990, the size of the welfare package available to single-parent families did not rise much if at all, yet illegitimacy continued to increase sharply over this period. Some analysts contend that this proves that welfare could not be the cause of increased out-of-wedlock births because illegitimacy increased significantly over this period when welfare benefits were not rising.

This experience does suggest that there is not a simple one-to-one correspondence between current welfare benefits and current illegitimacy. But a somewhat more nuanced view of how welfare influences illegitimacy is consistent with the historical experience. Specifically, let us suppose that current illegitimacy depends on two factors: today's welfare benefits and the social acceptability of unwed motherhood. By *social acceptability,* I mean the social norms and peer group effects that characterize a community and can exert an independent influence on whether an unmarried woman chooses to have a child.

Now consider this scenario. Welfare benefits increase this year and thereafter stay at the higher level. In the first year, that may induce some unmarried women to have children. In the following year the community will have more unmarried mothers, leading to a reduction in the social stigma attached to that lifestyle, and other young women who are friends with these welfare recipients see no immediate great disadvantages to their choices. In this way the social climate changes in a way that encourages (or reduces the discouragement of) more women in year two to have children out of wedlock even though welfare benefits have not risen in that year. In short, welfare can be the instigating factor that contributes to a change in social norms and that contributes to illegitimacy in subsequent years independently of further increases in welfare. Or, as economists might put it, the short-run, or immediate, effects of policies are generally not as large as the longer-term effects; the longer-term effects take time to fully materialize.

This explanation appears to be broadly consistent with the historical experience, but that does not mean it is necessarily correct. Clearly, *something* has caused a massive increase in the percentage of children born to unmarried women, and if not welfare, what is it? Apologists for the welfare system often argue that broad social changes, like a reduction in the stigma associated with single motherhood, are responsible. That this amorphous factor has contributed to rising illegitimacy seems probable, but it is simply not credible that it alone has produced the enormous increase in illegitimacy we have seen.

Changes in social stigma, or social norms, can exert effects on illegitimacy, as I explained above. (It may also be that welfare is partly responsible for the change, again as mentioned above.) But if this were the whole story, we would expect to see illegitimacy increase dramatically among all groups of women. We don't. In 1992, for example, women with incomes below $20,000 accounted for 73 percent of all illegitimate births; women with incomes above $75,000 contributed only 2 percent.[13] In 2002, the illegitimacy rate for women without a high school diploma stood at 63 percent; for those with a bachelor's degree it was 6 percent.[14] That illegitimacy is heavily concentrated among women with limited labor-market skills and low incomes is consistent with the welfare story, but not with the "broad social changes" story. A $15,000 welfare package is a more powerful inducement for a woman whose options don't extend much beyond a minimum-wage job than for women who can command a high salary, so if welfare is the culprit, we expect illegitimacy to be higher among those with limited opportunities. And it is.

That unspecified broad social changes have made some contribution toward increasing illegitimacy I don't doubt, but it is hard to believe that they are independent of the huge increase in welfare spending. Furthermore, we should not forget that there have also been broad social changes that should have reduced illegitimacy. I am referring to the increased availability of effective birth control techniques and the legalization of abortion, both dramatic changes in the past 50 years that would be expected to reduce illegitimacy. Yet illegitimacy increased. *Something* potent has changed to produce this outcome, and the vast expansion in the welfare system that began in the mid-1960s seems the most likely culprit.

I have not referred to any statistical studies of this issue, but there is no shortage of such studies. Writing in 1998, Moffitt summarizes this literature: "I argue that the consensus in the research community shifted over time from the 1970s, when it was generally believed that the welfare system had very little effect on marriage and childbearing, to the 1980s and 1990s, when most analysts came to believe that there is an effect. But the magnitude of any effect that is present is highly uncertain and unresolved; some researchers argue that the effect is small and others argue that it is sizable."[15] Research since 1998 continues in the same vein, with perhaps a tendency toward finding larger effects than earlier studies.

Why is this issue so important? Why should we care if women choose to have children out of wedlock? Part of the reason is obviously cost; the more single-parent families on welfare, the greater the cost to taxpayers. But the more fundamental reason for concern, I believe, is that we know that the decision to have children out of wedlock is often unwise, and that to have children out of wedlock is not in the long-term interest of the child or perhaps even the mother. A 15-year-old girl who has a child out of wedlock and drops out of school is acting contrary to her own long-term interest and certainly that of her child, regardless of what she thinks. If welfare encourages or supports these decisions, it may be harmful to the very people it is intended to help.

Perhaps our greatest concern is with the impact on children. And here the research community has once more finally caught up to reality (as it has with respect to the link between welfare and illegitimacy); it is now widely agreed that children raised in single-parent homes, especially those headed by never-married women, suffer a number of disadvantages. Maggie Gallagher and Linda Waite provide a convenient summary of this literature: "Children raised in single-parent households are, on average, more likely to be poor, to have health problems and psychological disorders, to commit crimes and exhibit other conduct disorders, have somewhat poorer relationships with both family and peers, and as adults eventually get fewer years of education and enjoy less stable marriages and lower occupational statuses than children whose parents got and stayed married. This 'marriage gap' in children's well-being remains true even after researchers control for important family characteristics, including parents' race, income, and socioeconomic status."[16]

For these reasons, the effects of welfare's subsidization of single-parent families are arguably more important than those flowing from the well-documented work disincentive effects of welfare.

MATERIAL RESOURCES

When egalitarians emphasize the benefits produced by welfare programs, they invariably refer to effects such as improvements in nutrition, health care, education, housing, and so on. For such benefits to occur, it is necessary that the goods, services, and/or cash—what I will refer to as *material resources*—available to low-income households be increased. Whether our concern is with health, nutrition, job skills, or housing, beneficial effects depend on (but are not necessarily proportionate to) increasing the material resources at the bottom of the income distribution. So a fundamental question is: How much has the welfare system increased the material resources of these households?

Government spending on transfers to the low-income population does not translate dollar for dollar into increases in their material resources. One reason for this is that recipients of transfers reduce their own work effort and earnings in response to the policies. Suppose, for instance, that a transfer of $100 to a family leads that family to work less and earn $100 less. Then its total cash income (material resources) has not been increased at all by welfare, and so there would be no improvement in food, housing, health care, or other materialistic trappings. Although the family is better off by its own standards, I do not think that most taxpayers, or people concerned with the status of the disadvantaged, would find this outcome of welfare highly desirable. Most of us would like welfare to improve the material standard of living of the poor and not just increase nonwork. That is why I think it appropriate to think of welfare's benefits as related to how material resources are affected, and that in the case of the above example it is reasonable to conclude that the $100 in welfare assistance has no benefit at all.

Why is it that material resources transferred to the poor may fail to improve the material standard of living of recipients? We have seen how a reduction in the recipient's own earnings can have this effect, but there are other consequences of welfare that produce the same outcome. One not-so-obvious way involves welfare's effect on family structure: If welfare leads to the formation of more single-parent families, its impact on the material standard of living is diluted even if work effort (earnings) doesn't fall at all. The reason is that there are economies of scale as family size increases. A four-person family does not require twice as much in material resources to attain the same standard of living as a two-person family.

This is implicit in the poverty thresholds: $19,971 for a family of four, $15,577 for a family of three, and $9,973 for a family of one (in 2005). Suppose that welfare causes a potential four-person family to become instead two family units of three and one persons. Then it requires $5,579 *more* in material resources just to attain the *same* material standard of living. (To attain the poverty thresholds now requires $9,973 plus $15,577, or $25,550, which is $5,579 more than required to attain the threshold for a four-person family.) Thus, if welfare produces this effect, in this case $5,579 of the welfare expenditures is wasted as it does not improve the material standard of living of the recipients. And of course if welfare causes welfare recipients to have more children, it may not increase the material resources available per person.

There are still other ways government transfers can be diluted in their effect on material resources of recipients. For instance, most transfers reduce the incentive to save. Both welfare programs and Social Security result in lower saving, so provision of retirement benefits through Social Security (as we will see in the next chapter) does not increase the material resources of retirees by the amount of the government pension (because their own contribution to retirement income is reduced). Yet another way is by reducing incentives to upgrade job skills to attain better-paying jobs. The high marginal tax rates in welfare programs reduce the payoff not only of earning more by working more but also of earning more by improving skills. Welfare may thus play a role in diminished school performance and school dropouts, once again diluting the extent to which welfare raises material standards of living.

Immigration also results in a dilution of the extent to which welfare expenditures raise the material resources available to native Americans. Immigrants, even illegal immigrants, receive benefits from welfare-state policies, absorbing some of the spending that would otherwise be available to improve the material resources of natives.

Finally, recall that the administrative costs of operating welfare-state policies act as a direct wedge between the total expenditures and the amount available to the low-income population.

When all these factors are considered, it should be no surprise that the trillion dollars spent on programs that benefit the low-income population do not increase their material resources by anything like a trillion dollars. How much slippage there is is perhaps suggested by the fact that the aggregate money income of the lowest quintile of households was only $246.5 billion (one-fourth of a trillion dollars) in 2005, according to the Census Bureau. Making allowance for the fact that many welfare benefits are not counted in this figure (which partly accounts for the fact that consumption expenditures of the lowest quintile are twice its income), it is apparent that the trillion dollars spent do not increase material standards of living of the low-income population by anything like a trillion dollars.

I know of no research study that even attempts to answer the important question of how much the expansion in government transfer programs over the past half century has improved material conditions at the bottom. Nonetheless, I think the available evidence suggests that a substantial part of the potential trillion-dollar improvement has been dissipated through the avenues described above. My best guess is that every dollar of welfare-state expenditures intended to help the low-income population adds at most 50¢ to the material resources of this group. In other words, it costs taxpayers at least two dollars to add one dollar to the material resources of those at the bottom of the income distribution.

I have predicated this discussion on the assumption that the benefits of welfare programs, whatever they are, are related to material resources. More material resources are required to produce better outcomes, whether the specific desired outcomes be improved nutrition, better housing, better health, or whatever. This correlation between material resources and beneficial outcomes may not be true in all instances (think of welfare that finances a drug habit), but it is worth considering the relationship in at least one important case: the effect of material resources on children.

It is surely the case that much of the support for welfare spending is based on the belief that it benefits children when their families have higher incomes. But does raising the income of a family really benefit the children? It is certainly widely believed. As Susan Mayer describes the conventional wisdom when she wrote her important book, *What Money Can't Buy:* "No social scientist believes that income is the sole determinant of how children turn out, but most believe that parental income has an important influence on children, and some believe it is the single most important influence on children's life chances."[17]

To her own surprise, Mayer's research led her to a very different conclusion: "I argue that when parents' income increases, children's material standard of living improves. But this improvement has little influence on children's test scores or behavior, on their educational attainment or labor-market success, or on teenage girls' chances of having a baby or becoming a single mother. *We therefore have little reason to expect that policies to increase the income of poor families alone will substantially improve their children's life chances* [italics added]."[18] She supports these conclusions with substantial evidence, and there is other research that points to the same outcome. In summarizing a review of the literature by Janet Currie, Moffitt says the research "yields one striking finding: unrestricted transfers such as AFDC and the Earned Income Tax Credit have relatively few discernible effects on children."[19]

These studies do not deny that some welfare programs, such as perhaps Head Start and educational interventions, can have long-term benefits for poor children. But they do strongly suggest that raising the income (material resources) of poor families does little to improve outcomes in later life for the children. That is consistent with the thrust of our discussion in chapter 1, which emphasized the importance of genetic endowments and early childhood environments on later outcomes. Providing welfare to poor families will not change the genetic endowments of the children nor is it likely to greatly improve the parenting skills of the parents, and therefore welfare would be expected to have rather limited (but not necessarily zero) effect on children's lives.

One does not need to pore over a multitude of statistical estimates to see that this finding is probably true. Recall that the welfare system had already been greatly expanded by 1980, so young people in their teens and twenties today grew up in a world where material resources of low-income households had already been significantly augmented (unless the offsetting factors discussed above are even larger than I believe). Did this lead to improved outcomes for these young people? Anyone familiar with evidence concerning educational attainments, illegitimacy, labor-force participation, poverty, and crime knows that in most of these areas outcomes appear no better than before the expansion of welfare. If transferring income downward enhances life prospects for children, it is hard to see this in the present generation of young people raised in low-income families, as we should if there were size-able effects.

CAN WELFARE HARM THE POOR?

Nothing said here implies that welfare actually harms the poor. Indeed, according to conventional economics, it is nearly impossible for a policy that *offers* assistance to people to make them worse off. How could it? If participation in the program were actually to harm someone, he or she could simply decline to accept the assistance. That is what the tenets of economics imply would happen for potential welfare recipients who might be harmed by some policy. In general, we expect potential recipients to weigh the benefits and costs associated with receipt of welfare assistance and to accept the proffered assistance only when the benefits outweigh the costs.

You will see that this sanguine conclusion depends on the assumption that potential welfare recipients are aware of the consequences of their choices. That is a fundamental assumption of economics, and in most cases it is probably reasonably accurate. But the emerging field of behavioral economics has accumulated evidence that some people—and not just the poor—regularly make systematic errors in certain choice situations. When people do not correctly perceive the consequences of their choices and actions, it obviously becomes possible for a government subsidy to harm the recipient.

Scott Beaulier and Bryan Caplan have recently argued that the findings of behavioral economics have particular relevance for the analysis of welfare programs.[20] They argue that however often the average person may make mistaken choices that turn out to be detrimental, such outcomes occur much more frequently for the poor. A common situation where a choice may end up harming one is when it involves immediate benefits but with uncertain costs in the future. Obviously, if the costs are not recognized, it is possible for one to opt for the immediate benefits even when the delayed costs are greater.

The poor do display a greater tendency to make choices that involve immediate gratification but delayed costs than do the nonpoor. Whether it is overeating, drinking, not exercising, smoking, drug use, crime, unprotected sex, or dropping out of school, the poor make choices that involve short-run benefits but long-run costs, and they do so much more frequently than the nonpoor. If the poor have a tendency to overstate immediate benefits and understate future costs, which these instances suggest, provision of welfare assistance could encourage behavior that has the unintended effect of harming them. An example given by Beaulier and Caplan describes how this might occur: "Women may underestimate their probability of pregnancy from unprotected sex. After becoming pregnant, they might underestimate the difficulty of raising a child on one's own, or overestimate the ease of juggling family and career. Policies that make it easier to become a single mother may perversely lead more women to make a choice they are going to regret."[21] (I would add that women who have unprotected sex may underestimate the damage to their future employment prospects following temporary withdrawal from the labor force.)

Arguing along these lines, some conservatives have concluded that welfare *generally* harms the poor. I don't think the logic of the argument or the limited evidence supports that strong a conclusion; however, it does seem likely that at least some of the poor are led by welfare programs to make decisions that they will later regret.

Social Security
and Medicare

Social Security is the largest government expenditure program in the world, with expenditures of $523 billion in 2005. That figure includes only the cash retirement benefits paid. Social Security's companion policy that covers medical expenses of the elderly, Medicare, had expenditures of another $299 billion. Taken together, the federally financed retirement benefits amounted to $822 billion.

Despite its vast size, and the fact that it affects almost everyone each year of their lives, the Social Security system is probably the most poorly understood government policy of all. The jargon alone is incomprehensible; we hear of unfunded liabilities, infinite and 75-year time horizons, AIME and PIA, trust funds and lockboxes, wage indexing versus price indexing of benefits, bend-points in the benefit formula, carve-outs and add-ons, replacement rates, covered and uncovered earnings, and on and on. There is, however, probably no policy more important to understand because the consequences for the way we live, and how well we live, are monumental.

This chapter will focus on what I believe to be the fundamental issues surrounding the design of a system to provide retirement benefits to the elderly. We will begin by explaining how Social Security works.

SOCIAL SECURITY BASICS

The retirement benefits provided to the elderly by Social Security (and Medicare) each year are financed by taxes on the earnings of workers. The benefits received by those now retired do not come from a fund they accumulated by paying taxes during their working years. The taxes they paid in earlier years were all spent on providing benefits to those then retired. Similarly, the taxes paid by workers today do not go into a fund to finance their own retirement; they are spent providing retirement benefits to those retired now. Social Security is thus an income-transfer program, with income transferred each year from workers to retirees.

But, you will say, what about the trust funds we hear about all the time; doesn't the money go into the trust funds? It is true that there are trust funds, but they play a minor, even negligible, role in the operation of Social Security. They are temporarily playing a somewhat larger role right now than they did in the past or will in the future, but it is a minor factor even today. (In 2005, 84¢ of each dollar in workers' taxes were immediately paid out as retirement benefits; only 16¢ went into the trust funds.) We will discuss the trust funds later, but we can get a clearer understanding of how Social Security operates by first ignoring them.

A retirement system that finances retirees' benefits by taxing younger workers' earnings (as Social Security does) is said to be run on a *pay-as-you-go* basis. No fund is being accumulated on behalf of the taxpayers, so this arrangement is also sometimes called an *unfunded* system. I will use the pay-as-you-go terminology or PAYGO for short.

A PAYGO system bears an eerie resemblance to a Ponzi scheme (also known as a pyramid scheme), named after Charles Ponzi who apparently first utilized the device to swindle investors. In 1920, Ponzi began borrowing money from investors, promising them a return of 50 percent after only 45 days. (On an annual compound basis, this is comparable to a return of 2,500%!) He paid off the early investors by using the funds provided by later investors (as Social Security paid off early retirees by taxing later retirees, i.e., young workers); he did nothing with the funds to actually generate such fantastic returns (as Social Security does not invest the taxes paid by workers). Like most pyramid schemes, it collapsed, leaving the later investors with nothing since their funds had been used to pay off the early investors. The entire swindle lasted less than a year, with Ponzi pleading guilty to mail fraud and spending four years in jail. Since that time, pyramid schemes have been illegal.

Pyramid schemes are illegal, that is, unless they are run by the federal government, as with Social Security. But there are differences between privately operated Ponzi schemes and publicly operated PAYGO retirement programs that enable Social Security to be a viable system for providing retirement benefits. Notably, the government can force current and future workers to contribute money (by collecting taxes from them), so that retirees can always be assured of incoming funds supplied by younger workers.

Saying that a PAYGO system is a feasible way to provide retirement benefits is not the same as saying it is desirable, so let's consider how it affects people over their lifetimes. To understand how it operates in the simplest way, suppose we imagine people living for only two years, working in the first year and retired in the second. When working they pay a tax on their earnings of, say, 10 percent, and that 10 percent finances retirement benefits to those retired. What can you expect to get from such a system when you retire?

When you retire, you get the proceeds of the 10 percent tax on the earnings of those then working. That means that if their earnings are greater than the earnings you had when you paid the 10 percent tax, you will get back more in retirement than you paid in taxes when you were a worker. All retirees can potentially get back more than they paid in taxes as long as the earnings of workers are growing over time, and the number of workers per retiree doesn't change.

This suggests a link between growth in earnings and the returns that can be generated by PAYGO Social Security. Indeed, more elaborate calculations show that Social Security can provide over the long term an implicit (annual) rate of return on taxes paid that is equal to the annual rate of growth in (taxable) earnings. So all generations of workers can get back more than they paid in as long as earnings rise over time. As it is sometimes expressed, Social Security allows people to "share in the growth of the economy" because economic growth and earnings growth are pretty much the same thing.

What you can expect to get back (or more precisely what people on average can expect) is therefore tied to the growth in earnings. Over the past 50 years or so the annual growth in total *real* earnings has averaged about 2.5 percent. For reasons to be discussed later, future growth is expected to be somewhat lower, perhaps 1.5 to 2.0 percent per year. This means that the implicit real rate of return on taxes paid into Social Security will likely average around 1.5 percent or so in the foreseeable future. We will be comparing that return to the returns available from other ways of providing for retirement in the next section.

All of the rates of return (or interest rates) discussed in this chapter will be *real* rates, that is, adjusted for inflation. If the nominal (or monetary) rate of return is 10 percent but prices are rising by 10 percent a year, then the real rate of return is zero—because the purchasing power of the $1.10 you get back one year after investing a dollar has the same purchasing power as the $1.00 you started with. Real returns are what determine living standards, and that is why the growth rates in earnings cited above are expressed in real terms, that is, in terms of dollars of constant purchasing power.

One other matter deserves emphasis. We have explained that over the long haul a PAYGO system offers an implicit real rate of return equal to the rate of earnings growth. The "long haul" here refers to people who spend their entire lifetimes under the full-blown system, paying taxes over all their working years and then receiving retirement benefits. In a PAYGO system some people will do much better than this long-haul return. They are persons who retire in the early years of the operation of the system, and who did not pay taxes for all their working years, or who paid taxes when rates were lower. To see this, imagine that we start a PAYGO system with a 10 percent tax rate this year. People who are retired this year will receive the tax revenues as retirement benefits (remember it is PAYGO) even though they paid no taxes at all during their working years since the system didn't exist then. They get a really sweet deal, benefits at no cost to themselves, clearly faring much better than young workers just starting out who will pay taxes and only receive a return equal to the rate of growth of earnings. People who are near retirement age also do extremely well because they will pay taxes for only a small proportion of their working years.

Therefore, we expect those retiring in the early years of a PAYGO system to fare much better (receive a much higher rate of return) than those retiring later. They receive windfall gains, just as the early participants in Ponzi's scheme who were paid off before the operation collapsed did excessively well. In contrast to Ponzi's scheme, however, Social Security can, as we have seen, continue to pay later generations of retirees an implicit rate of return equal to the rate of earnings growth.

The windfall gains received by early retirees are one of the major differences between a PAYGO system of providing retirement benefits and using a funded system. In a funded system, what you get back is strictly linked to what you put in; if you put nothing in you get nothing back. Some generations of retirees do not automatically get much higher returns than other generations in a funded system as they invariably do in a PAYGO system.

Is Social Security a Good Deal?

We have seen that not all generations of retirees will receive the same rate of return on their Social Security taxes. Generations retiring earlier do better than later generations. In contrast to our earlier heuristic discussion, however, Social Security did not emerge full blown after its enactment in 1935. Benefits were first paid in 1940, and not all the elderly received benefits because of the specific legislative restrictions on eligibility. In fact, in 1950 only one of six people over the age of 65 was receiving benefits. That figure rose to 62 percent by 1960 and 86 percent by 1970. Today, more than 95 percent of the elderly receive Social Security pensions. Tax rates also rose gradually, starting at a rate of 2 percent in the 1940s, rising to 4 percent in the 1950s, reaching 9.6 percent in 1970, and finally attaining its current level of 15.3 percent in 1983.[1]

The gradual expansion of Social Security, together with complicated and changing rules determining individual benefit payments, makes it difficult to determine exactly what kind of deal people get from the policy. There have been, however, a number of careful studies that provide estimates for both past generations as well as future generations. Table 7.1 has culled some of the findings from three of these studies to present an overview of the rates of return that have been generated in the past and likely will be (if Social

TABLE 7.1A
Implicit Annual Rates of Return on Social Security Taxes Paid

Demographic Status	Earnings Profile	Rate of Return by Year in which Household Head Becomes 65 (%)							
		1970	1980	1995	2008	2020	2038	2050	2068
Single Male	Low	7.5	5.3	3.1	2.4	2.5	2.3	2.2	1.8
	Average	6.3	4.5	1.9	1.3	1.4	1.3	1.1	0.8
	High	5.4	4.0	1.5	0.8	0.8	0.6	0.4	0.2
Single Female	Low	10.7	7.7	3.7	2.9	2.9	2.7	2.6	2.2
	Average	9.1	6.6	2.7	1.9	2.0	1.7	1.6	1.3
	High	6.7	5.1	2.3	1.5	1.4	1.1	1.0	0.7
One-Earner Couple	Low	9.7	7.4	6.1	4.9	4.8	4.6	4.4	4.0
	Average	8.5	6.7	5.0	3.9	3.9	3.6	3.4	3.0
	High	7.5	6.0	4.7	3.4	3.2	3.0	2.8	2.4
Two-Earner Couple	L/L	8.8	6.4	3.9	3.1	3.1	2.9	2.8	2.4
	A/L	7.7	6.0	3.5	2.7	2.8	2.6	2.4	2.0
	A/A			2.7	2.0	2.1	1.9	1.7	1.4
	H/A	6.7	5.1	2.7	2.0	1.9	1.7	1.5	1.2
	H/H			2.3	1.5	1.4	1.2	1.0	0.7

Sources: 1970 and 1980 figures from Michael D. Hurd and John B. Shoven, "The Distributional Impact of Social Security," in *Pensions, Labor, and Individual Choice*, ed. David A. Wise (Chicago: University of Chicago Press, 1985), pp. 193–207. All other data from *Report of the 1994–1996 Advisory Council on Social Security* (Washington, DC: Government Printing Office, 1997), pp. 219–22.

TABLE 7.1B
Average Implicit Annual Rates of Return on Social Security

	Rate of Return by Year in which Household Head Becomes 65 (%)					
	1960	1970	1980	1990	2000	Long Run
Unadjusted	14.7	9.2	6.0	4.8	3.5	2.5
Adjusted	14.3	8.2	4.1	2.1	-0.4	-1.1

Source: Jeffrey C. Edwardson, *Social Security Money's Worth Measures in a Life Cycle Context* (Ph.D. diss., Texas A&M University, College Station, 2000).

Security continues unchanged[2]) provided in the future. All of the figures represent the implicit annual real rate of return on Social Security taxes paid. In other words, they show what interest rate would have to be earned if the taxes were invested to produce a pension equivalent to that provided by Social Security.

You will note that estimates are provided for 14 (or only 12 in two years) different family types. The reason for this is that Social Security has complicated rules for the determination of individual benefits. If all people were given pensions that were strictly proportionate to the taxes they paid, then the rates of return (in a given year) would be the same for all of these family types. But they are not; some family types do significantly better than others. This is deliberate and represents another instance where egalitarianism has affected the design of policy as the government gives higher returns to those deemed more needy.

There are a lot of numbers in the table, but sense can be made out of this potpourri by noting that there are two definite patterns. The first pattern can be seen by looking across any row. This shows the rate of return received (or to be received) by a given family type retiring in different years. In all cases, the rates decline over time. For example, a two-earner couple where one earner has high lifetime earnings and the other average earnings received a 6.7 percent rate of return in 1970, but in 1995 received only 2.7 percent. By 2050 the rate of return declines to 1.5 percent and then to 1.2 percent by 2068. The same pattern, lower rates for those retiring in later years, holds for all family types.

This pattern reflects the PAYGO nature of Social Security. As explained in the last section, a PAYGO system invariably treats earlier retirees much better than later retirees, who receive (on average) only the rate of growth in total earnings. An overview of this pattern is provided in table 7.1B, which shows the unadjusted (ignore the adjusted figures for now; they will be explained later) average rates of return for all those retiring in different years. They declined from 14.7 percent for those retiring in 1960 to 3.5 percent in 2000, and in this study the unadjusted average rates of return are *assumed* to ultimately stabilize in the future at 2.5 percent (somewhat higher than most economists today expect).

The second pattern displayed in table 7.1A is the variation in rates of return received by different household types retiring in the same year. Looking down the column for 2008 we can get a good idea of this variation for people retiring now. The rates of return vary from a high of 4.9 percent to a low of 0.8 percent. As mentioned earlier, this variation is the result of specific rules for determining individual benefits. Some groups can receive rates higher than the overall average, but of course this must come at the expense of other groups receiving lower-than-average returns. In general, these differences reflect egalitarian concerns to provide higher benefits to families in greater need. Thus, low-earning households systematically receive a higher rate of return than higher-earning households.

We still need to consider whether, and for whom, Social Security has represented or will represent a good deal. To evaluate this, we must remember that the rates of return shown in table 7.1 are compound annual rates of return that apply over long periods of time (lifetimes). As Albert Einstein once said (perhaps apocryphally), compound interest is the eighth wonder of the world. By this he meant that small differences in rates can produce big differences in outcomes when compounded over long periods of time.

Consider a person who contributes (or pays Social Security taxes) in an amount equal to $200 every month ($2,400 a year) to a retirement fund, and does so for 45 years (say, from age 22 to age 66). How much will he have accumulated when he retires at age 66? The following numbers show how the accumulated amount depends on the rate of return, and the figures in parentheses approximate the annual pension that such an amount can finance.[3]

```
At 1% . . . . . . . . . . . $136,438 ($8,868)
At 1.5% . . . . . . . . . $154,305 ($10,030)
At 2% . . . . . . . . . . . $175,223 ($11,389)
At 3% . . . . . . . . . . . $228,645 ($14,861)
At 4% . . . . . . . . . . . $302,900 ($19,689)
At 5% . . . . . . . . . . . $406,976 ($26,453)
At 6% . . . . . . . . . . . $553,954 ($36,007)
At 7% . . . . . . . . . . . $762,943 ($49,591)
```

The specific case we are examining here is analogous to a worker earning around $22,000 a year since such a worker pays Social Security taxes of about $2,400 a year. With that in mind, we see that if he gets a 1.5 percent return (which, recall, is the long-run average prospect for Social Security), he will accumulate a total of $154,305 at age 66. That can provide an annual pension for the remainder of his life equal to $10,030, which is only 45 percent as large as his pre-retirement earnings. On the other hand, if he achieves a 5 percent return, his accumulation is $406,976, which can provide a pension of $26,453—20 percent more than his earnings before retirement. And if he gets 7 percent, his accumulation is more than three-quarters of a million dollars, with an annual pension of $49,591. His pension is nearly *five times* higher if he receives a rate of return of 7 percent rather than 1.5 percent. Such is the power of compound interest over a working lifetime.

These examples demonstrate that even seemingly small differences in rates of return can make huge differences in the pensions, and thus living standards, of retired workers. With that background, we return to the central question: How good a deal is Social Security? We now see that the answer depends on what family types (high or low earnings, etc.) we are considering and on their year of retirement. Families retiring in the earlier years (roughly, the 1980s or before) typically did much better than those retiring later.[4] Future retirees, as we see from table 7.1A, can expect lower returns that decrease over time and bottom out at around 1.5–2.0 percent on average.

Our assessment of Social Security must also reflect what alternative means of providing retirement income exist and the returns expected from these alternatives. The obvious alternative is for people to save individually for retirement (or through company-sponsored pension plans), accumulating assets in the form of stocks and/or bonds that then finance retirement income. According to Jeremy Siegel's definitive study *Stocks for the Long Run*,[5] the real compound annual rate of return on stocks has averaged 6.9 percent over the past 200 years (1802–2001). The returns have been remarkably stable over shorter (but still quite long) subperiods, averaging 6.9 percent since 1926 and 7.1 percent since World War II (1946–2001), for example.

Stocks do involve risks, and returns vary greatly over short periods. For those who want a guaranteed rate of return, bonds are normally the choice. Since World War II, corporate bonds have generated real returns that average around 4 percent. Many investors choose portfolios involving both stocks and bonds. Martin Feldstein and Andrew Samwick point out that a portfolio composed of 60 percent stocks and 40 percent bonds has generated a yield of about 5.5 percent since 1946 and also over the entire period since 1926.[6]

These yields (stocks, 7%; bonds, 4%; and mixed, 5.5%) that have resulted from private savings in the past provide a perspective on the deal provided by Social Security. Certainly, for those retiring now and even more so for future retirees, the returns implied by Social Security pensions pale in comparison with private investments. Recall from our earlier example that the pension generated by a 7 percent return (stocks) is five times as large as that produced on average in the long run by Social Security (a 1.5% rate of return). A 4 percent return (bonds only) will produce a pension about twice as large as Social Security, and the 5.5 percent return from a portfolio of stocks and bonds will produce a pension three times as large as Social Security.

Everyone "knows" that private investments yield higher returns than Social Security. Few know that the differences in returns compounded over a working lifetime imply huge differences in the pensions available to retired persons. Do persons retiring today realize that they would have a pension two, three, or more times the size of their Social Security pension if they had been able to invest their taxes in stocks? While we must recognize that future yields on private investments may differ from past yields, it is difficult to avoid the conclusion that Social Security is a bad deal for present and future workers. Surprisingly, however, these comparisons *overstate* the benefits from Social Security, as we will see in the next section.

THE HIDDEN COSTS OF SOCIAL SECURITY

Comparisons like those in the previous section are commonplace in evaluations of Social Security. Yet such comparisons invariably make Social Security look better than it really is because they ignore two of the important economic consequences of PAYGO Social Security: how it affects private saving for retirement and how it affects work effort (labor supply) of workers. Let's examine these consequences.

Most people intuitively understand that Social Security leads workers to save less for their own retirement. It does so in two ways. First, by taking 15 percent of the earnings of workers, it reduces their ability to save. Second, and more importantly, Social Security reduces the need to save by providing a pension to workers when they retire. To see this second point most simply, imagine a worker whose goal is to maintain his pre-retirement standard of living over his retirement years. In the absence of Social Security, he will save and accumulate assets sufficient to produce the required pension. Now suppose Social Security promises the worker a pension of this amount. He no longer has any reason to save and will reduce his savings (for retirement purposes, at least) to zero.

Clearly, we do not expect all workers to reduce retirement saving to zero. Depending on the size of the expected Social Security pension, some will want to supplement it by saving privately. But they will be saving less than they would have if there were no Social Security pension. And do not make the mistake of thinking that the government is saving for you when it collects the taxes. Those taxes are not saved in any economic sense; they are transferred directly to retired persons (PAYGO), who spend the proceeds.

Economists are in wide agreement that PAYGO Social Security decreases private saving for retirement for these reasons.[7] Why is this important? Remember that private saving usually involves purchases of stocks or bonds, which provide funds that finance investments in such things as buildings, vehicles, equipment, computers, and software. Saving thus ultimately finances the acquisitions of real productive assets, that is, *real capital* in economist lingo. Sometimes, as when a person uses his savings to finance a small business, the link between saving and the subsequent investment in real productive assets is even clearer.

An important point here is that real capital is productive, that is, it adds to the economy's output. When a business has new or better machinery or facilities, its output is greater even with an unchanged labor force. For the economy as a whole, then, additional saving leads to additional capital accumulation and that in turn leads to higher output in later years. Capital accumulation financed by saving is one of the reasons economies grow over time. And growth in GDP means growth in personal incomes, because, as we saw in chapter 1, output equals income for the society as a whole.

Thus, when Social Security leads to reduced saving by workers, a set of further outcomes is produced. Less saving means less investment, and less investment means output will be lower in later years (than it would have been had saving not fallen). And that means that personal incomes will be lower in later years. We end up with a lower stock of real capital, so there is less capital for each worker to use, which means the productivity of labor will be lower and wage rates will be lower. This does not mean lower than in previous years, but lower than wage rates would have been if saving had not fallen. Even with Social Security's effect on saving, there is still saving going on, and this plus other factors contributing to economic growth generally are enough to continue to raise wage rates over time, only less rapidly than they would have risen if saving had not fallen.

The second significant economic consequence of PAYGO Social Security flows from its taxation of labor earnings. Currently, the tax is levied at a rate of 15.3 percent on earnings up to a ceiling amount ($97,500 in 2007, indexed to grow automatically over time). This tax can affect workers' decisions regarding whether and how much to work, when to retire, whether to work overtime, and how diligently to perform on the job. In general, the tax can be expected to reduce the amount of effective labor supplied to the American economy. Less labor means lower output (lower GDP) and lower *before-tax* incomes for workers.

To summarize these two consequences: PAYGO Social Security leads to lower quantities of productive capital and lower quantities of labor employed in the economy. Both imply lower output and hence, lower average incomes for Americans. This represents a real cost borne by people over and above the taxes directly paid to finance Social Security. They have lower before-tax incomes prior to payment of their Social Security taxes.

These hidden costs are not incorporated in the rates of return for Social Security reported in table 7.1A. Those rates are calculated by comparing Social Security's pensions with the taxes paid when working. As we now see, workers bear costs in addition to taxes paid; their earnings are lower before they confront the tax collector. What this means is that these rates overstate how beneficial Social Security is (or understate how harmful it is). While the magnitude of this overstatement is difficult to pin down, there is no question that the "deal" provided by Social Security is worse than suggested by the comparisons in the last section.

But it is important to have a rough idea of the magnitudes involved. Economists have, of course, studied this issue, but there is no consensus that would allow us to say precisely how much lower GDP is than it would be if Social Security had never existed. Nonetheless, the available evidence suggests that Social Security has reduced GDP by somewhere between 5 and 10 percent.[8] Most of these studies, however, examine only the effects of Social Security; they do not consider Medicare. Because Medicare can be expected to reduce saving for retirement just as does Social Security, it seems reasonable to conclude that the system as a whole results in at least a 10 percent reduction in GDP.

It is also important to understand that this 10 percent reduction is the cumulative effect of a seemingly small annual reduction in the rate of economic growth over a long period; it did not occur all at once. The reduction in annual saving caused by the Social Security system might have reduced the growth rate of GDP by perhaps 0.3 percentage points per year, say from 3.0 percent to 2.7 percent.[9] Given the normal year-to-year variations, that would hardly be noticeable, but after 32 years the level of GDP would be 10 percent lower than it would have been if the long-term trend had remained at 3.0 percent.

With 2005 GDP at $12.5 trillion, a 10 percent reduction means that GDP (and personal incomes) would have been about 11 percent higher had Social Security (and Medicare) never been enacted. To bring this to a more personal level, it implies that the average household in the United States would have had an income that was $12,175 higher than their actual income in that year. The average household thus loses more than $12,000 from Social Security each year, and that is before they pay their Social Security taxes.

This is an immense effect and would be huge even if the effect on GDP is only half as large as I assumed it to be. Look at it this way: Expenditures on Social Security and Medicare now run at 7.3 percent of GDP. A 10 percent reduction in GDP from these programs means that each dollar spent on them reduces GDP (and personal incomes, of course) by nearly $1.40 before the taxes are collected.

We now see why discussions of Social Security that do not go beyond comparing its implicit rates of return to private investment returns, as we did in the last section, are seriously incomplete. The implicit returns calculated for Social Security are based only on the taxes paid, treating the taxes as if they were the only cost of the program. But workers not only pay taxes to finance Social Security retirement benefits, they also have lower before-tax incomes because of the impact on private saving. We have ignored a large portion of the cost of providing Social Security retirement benefits.

Let's revise our conclusions from the last section to incorporate the effects of Social Security on GDP. We saw that early retirees (retiring in the 1980s or earlier, roughly) did extremely well. That remains largely true even when we consider the growth-retarding effects of reduced saving because these effects start out small and only slowly accumulate over time. By 1970, the effect of Social Security on GDP was probably no more than 1 or 2 percent, and people retiring that year would have been working in years when the effect was even smaller. Thus, we can reaffirm our earlier conclusion that early retirees fared extremely well under Social Security because they avoided most of the GDP-reducing effects.

Later retirees do not do so well. It is probable that by the present time GDP is 10 percent lower, so people retiring today had significantly lower before-tax earnings during their working years. For people retiring now, and certainly in future years, the implicit rates of return reported in table 7.1A greatly overstate the benefit of the program. In fact, when we account for the hidden costs of Social Security, it is evident that most, if not all, current and future retirees are worse off than if the system had never begun.

Results from Jeffrey Edwardson's study, reported in table 7.1B, confirm these conclusions.[10] Edwardson developed an elaborate simulation model to track how Social Security evolves and affects people over time. The unadjusted-rates-of-return row shows the average implicit returns from Social Security when calculated in the conventional way (benefits relative only to taxes paid); they are quite similar to the figures from other studies in the upper part of the table. However, the adjusted rates of return show the retirement benefits relative to all the costs borne by younger workers, the lost before-tax wages as well as taxes. They are, of course, lower, but note that in the early years the adjusted returns are only slightly lower than the unadjusted returns and then the difference becomes greater over time.

By the year 2000, Edwardson finds that the adjusted rate of return to Social Security is negative, implying that retirees at that time got back less in Social Security benefits than the costs they bore as workers (taxes and lost earnings). All later generations are estimated to receive negative returns as well. Since Edwardson's study does not include Medicare and is based on an ultimate reduction in GDP of only 8 percent, actual outcomes from the system are likely even worse than he estimated.

Is Social Security a good deal? Our analysis suggests that the answer to this fundamental question is: It was a good deal for early retirees, but for present and future retirees it represents a very bad deal. Put differently, with PAYGO Social Security, early retirees gained at the expense of all later generations. This result, it should be emphasized, is the consequence of the PAYGO nature of the Social Security system. With a funded system of providing retirement benefits, as with private saving supporting retirees, future generations do not lose out.

The Future of PAYGO Social Security

A PAYGO system of providing retirement benefits can operate indefinitely with no change in the tax rate necessary to finance pensions under certain conditions. The primary condition that must hold is that the number of workers per retiree not change over time. Today there are 3.3 workers paying taxes for every retiree receiving benefits.[11] The average worker must therefore pay a tax that will provide about 30 percent of the average retiree's benefits. If the 3.3 to 1 ratio of workers to retirees does not change, a given tax rate on workers' earnings can fund benefits indefinitely.[12]

However, the worker/retiree ratio is on course to decline sharply in the foreseeable future. According to the Social Security's Board of Trustees, there will be only 2.6 workers per retiree in 2020, and the ratio continues to decline to 2.0 workers per retiree in 2040, finally reaching 1.9 workers per retiree in 2065. Most of the future financial difficulties that are much in the news stem directly from this large decline in the worker/retiree ratio.

This projected decline is driven by population trends that have been in progress for several decades: People are having smaller numbers of children and are living longer. Of particular note is the baby boom that occurred after World War II, followed by a continuing baby bust. In the baby boom period (1946–1964), the number of children the average woman had over her lifetime peaked at 3.7 in 1957 and then began a steady decline bottoming out at 1.7 in 1976. It has remained low since then, varying in the narrow range 1.82–2.07 since 1980. (These numbers measure the so-called total fertility rate, which must be 2.1 to result in zero population growth over the long term.)

As a result, the labor force is now awash with workers from the baby boom generation (yielding 3.3 workers per retiree), but when they retire the labor force will be populated only by the baby bust generations. This, combined with slowly improving life expectancy for the retirees, produces the dramatic change in the worker/retiree ratio that will occur in the near future.

Social Security and Medicare will both be affected by the coming decline in the worker/retiree ratio because they are both funded on a PAYGO basis. An additional factor, however, influences Medicare's future: the rising costs of medical treatments. If medical costs continue rising faster than overall prices, as they have for the past half century, then in the future Medicare will have to deal with fewer workers per retiree *and* higher medical costs per retiree. This double whammy makes the future financial condition of Medicare much worse than Social Security alone.

There are many ways to try to quantify the approaching financial problems confronting Social Security and Medicare. I believe the easiest to understand is to consider the taxes required to balance income and outgo in the PAYGO systems in the future if currently scheduled benefits are to be paid. In 2006, outlays on Social Security were 4.2 percent of GDP and outlays on Medicare were 3.1 percent (7.3% total). In 2040, outlays on Social Security are projected to reach 6.6 percent of GDP while Medicare's outlays will be 8.6 percent. Total outlays on the PAYGO programs will thus more than double as a percent of GDP, rising from 7.3 percent to 15.2 percent. After that date, Social Security's costs stabilize at around 6.6 percent of GDP (because the worker/retiree ratio doesn't change much after 2040), but Medicare's costs keep rising. By 2078 Medicare's cost is estimated to reach 13.8 percent of GDP.[13] Thus, while Social Security's costs are projected to increase (as a percentage of GDP) by about 50 percent, Medicare's costs more than triple by 2040 and more than quadruple by 2078.

It is evident that these scheduled future benefits cannot be paid without a huge increase in taxes. As long as we stay with PAYGO financing, we have basically two ways of dealing with this situation. First, we can reduce scheduled benefits to match taxes generated by unchanged tax rates. This would require scheduled benefits to be reduced by about 50 percent in 2040. (Reductions in benefits would have to begin before 2040, of course, but they would have to reach a 50% reduction in that year.) Second, we can double the tax rates that finance these programs and continue to pay scheduled benefits. The payroll tax rate would become at least 30.6 percent (higher if taxpayers respond by earning less), which in combination with the federal income tax and other taxes would confront most Americans with marginal tax rates in excess of 60 percent. Further benefit cuts or tax increases (or both) would be required after 2040.

These are unappealing options, but there are no other possibilities (apart from a combination of both tax increases and benefit cuts) as long as we stick with PAYGO retirement programs. These programs have simply promised much more than they can deliver in the future, and something has to give.

In all the discussion to this point, I have neglected the trust funds, and it is time to repair that omission. Social Security and Medicare have always had trust funds, but until recent years they had the equivalent of only a few months worth of benefit payments, which were used primarily to ensure continued benefit payments during recessions when taxes temporarily declined. Fundamentally, the system was purely PAYGO. That changed in 1983 when Congress scheduled increases in payroll tax rates producing the 15.3 percent rate we have today. Shortly thereafter, revenues began to exceed outlays on Social Security and Medicare, and the surpluses have been credited to the trust funds.

The idea behind the 1983 reform was to delay the day of reckoning when taxes would have to be increased or benefits cut. It was already known at that time that the system was in long-run trouble (how much trouble was not fully appreciated). With assets in the trust funds, when annual revenues first begin to fall short of benefit outlays (the date this happens for Social Security is 2017; for Medicare it is 2007), the shortfall can be made up by drawing down the trust fund assets. The annual shortfall grows greater each year, and ultimately the trust funds will be depleted. That date is projected to be around 2041 for Social Security and 2019 for Medicare. On those dates, if not before, taxes must be increased or benefits cut.

At best, it appears that the trust funds have bought us a little time. Yet even this is misleading because the trust funds do not contain any real assets. When the trust funds receive the surplus funds, the money is not used to purchase stocks or corporate bonds—claims on real assets. Instead, the money is turned over to the Treasury Department, which uses the funds to pay for other government programs, and the trust funds are given special government bonds that say the Treasury Department owes them money. What the trust funds contain is promises from one government agency to another.

Consider how the trust funds affect the options available in 2017 when tax revenues are insufficient to finance Social Security benefits. What can we do to make up the shortfall? We have the options of increasing taxes or reducing benefits, just as we would have with nothing in the trust funds. We also have the option of selling the pieces of paper in the trust funds to the public and using those revenues to finance the shortfall. In other words, we can use deficit finance (borrowing from the public) to finance the shortfall. But the option of borrowing to finance Social Security benefits exists whether or not there are any pieces of paper in the trust funds. Thus, the trust fund so-called assets do not give us any new options that we didn't already have. Deficit financing is always an option, but it is arguably worse than either raising taxes or cutting benefits. Yet that is exactly how Social Security is scheduled to balance its accounts until 2041, and Medicare until 2019.

The trust funds have acted as a major distraction that has permitted people to mistakenly believe the future financing problems with Social Security and Medicare are smaller, and further in the future, than they actually are.

WHY HAVE SOCIAL SECURITY AT ALL?

Any serious consideration of Social Security and its potential reform should include an examination of the rationales for government involvement in the provision of retirement benefits. Only if we know what we are trying to achieve with the program are we able to ascertain whether it is working, or whether some reform option is preferable.

The three most common justifications given for Social Security are:[14] First, many people are too short-sighted to anticipate their retirement needs and will not save enough to provide for their own retirement. Second, some people will consciously decide not to save in the expectation that society (i.e., government welfare programs) will take care of them in retirement, thereby "gaming the (welfare) system." Third, it is desirable to redistribute income from high-income retirees to low-income retirees.

Let's briefly examine these arguments. The first two can be dealt with together since they both simply argue that a lot of people will reach retirement age without sufficient assets to support themselves in retirement. That could be true, although I think it is easy to overstate how many people are likely to be improvident. But do we have to have a government retirement program to take care of these people? There is another option: They can keep working. If someone hasn't accumulated enough to retire at age 65, is it unreasonable to expect him to work a few more years until he has accumulated enough? Most people are perfectly capable of working into their seventies, and for those who aren't there are disability benefit programs. It is not clear why the government has to guarantee people a retirement at age 65.[15]

Reservations about the third argument, that Social Security is needed to redistribute income among retired persons, also abound. Redistribution may be desirable, but we don't need Social Security to do it. We could, for example, tax the elderly wealthy to benefit the elderly poor without concealing this operation in Social Security's complicated benefit rules, and indeed without having a government retirement program at all. Some defenders of Social Security acknowledge this, but fall back on the contention that the public would not permit as much redistribution if it were done openly. Maybe so, but if the voters wouldn't support this policy if it were in the open, is it acceptable to impose it on them in concealed form? Many egalitarians answer this question affirmatively; I do not.

Related to the redistribution argument is the contention that one of Social Security's great benefits is that it has reduced poverty among the elderly. It is true that the (official) poverty rate among the elderly has declined pari passu with the expansion of Social Security spending: The rate declined from 24.6 percent in 1970 to 10.1 percent in 2005. But that rate would have gone down without Social Security because of the growth in earnings that occurred over this period. Perhaps it would have declined even more without Social Security.

In principle, Social Security affects poverty among the elderly in two opposing ways. First, it *increases* poverty by reducing the accumulated assets people bring to retirement (reduced saving),[16] and then it *reduces* poverty by providing the government pension. Which effect is larger is by no means clear. Consider this: Retirees in the lowest earning categories in table 7.1A will receive an implicit rate of return on taxes paid of around 3 percent (a bit higher for one-earner couples) in 2008. Had they invested these same taxes in a balanced portfolio (60% stocks and 40% bonds), they would receive a return of around 5.5 percent. In view of the calculations reported earlier in the chapter, this implies that their retirement income would be more than twice as great had they invested the funds privately. There would likely be fewer poor among the elderly today if they had been permitted (or required) to save privately when younger rather than participating in Social Security.

Despite these reservations about the practical significance of the three arguments for Social Security, they do provide logically valid positions. But do they justify PAYGO Social Security? As is I hope apparent, they may argue for some sort of government retirement policy, but they do not provide *any* justification for that policy to be a PAYGO program, transferring income each year from workers to retirees. As the President's Council of Economic Advisers puts it: "An essential part of this debate [on Social Security] is that none of these rationales require that Social Security be operated on a pay-as-you-go basis."[17] This important point is little understood, as evidenced by the fact that it is difficult to find any explicit argument favoring PAYGO over funded methods of providing retirement.

Can a PAYGO system be defended? To see how one must argue to justify PAYGO financing, recall that the defining characteristic of this policy, the one that distinguishes it from funded alternatives, is that it benefits the early retirees at the expense of later generations. Why should we have a policy that harms all future generations in order to benefit those who retired in the early years of the Social Security system? It is not easy to give a good reason for this type of redistribution.

Indeed, it is widely accepted that this type of redistribution is immoral. One of the major arguments against use of government deficits is that it unconscionably imposes costs on our children and grandchildren. Yet that is exactly what PAYGO government retirement programs do. This similarity between deficit finance and PAYGO Social Security is not accidental: Social Security, when operated on a PAYGO basis, is just like an elaborate deficit-financed pension program (that's what all the talk about so-called unfunded liabilities is about). If deficit finance is unwise or immoral, so is PAYGO Social Security.

I think that these points, together with the absence of any convincing (or even articulated) argument for PAYGO in the mountains of material written on Social Security, is sufficient for us to conclude that there is not a very good case to be made for the government operating retirement programs on a pay-as-you-go basis.

WHAT COULD HAVE BEEN

I have asserted that it is not necessary to have a PAYGO system to accommodate the three arguments most commonly made in support of Social Security. I will now back up that claim. The following is the outline of a policy that is capable of satisfying all of these rationales.

Suppose that in 1940 we had begun a retirement program along the following lines (with figures in today's dollars). Each worker is required to contribute 10 percent of the first $12,000 in earnings to a retirement account. These contributions must be invested in a balanced portfolio of stocks and bonds containing 60 percent stocks and 40 percent bonds (chosen from index funds to assure diversification and low administrative expenses). At the age of 66 (or later if he chooses) the individual is required to use the accumulated assets to purchase an annuity, or annual pension, that will continue as long as he lives. The annual benefits will be indexed to inflation to assure no deterioration in purchasing power over the retiree's last years. In bare outline, that is all there is to it.

Note how this can satisfy all three of the common arguments for Social Security. Because people are required to save for retirement, no one will reach retirement age without adequate (as we will see) assets to provide a pension. Redistribution can be accommodated (if it is desired) simply by taking some of the assets in some people's accounts (presumably those who are well off) at age 66 and adding them to other people's accounts (presumably those who are poor). It is not clear that this is desirable, but it could easily be done.

Let's look a little closer at what we could expect from such a policy. Note that everyone who earns in excess of $12,000 a year, which is just about everyone who works full time, makes the same contribution of $1,200 a year. That will entitle them to (roughly) the same government pension—not exactly the same since people who retire in different years will realize different returns. This pension, as we will see, will not be particularly generous, and most people will choose to save privately to supplement it. But it will provide a guaranteed floor of income support for the elderly.

What kind of pension will this policy provide? As we have seen, since 1946, this type of investment portfolio has generated a rate of return of 5.5 percent. So if people contribute $1,200 a year for 45 working years (as in our earlier examples), at that rate of return the accumulated assets at age 66 would be $237,038. That can provide an annual pension of $15,407 to every individual worker. That pension exceeds the poverty line for an elderly single person

($9,367 in 2005) and also for an elderly couple ($11,815) by a comfortable margin. So this policy ensures that the poverty rate among the elderly will be close to zero.[18]

Most elderly people would not be, of course, relying solely on this pension. They would save privately to provide additional retirement income, just as many people do today. Importantly, the saving that they do would yield the higher returns available to private investments rather than the 1.5 percent return of Social Security. This retirement policy thus effectively places a floor below which retirement income cannot sink, guaranteeing a minimum amount above the poverty line. Because this effectively eliminates poverty among the elderly, it is not clear that we would want to redistribute assets among the retired population, but as stated earlier, that is easily done if it is desired.

The returns generated by this policy could also be used to finance health insurance for the elderly. Indeed, the $15,407 pension exceeds the $9,367 poverty line by enough to provide a basic health insurance policy to the retired person and still leave him with cash income above the poverty line. If we wished to ensure fuller insurance coverage it would be necessary to increase the contribution rate, say to 14 percent. That would yield an annual pension of $21,570, nearly $12,000 above the cash poverty line and more than adequate to finance a comprehensive health insurance policy and also provide cash benefits exceeding poverty.

If we had adopted this type of government retirement policy in 1940 instead of PAYGO Social Security, it is probable that all Americans alive today would be better off. There would be no poverty among the retired. Saving and capital accumulation would have been greater, so GDP and wage rates would be higher. This means that low-income (and other) young workers would also be better off. Retirees would, of course, be better off because they would have realized the much higher returns available on private saving. Tax rates would also be lower. Note that the *marginal* tax rate is zero for those earning above $12,000, so that effectively means that marginal rates for most workers would be 15.3 percentage points lower than they are today. Higher-wage workers would have more after-tax income from which to save and increased incentive to save to supplement the basic pension. And all this without raising taxes on low-wage workers—the 10 or 14 percent contribution rate is lower than the 15.3 percent tax they now pay.

The major objection to this type of retirement policy is that it exposes people to the great risks in the stock market. It is true that the 5.5 percent historic return on stocks plus bonds, as well as the 7 percent return on stocks only, are not guaranteed returns. They are averages over long periods of time. Some retirees will do better and some worse, depending on their investments and when they convert their assets to pensions. There is risk in that sense. But if historical experience is any indication, the risks are far smaller than generally imagined.

Between January 2000 and July 2002 the stock market declined by 37 percent as measured by the Standard and Poor 500 index. Suppose you had been investing totally in stocks over the preceding 35 years, and were unfortunate enough to have to convert your assets to a pension in July 2002 at this low point. Scary, isn't it? But what would have been the compound annual real rate of return you would have realized if you cashed out at this most unfortunate time? It would have been 7.35 percent, even *higher* than the historic long-run average for stocks. You would have been even better off if you had cashed out at the high point for stocks in January 2000 (garnering a rate of return of 9.74 percent!), but a 7.35 percent return would finance a comfortable pension, certainly better than the 1.5 percent return of Social Security.

Another downturn in the stock market occurred in 1987, with stocks falling 26 percent between August and November 1987. If you had cashed out in November 1987 after investing for 35 years, you would have realized a rate of return of 4.88 percent (6.64 percent if you had gotten out in August). Not as good as 2002, but still three times the rate of return for PAYGO Social Security. Another large downturn occurred between January 1973 and December 1974, a decline of 43 percent. If you cashed out at the low point in 1974, your rate of return would have been 5.77 percent. Still another downturn occurred between February 1966 and May 1970, a decline of 18 percent. Retiring in 1970, your return would have been 8.1 percent.[19]

These, and numerous other examples that could be given, show that returns are variable in the stock market, but when considering long-term investing they vary over a narrow range that at its worst is much better than PAYGO Social Security. There is large short-term variability (which is why stocks are too risky for short-term investing), but much smaller variability over the long term, which characterizes saving for retirement. They would be even less variable over a 45-year lifetime of investing than for the 35-year time span reported in the study cited above.

Thus, there are risks associated with private saving for retirement, but there are also risks with the existing PAYGO Social Security program. These are the political risks related to how the government chooses to deal with the impending financing problems confronting the system. Will the government raise taxes or cut benefits (or both), and by how much and for whom? Your rate of return from PAYGO Social Security is by no means risk free; all you can be assured of is that it is a very low or negative return.

Although many details would have to be filled in, the plan I sketched above certainly seems preferable to PAYGO Social Security. Why not put it, or something similar, in place immediately? Why would anyone oppose such a plan? The answer is that it is very difficult to extricate ourselves from a PAYGO system without harming some people.

Suppose we try to implement my plan by having workers divert $1,200 from their current Social Security taxes into the investment accounts I described. The problem is that this reduces tax revenues that finance benefits to current retirees (remember it's PAYGO). We could cut benefits to retirees (about a 20 percent cut in both Medicare and Social Security would be required), but that would harm the elderly. Those near retirement would also be harmed because the accumulations in their investment accounts for only a few years will not offset the 20 percent lower Social Security benefits in retirement. While the young and future generations all benefit, the middle-aged and already retired would bear costs.

This scenario illustrates what is referred to as the *transition costs* of replacing one policy with another. Although an investment-based retirement system is superior to PAYGO Social Security in the long run, there will invariably be some people harmed in the short run while we substitute one policy for the other. Policy analysts have suggested different ways to cope with this problem, but it is difficult to design a transition plan that does not harm some people. Typically, most proposals begin by guaranteeing that the currently retired population will not be harmed (their Social Security benefits will not be cut), but that means the middle-aged population will bear all of the transition costs.

Because of the much higher returns available from private investments than from the PAYGO system, these transition costs, while real, are not as large as you might suppose. It is possible to move to a system of private accounts in a way that does not impose annual costs in excess of 2 or 3 percent of earnings on anyone, and even those costs decline over time.[20] The details need not detain us; what is important is understanding the inherent superiority of investment-based (funded) methods of providing retirement income over our PAYGO system. If we selfishly try to shore up the PAYGO system to avoid the modest transition costs, we will consign our children and grandchildren (and their children and grandchildren) to substantially lower standards of living.

THE MOST SUCCESSFUL PROGRAM?

It is surprising how often one encounters defenders of our PAYGO Social Security system making statements like: "Social Security has been the most successful domestic government social program of the twentieth century."[21] A charitable interpretation of such accolades is that the program has been politically popular (probably true), but it is difficult to argue that it has produced desirable consequences. A policy can be politically popular and yet have deleterious consequences.

There are a number of features that combine to make Social Security look good on a superficial examination and therefore account for its political appeal. Among them are:

- The nominal splitting of the payroll tax into employer and employee portions. The 15.3 percent tax is composed of equal rates of 7.65 percent that are collected from the employee and employer. Economists know that workers bear the full burden of both levies, but many workers are unaware of even the existence of the employer portion of the tax, much less that it is a cost to them. The true cost to workers is double what they believe it to be. (See the first note for this chapter.)

- The taxation of income from private investments. The U.S. tax system imposes severe taxes on the return to private saving (income taxes, capital gains taxes, corporate profits taxes, and property taxes). The after-tax returns that savers receive are much lower than the before-tax returns, and this leads them to understate the benefits from private saving. It is the before-tax returns that measure the contribution that capital accumulation makes to the economy. This before-tax return is around 9 percent, even higher than the long-run returns of 7 percent in the stock market. (Investors receive 7 percent because businesses must pay corporate and property taxes from the 9 percent return before investors receive what is left.)
- The windfall gains to early retirees. As we have seen, early retirees did fare very well, and people who base their assessments of Social Security on that fact will conclude that it is a successful policy. These returns were temporary, but it is necessary to understand how PAYGO systems operate to appreciate that.
- The hidden costs of PAYGO on saving and labor supply. There is no doubt that Social Security has decreased saving, capital accumulation, labor supply, and thus GDP. Very few people see these costs and can easily believe that they do not exist. (Try convincing someone that their *before-tax* earnings are 10 percent lower due to Social Security.)

These factors conspire to make it difficult for the average person to understand what a truly bad deal our PAYGO Social Security system really is. In turn, many politicians find it easier to play on these misperceptions than do the hard work of educating the public. That is why we have PAYGO Social Security, and why it is so difficult to achieve a meaningful reform.

Franklin Delano Roosevelt, who signed the legislation establishing Social Security in 1935, is often referred to as the father of Social Security. Yet there is convincing evidence that although he favored a funded system rather than a PAYGO program he was overridden by Congress.[22] Perhaps we would make more progress in reforming the system if we acknowledge Charles Ponzi as the true father of Social Security.

More Transfers

We have now examined the two largest categories of government expenditure policies that transfer income from some people to others: welfare programs and the Social Security system. There are many other welfare-state policies that also redistribute income, some not involving government expenditure programs at all, and in this chapter we take a look at four of them. In all these cases, I invite the reader to consider whether these policies contribute to social justice, as egalitarians tell us they do.

UNEMPLOYMENT INSURANCE

The unemployment rate is perhaps the most widely cited of all economic statistics. We would like that rate to be as low as possible, but the government policy that most directly affects that rate, unemployment insurance, has the effect of *increasing* it. Before explaining how it does this, a few basic facts about the nature of unemployment will be helpful.

Unemployment is sometimes portrayed as a pool of workers who will remain without jobs until the overall unemployment rate is reduced. This is very far from the truth. The most important fact about unemployment is that most unemployment is short term (at least in the United States). Even though the unemployment rate may remain unchanged month after month, that does not mean the same people remain unemployed; there is turnover in this statistical category just as in others (like poverty) we have examined.

During the 1990s, the median amount of time an unemployed person was out of work was 7.6 weeks. In other words, half of the people who become unemployed find jobs in under two months even if the unemployment rate remains unchanged. Indeed, more than a third of the unemployed find work in less than five weeks! Fewer than one in six unemployed workers takes 27 or more weeks to find a job.[1] In reality, achieving a low unemployment rate is primarily a question of shortening how long people are unemployed, not putting people from a fixed pool back to work.

Unemployment insurance (UI) increases the nation's unemployment rate by encouraging those who lose their jobs to stay unemployed longer than necessary so they can collect more in UI benefits. UI provides weekly cash benefits to workers who have lost their jobs while they remain unemployed up to a maximum that is typically 26 weeks. Generally, the weekly benefit is about 50 percent of previous earnings, subject to minimum and maximum payments that vary among the states. Normally, the minimum weekly benefit is around $50, and the maximum is in the $300–$400 range.

Outlays on UI are financed by payroll taxes on the earnings of employed workers. These taxes are collected from employers; workers may not even know of their existence, much less their size, although economists believe that the workers bear the burden in the form of reduced wages. Typically, the tax is applied at a rate of around 4 percent to the first $10,000 or so of earnings, with considerable variation in both the rate and the ceiling on taxable earnings among the states.

In broad outline, then, the UI system transfers funds from employed workers to unemployed workers. Why does this increase unemployment? Clearly, UI does not very often cause people to lose jobs; rather, it creates incentives for workers, once unemployed, to extend the duration of unemployment. Recall that UI typically replaces half of previous earnings. That means that it reduces the cost of remaining unemployed by about half (up to 26 weeks) and diminishes the need to promptly find another job. The law of demand tells us that this will lead to unemployed persons staying unemployed for longer periods.

How do we know it has this effect? There is a voluminous literature in economics that is almost unanimous in supporting this conclusion. But some simple facts may be more convincing than citing these statistical studies. Consider the rate at which people who have lost their jobs find new ones. Some will return to work (find a new job or return to the old one after a layoff) after one week, some after two weeks, and so on. It turns out that the percentage of the remaining unemployed who exit unemployment (get a job) generally varies between 5 and 7 percent each week. That is true for the first 25 weeks of unemployment. In week 26, however, the percentage that gets a job spikes to 16.5 percent.[2] What is special about week 26? That is the week that UI benefits run out. Apparently, a sizeable number of unemployed persons *choose* to stay unemployed as long as they can collect unemployment benefits.

A comparison with Europe is also telling. Unemployment rates in most European countries are much higher than in the United States. For example, the unemployment rate in France was 8.8 percent in 2001, 10.3 percent in Germany, 9.0 percent in France, but only 4.7 percent in the United

States. Economists believe these differing outcomes are, in part, related to the differences in UI systems. European countries pay higher unemployment benefits for longer periods of time. Although UI benefits terminate after 26 weeks in the United States, most European countries pay these benefits for more than a year, often more than two years. Probably as a consequence, long-term unemployment is much more common in Europe. "In 2000, the proportion of the unemployed who had been out of work for at least 12 months was 51.5 percent in Germany, 42.5 percent in France, and 60.8 percent in Italy. In contrast, only 6.0 percent of the unemployed in the United States were in these very long term unemployment spells."[3]

Thus, it is safe to conclude that UI has the effect of increasing the nation's unemployment rate, though thankfully not as much as European programs do. How much it adds to our unemployment rate is debatable. After surveying the evidence, Daniel Hammermesh conjectures that UI adds 0.7 percentage points to the unemployment rate, while Martin Feldstein's best guess is that it adds 1.25 percentage points.[4] More recent evidence also supports the view that UI adds about one percentage point to the unemployment rate.[5]

With unemployment running at around 5 percent, that means that 20 percent of the nation's unemployment is due to the UI system. And that substantially understates its importance because some unemployment is necessary and unavoidable. People require time to find the best jobs available when they are unemployed, and so there will always be what economists call *frictional unemployment*. Frictional unemployment probably can't and shouldn't be reduced below 3 percent or so. If that is approximately correct, then UI is responsible for half of avoidable unemployment (and other government policies, like the minimum wage and Davis-Bacon Act, are responsible for some of the remainder).

If this were the whole story (that UI increases unemployment), no one would favor this policy. But there are also benefits from the provision of unemployment compensation. UI provides insurance against the risk of becoming unemployed and helps unemployed workers maintain their standards of living while they search for a new job. Economists often claim that the determination of the optimal UI policy involves weighing these benefits against the costs associated with higher unemployment. Attach enough weight to the importance of supporting spending by unemployed workers, as egalitarians do, and UI might seem like a reasonable bargain.

This evaluation, however, misses the critical point that there are other ways consumption spending by unemployed workers can be supported. In particular, workers can self-insure by accumulating savings to support themselves during periods of unemployment. That many workers don't do this now is no reason to think they wouldn't, or couldn't, do so in the absence of UI. Just as Social Security reduces saving for retirement, UI reduces saving for short-term contingencies like unemployment. Could people afford to accumulate a nest egg sufficient to support themselves during periods of unemployment? In answering this, it is important to recall that most unemployment is of short duration (and would be of even shorter duration without

UI). The majority of people who become unemployed are unemployed for less than 7.6 weeks, and UI provides benefits only after a one-week waiting period. Thus, since UI benefits are only half of earnings, a worker would require savings equal to 3.3 weeks wages to support spending equal to or better than UI in the majority of cases. To provide support for 26 weeks at UI levels, of course, would require accumulated savings equal to 13 weeks wages, hardly an insurmountable obstacle.

In contemplating the elimination of UI, egalitarians automatically think of poor workers who may be unable to afford saving enough even for short spells of unemployment. But these workers are already paying UI taxes to support the current system, and in the absence of these taxes they would have higher earnings from which to save. Consider a minimum-wage worker in a state with a 4 percent tax on the first $10,000 in earnings. Working full time in 2006, this worker earns $10,712 a year, so the UI tax would be $400 a year. Without UI, that worker would have $400 more a year, and if this sum was saved for just two years, it could be used to support eight weeks of unemployment at half pay. Obviously, poor workers *are able* to accumulate enough to cover spells of unemployment, but perhaps they *would not* do so. If that is viewed to be a serious problem, then we could proceed in a way similar to that proposed in the analogous case of Social Security: Require people to accumulate savings that can only be used when they are unemployed.

But in any case most workers who receive UI benefits are not poor. Feldstein has pointed out that only 17 percent of total UI benefits go to families with incomes below half the median level. Indeed, more than half the benefits go to families with incomes (even before counting UI benefits) that are greater than the median.[6] UI is no welfare program; all workers are covered, and higher-paid workers get larger benefits when they are unemployed. It is clear that most of the people who receive UI benefits would have little difficulty accumulating savings that afford the same or better protection against the risk of unemployment than is provided by UI. There would certainly be hardship cases (low-wage workers who lose jobs before they have had time to accumulate much savings), but it does not seem wise to base the entire edifice on the rare cases that could be handled in other ways.

Egalitarians portray UI as a policy that provides assistance to unfortunate families when they need it most, but it actually increases their need by encouraging lengthy unemployment spells and taxing them when they are working, all the while providing most of its benefits to those who are nonpoor. This is social justice?

THE MINIMUM WAGE

Egalitarians see a problem: Some people are paid low wages. To them, the obvious solution is to pass a law requiring those wages to be increased. Such a law has been in existence since 1938; it is called the minimum wage. Set originally at 25 cents an hour, it now (2007) stands at $5.85 and is scheduled to rise to $7.25 in 2009.

One of the lessons of economics is that obvious solutions often have bad consequences, and few policies better illustrate this than the minimum wage. Here, the principal bad consequence follows from the law of demand: Raise the price of something and less will be bought. Activists recognize the law of demand as it applies to commodities. For example, when they advocate higher gasoline and cigarette taxes, they believe (correctly) that the resulting higher prices will lead to reduced consumption. But the law of demand also applies to labor. If you raise the price (wage) of labor, employers will cut back on their employment of workers. The result is decreased employment and increased unemployment.

How do we know that the minimum wage reduces employment among low-wage workers? For economists, part of the answer is our belief in the universality of the law of demand, but the other part is the voluminous empirical literature supporting this conclusion. Because the minimum wage in the United States is low relative to the wages of most workers, however, it directly affects only a small share of the labor force (1.2 percent of full-time workers were paid the minimum or less in 2005; about 2 percent of all workers), so the effects are often quite small relative to the total labor market and thus hard to detect.

In at least one instance, however, the minimum wage was increased so much that its effects were obvious. Historically, the minimum wage in Puerto Rico was set significantly lower than in the United States in recognition of the lower general level of wages there. But in 1974, the Congress began to gradually increase the minimum wage for Puerto Rico until it equaled that in the United States in 1987 at $3.35 an hour. This wage was 34 percent of the average manufacturing wage in the United States, but it was 63 percent in Puerto Rico. As a consequence, a much larger share of the labor force was affected in Puerto Rico. This increase in the Puerto Rican minimum wage to U.S. levels reduced total employment in Puerto Rico by 9 percent![7] Of course, the percentage reduction in employment was even greater for the minority of lower-wage workers who were directly affected.

In addition to reducing the number of persons employed, the minimum wage also gives firms incentive to reduce hours of employment for those who are employed and to reduce fringe benefits (e.g., on-the-job training and health insurance) in order to comply with the higher cash wages mandated by the law. Workers are harmed by these changes as well as the diminished job opportunities.

It is important to understand that the adverse employment effects will strike most strongly those who would otherwise have the lowest wages. Workers, for example, who would earn $4.00 an hour in the absence of the minimum wage will be harder hit than those who would earn $5.50 an hour. That is because a $5.85 minimum represents a 46 percent increase in wages for $4.00 workers but only a 6 percent increase for $5.50 workers, so employers will cut back employment more for the former group. This means that the most unskilled, disadvantaged workers will be the hardest hit with reduced job opportunities, and presumably this is the group egalitarians would most like to help.

For many workers, a minimum-wage job is the first job they get. They may not be paid much, but they gain experience, develop good work habits, perhaps gain skills on the job, all of which means they will have higher wages later on. (About two-thirds of those who start work at the minimum wage are earning more than the minimum within a year; 85 percent within three years.) The minimum wage makes it more difficult for the most unskilled workers to obtain these advantages, and making it more difficult for unskilled workers to get needed work experience can have lasting adverse effects. As some have put it, raising the minimum wage is like cutting off the bottom rungs of the employment ladder, making it all the harder for disadvantaged workers to get those first crucial jobs that help them move up the ladder. A recent study[8] documents this effect by showing that teenagers who grow up in states with minimum-wage rates higher than the federal standard have lower earnings and work less a decade later when they are in their twenties (and earning above the minimum wage).

If the only effect of minimum wages were to eliminate entry-level jobs for low-wage workers, no one would be in favor of it. But an increase in the minimum wage does provide benefits to those who retain their jobs, although some of these may have their hours of work curtailed. A higher minimum causes employment among unskilled workers to decline but not to zero. Indeed, as long as the minimum is kept relatively low, there will be more workers who get a pay raise and keep working than those who become unemployed. Proponents of the minimum wage emphasize this benefit for those who continue working.

So let's take a look at the benefits to low-wage workers lucky enough to keep working. Although often promoted as assistance to the working poor, we have already seen why this is misleading. Recall that only one in seven working-age poor adults works full time; more than half do not work at all. So most of the poor will receive no benefit at all from the minimum wage. But even for the 44 percent of poor adults who work part or full time, the minimum wage provides little or no benefit because most of these workers earn well above the minimum wage and would not be affected at all! Only 5 percent of minimum-wage workers are from households below the official poverty line; 95 percent of minimum-wage workers are from nonpoor households.

A recent study provides insight into just who likely benefits from the minimum wage. Richard Burkhauser and Joseph Sabia examined the effects that would result from an increase in the minimum wage from $5.15 to $7.00 in 2003. What they found is that 70.7 percent of the workers in poor families already earned more than $7.00 an hour in 2003, so only a minority of the working poor stands to benefit at all. Indeed, they found that 85 percent of minimum-wage workers (which they define as those initially earning less than $7.00) are in families with incomes above their respective poverty lines. Thus, "the majority of the working poor are not helped by a minimum wage hike and the vast majority of those who are helped do not live in poor families."[9] In fact, they find that there are nearly three times as many minimum-wage workers in families with incomes more than triple their poverty lines than there are in poor families. Close to half of all minimum-wage workers are in families with incomes in the upper half of the income distribution.

How can it be that there are so many minimum-wage workers in families that are not even close to being poor? Basically, it is because many families have multiple earners. Nearly two-thirds of minimum-wage workers are in families with other earners who earn more than the minimum (that is, more than the simulated minimum of $7.00). More than 30 percent of minimum-wage workers are teenagers. To a significant extent, the minimum wage is a subsidy to the teenage children of middle- and upper-income families.

Therefore, the minimum wage is not a very effective antipoverty policy. Its benefits are not concentrated on the neediest people. If we truly wanted to transfer more income to the poor, increased spending on welfare programs would be more effective.

We have discussed one major cost (reduced employment) and one major benefit (higher earnings for those who remain employed) of the minimum wage. There is another significant cost which results from the fact that someone has to pay for the higher wages of those who remain employed. But exactly who does bear the cost of higher wages? It is often implied that employers absorb these costs out of profits, but economists believe the costs are spread far more widely.

It is not entirely clear how the costs of higher mandated wages are shifted throughout the economy, but we won't go too far afield by thinking of these costs taking the form of higher prices.[10] After all, a higher minimum wage increases production costs for those who employ minimum-wage workers, and that is likely to lead to higher prices of goods for which minimum-wage labor is an important cost. Higher prices for goods and services affect all consumers, rich and poor alike. In particular, the large majority of poor families with no workers who benefit from the higher minimum will be worse off because of the higher prices they have to pay. As Donald Deere, Kevin Murphy, and Finis Welch put it: "A higher minimum wage essentially takes money from people in front of the counter at McDonald's and gives it to the people behind the counter. At first glance, these two groups of people appear similar."[11]

In a more recent paper, Burkhauser and Sabia examine (using 2003 data) the effects of raising the minimum wage to $7.25—the level it is scheduled to reach in 2009.[12] They find that if there is no adverse employment effect this will raise the earnings of low-wage workers by $18.4 billion, but most of those benefits go to the nonpoor for the reasons discussed above. They estimate the earnings of the poor will rise by only $2.3 billion. However, this overstates the increase in the income of the poverty population for three reasons. First, there will be some reduction in employment, that is, some job losses. Second, the poor will bear part of the cost from the higher consumer prices produced by the increase in the minimum wage. Third, whatever increase in gross earnings is realized, it will be taxed at a high rate due to the marginal tax rates implicit in the welfare benefits the poor receive and the taxes they pay (as discussed in chapter 6).

Taking these three offsets into account, I estimate that the increase in the minimum wage to $7.25 will not increase the net real income of the poverty population at all, and may actually reduce it by a small amount.[13]

Overall, it is not hard to see why the minimum wage is held in such low regard by economists. It harms the least skilled workers among those directly affected, benefits at best a small minority of poor families with most of the benefits going to families that are not poor, and transfers income in a capricious way from consumers to a small number of families who have (employed) minimum-wage workers. If there were no other way to help the poor, it is conceivable that we might conclude the minimum wage is better than nothing. But there are other options: the multitude of welfare programs that transfer money from taxpayers to low-income families. We have noted that these welfare programs themselves have significant deficiencies, but even so, they are probably better than the minimum wage.

So egalitarians must think social justice entails harming the least skilled workers, harming most of the poor through higher prices, and benefiting primarily middle- and upper-income families with secondary workers employed part time.

PREFERENTIAL ADMISSIONS IN HIGHER EDUCATION

Affirmative action policies are intended to redress group inequalities of the sort discussed in chapter 3. These policies are probably more firmly entrenched in the academic world than anywhere else in society. Among other things, affirmative action in academia takes the form of using different admission standards for members of different groups. In this section, we will examine how this policy affects African American students as compared to white students.

At selective schools, admissions depend primarily on high school grades and standardized test scores, especially the SAT. That many schools admit blacks with lower academic credentials than whites is now well documented. Robert Lerner and Althea Nagai, for example, investigated a sample of 47 public colleges and universities across America and found that almost all of them gave preference to blacks in their admissions.[14] This can be seen in the differences between median black and white SAT scores at the various schools. To give a few examples: at the University of Michigan (Ann Arbor), the median black combined SAT score was 230 points below the median white score; at the University of Virginia the disparity was 180 points; at

Washington State University, 180 points; at the University of North Carolina (Greensboro), 130 points; at Old Dominion University, 80 points. Comparable differences were also found with respect to high school grades.

Schools differ greatly in how selective their admission policies are, and there is a tendency for the most selective schools to give larger preferences to black students. This is necessary if they are committed to attracting a substantial number of black students. Consider that the nation's 25 or so highest-ranked universities typically require their students to have SAT scores of 1400 or more (on the 400–1600 scale). In 2002, 0.7 percent of all black SAT test takers scored at least 700 on the verbal portion, compared to 5.1 percent of whites; on the math portion, 0.7 percent of black students scored at least 700 compared to 6.2 percent of whites. Put differently, blacks make up 1.0 percent of all those who scored above 700 on the verbal portion and 1.4 percent of those scoring above 700 on the math portion.[15]

What these differences mean is that if these highly selective schools admitted students solely on the basis of SAT scores, they would have student bodies that were only 1 to 2 percent black. In fact, blacks make up around 6 percent of their student bodies, an indication that lower standards are applied to black applicants.

Preferential admissions policies do *not*, however, necessarily lead to more blacks attending college. What they do is change *which* colleges blacks attend. When Harvard and Princeton admit blacks with 1200–1300 SAT scores, they are drawing from the pool of blacks who would meet the normal (not preferential) admission standards of the good state universities (like Michigan and Virginia). That makes it harder for Michigan and Virginia to find enough blacks that meet their normal admission requirements, so they are led to lower their standards. The University of Virginia may, for example, end up admitting blacks with 1000–1100 SAT scores, well below their normal level, but this depletes the pool of black students who meet the normal standards of the next lower tier of colleges.

Preferential admissions policies produce a *mismatching* of black students and the schools they attend. This is the most important effect to keep in mind in evaluating the consequences of these policies. They probably do not lead to more blacks attending college in total, simply because a majority of institutions are not selective (i.e., they admit anyone with a high school diploma). Instead, these policies lead some blacks to attend schools where their academic credentials place them at the bottom of the student body at these schools, whereas in the absence of preferential admissions they would attend a less selective school where their academic preparedness would be similar to the other students.

Mismatching has significant implications for the college experiences of black students. Most importantly, some will have academic difficulties because their academic skills are below those of the majority of students, and instructors generally tailor their classes to fit the qualifications of the typical student. It is not surprising, then, that black students fail to complete college at higher rates than whites, and that the difference in dropout rates tends to be greater at schools that more aggressively practice preferential admissions. For example, at Harvard, with a 95-point difference in SAT scores, 5 percent of black students failed to graduate compared with 3 percent of whites, whereas at Duke, with a 184-point SAT score difference, more than three times as high a proportion of blacks dropped out, 16 percent compared to 5 percent.[16]

We would also expect mismatching to lead to lower grades for the blacks who do complete their college degrees. This, too, is borne out by the facts: those blacks who graduate finish, on average, in the bottom 25 percent of their classes.[17] It also seems likely that mismatching will induce more black students to select easier majors, but I am not aware of evidence bearing directly on that prediction.

Mismatching causes these artificial and unnecessary failures for black students. Black college students are capable of graduating at the same rate as other students, and of attaining similar grades, if they attend institutions where their academic qualifications are in line with other students. Preferential admissions policies set some students up for failure by placing them in environments where they are ill-prepared to compete with other students.

The harm due to higher dropout rates and lower grades is not the only cost borne by blacks as a result of preferential admissions policies. Some black students, not just those who receive preferential treatment, suffer from the stigma that they may not really deserve their places at selective schools. And we can only speculate as to how the self-esteem of these students is affected when they find themselves struggling and often failing academically. White students' attitudes towards blacks may also be affected in unfortunate ways by seeing blacks bringing up the bottom in many classes, perhaps reinforcing the stereotype that blacks just can't make it.

There is a paucity of research on the consequences of preferential admissions policies because schools are reluctant to divulge the information necessary to investigate the issue. Recently, however, Richard Sander published a major study dealing with the effects of preferential admissions in the nation's law schools.[18] He had access to a unique database that tracked the careers of some 27,000 law students at 163 accredited law schools (95% of all accredited law schools) from their acceptance to law school until several years following graduation.

In many respects, Sander's findings mirror the conclusions drawn above with regard to undergraduate schools. For example, he was able to document extensive mismatching of black law students and law schools. But he was also able to examine the consequences of this mismatching to a degree no one has been previously able to. He found that 19 percent of black law students dropped out without completing law school, compared with 8 percent of white law students. Among those who completed law school, close to half of the black students ended up in the bottom tenth of their classes, and only around 8 percent were in the top half of their classes. The dismal outcomes did not end at this point. Law school graduates must pass their state's bar exam to practice law, and Sander found that 39 percent of black law graduates failed the bar exam on the first attempt, four times as high a percentage as for whites. Moreover, "The pass rate for blacks through five attempts [at passing the bar exam] was 77.6 percent; the black failure rate through five attempts was more than six times the white rate."[19]

Sander emphasizes that these failures are artificial and the result of the mismatching produced by preferential admissions: "Blacks and whites at the same school with the same grades perform identically on the bar exam; but since racial preferences have the effect of boosting blacks' school quality but sharply lowering their average grades, blacks have much higher failure rates on the bar than do whites with similar LSAT scores and undergraduate GPAs. Affirmative action thus artificially depresses, quite substantially, the rate at which blacks pass the bar."[20]

His conclusion is that "most black law applicants end up at schools where they will struggle academically and fail at higher rates than they would in the absence of preferences. The net trade-off of higher prestige but weaker academic performance substantially harms black performance on bar exams and harms most new black lawyers on the job market. Perhaps most remarkably, a strong case can be made that in the legal education system as a whole, racial preferences end up producing fewer black lawyers each year than would be produced by a race-blind system."[21]

Sander's conclusion that black law students are on balance harmed by the policy of preferential admissions is backed up with a great deal of data supporting the conclusions cited above. Of course, his work has been criticized, but it appears to have the ring of truth.[22]

Sander is willing to evaluate preferential admissions policies solely in terms of how they affect black students, but we should not forget that these policies also have effects on other students. After all, this is a transfer program that increases access to some schools for one group of students and therefore reduces access for other groups. In the world of preferential admissions, black and (to a generally lesser degree) Hispanic students comprise the former group while white and Asian students make up the latter group. Clearly, there is harm done to the better-qualified white and Asian students who are passed over in the admissions process to make room for less-qualified black and Hispanic students.

What is striking about preferential admissions policies is the strong likelihood that they harm much of the very group they are intended to help. Yet egalitarians continue to support this policy since it promotes social justice in their view. Social justice is obviously a very flexible concept.

IMMIGRATION

Over the past 15 years, the United States has absorbed about 1.3 million immigrants per year, composed roughly equally of legal and illegal immigrants. Immigration has, as is well known, increased greatly in recent decades. In the

1950s, for example, there was an average of about 250,000 immigrants per year, less than one-fifth the number of recent years. The surge in recent immigration, as well as its increased illegal component, has catapulted the issue of immigration policy onto the national agenda.

At first glance, it may seem strange to find immigration discussed in a book dealing with distributional issues. However, as we will see, immigration does produce a substantial redistribution of income, and that indeed is perhaps its major economic effect.

How does immigration affect the American economy? Its major effects flow from the ways labor markets are influenced. Immigration increases the number of people looking for jobs in the United States, that is, it increases the supply of labor. As explained in chapter 1, basic economics teaches us that this will lead to an increase in employment, but at lower wage rates; employers will hire larger numbers of workers but only at a lower wage. That is the central message of economic analysis, but implicit in this are a number of subtleties that influence how we evaluate immigration policy.

Is immigration good for America? That is the crucial question, and in addressing it I will interpret it to mean: Is immigration good for native-born American citizens? (That it is good for the immigrants goes almost without saying, otherwise they would not come and stay.) That the goal of U.S. policy should be to benefit American citizens (who I will refer to as *natives*), rather than citizens of other countries, is widely accepted.

The most direct effect of immigration on natives is that their wage rates are reduced as a result of the increase in the total supply of labor. It is not just the new immigrant workers who receive lower wages, but all the native workers who are competing with them for jobs. So native workers are harmed by immigration, but by how much? That issue has been much debated by economists, and I think the most reliable estimates have been made by Harvard University's George Borjas. In a recent study, he concludes that the *average* wage in the United States was 3.2 percent lower in 2000 as a result of the increase in labor supply due to immigration.[23] At that time, immigrants accounted for about 11 percent of the labor force in the United States. Because today immigrants are a larger fraction, around 15 percent, of the labor force, it seems certain that the effect on wage rates is larger. I will assume a 4 percent decline in wage rates is a reasonable estimate for today's economy.

If native workers are receiving 4 percent lower wages than they would have in the absence of the last 40 years or so of immigration, then their total labor earnings are about $330 billion lower *each year* as a result of immigration policy.[24] That sounds like a major loss to natives, but this is not the full story. Natives are also employers of labor and consumers of labor services, and in these roles they benefit from reduced wage rates. Indeed, economists recognize that this $330 billion is a *transfer* of income from native workers to native consumers and owners of capital. There is no net loss in income but just a sizeable redistribution of income from one group of natives to another (overlapping) group. For the nation as a whole, there is no net loss, and no net gain, from immigration's effect on the wages of natives.[25]

Not all workers are affected to the same degree, that is, with a 4 percent loss in wages. That is the average effect, but in some labor markets we expect the effect to be much larger. Immigrants add about 15 percent to labor supply in total, but the increase in unskilled labor markets is considerably larger. One of the significant changes in immigration has been that recent immigrants are far less skilled (relative to natives) than immigrants from the 1960s and earlier.[26] Although immigrants comprise 15 percent of the total labor force, they account for 45 percent of workers with less than a high school diploma, according to the Congressional Budget Office.[27] That means immigration has increased the number of poorly educated workers by a staggering 82 percent. It would be surprising if the influx of poorly educated workers did not significantly depress the wage rates received by unskilled native workers.

Borjas estimated that immigration produced a decline in the wages of unskilled workers of 8.9 percent, nearly three times as large as the overall average reduction in wage rates. Taking account of the larger immigrant population today, this suggests the decline is at least 10 percent now. Given the 82 percent increase in supply, I am surprised that the reduction isn't greater. Even so, it is a substantial loss for unskilled workers. Recall that the median male high school dropout earns about $27,000 per year, so immigration costs such workers about $3,000 a year. That loss will become larger if immigration continues at its current pace.

Immigration has thus made the distribution of market incomes of the native-born population more unequal. Those at the bottom suffer the largest losses in wages, while those at the top likely gain because they own most of the capital (businesses, stocks, and bonds). High-wage earners may also face losses in wages, but they are the indirect beneficiaries of the nationwide reduction in wage rates, which economists believe accrue mainly to capital owners. Unskilled workers typically own little capital and so have no offsetting gain to their wage losses.

We can get an idea of the impact of immigration on inequality by comparing the HiLo ratios[28] across states. In the latter 1990s the five states with the most unequal income distributions (highest HiLo ratios, with highest first) were New York, Arizona, New Mexico, Louisiana, and California. For these states the HiLo ratios ranged from 14.1 to 11.9. Four of these five states (Louisiana is the exception) had immigrant populations that were above the national average (as a percentage of the state's population). Indeed, New York and California had immigrant populations that were nearly two and two-and-a-half times, respectively, the national average.[29]

In sharp contrast, the five states with the most equal income distributions all had immigrant populations that were lower than the national average, in fact averaging less than half the national average. These states are Utah, Indiana, Iowa, North Dakota, and Colorado. HiLo ratios for these states ranged from 6.9 to 8.1, significantly lower than the high-immigrant states.

While immigration is not the only feature that differentiates these states, it surely played a significant role in accentuating income inequalities in those states with large immigrant populations.

Immigration affects most measures of the distribution of income in two distinct ways. First, even if there were no effect on the wages of native-born workers, immigration increases the number of low-income families and would increase inequality (as measured by HiLo ratios or quintile shares) even in this case. Second, immigration of course does decrease the wage earnings of native workers, especially unskilled workers, and so increases inequality in that way as well.

Given that few people openly advocate transferring income from the poor to the well-off, why do some people, and most egalitarians, support immigration and often call for even more? An examination of the most common arguments may offer a clue.

Consider the arguments suggested by columnist Linda Chavez: "Without the more than 12 million immigrants who arrived in the 1990s—including some 5 million illegal aliens—*the U.S. would have created fewer jobs, experienced slower economic growth and maintained a lower standard of living for everyone*" (italics added).[30] Let's look briefly at each of these three familiar arguments.

It is true that there are more jobs (employed workers) created when there are more immigrants, but putting foreigners to work is not of obvious benefit to native workers. Jobs are not an end in themselves but a means to a higher standard of living, and the standards of living we should be concerned with are those of natives. Putting more and more immigrants to work does not raise the average standard of living of natives (with one minor qualification noted below).

It is also true that immigration adds to the growth rate of the economy. But the growth rate increases because of the added output produced by the immigrants, and they receive the value of the added output (their marginal value product, as explained in chapter 1) as wages. The higher output for the economy as a whole does not translate into any higher income for natives, and that is what matters, or should matter.

Finally, it is simply not true that immigration leads to a higher "standard of living for everyone." Some people are clearly harmed, as we explained. Indeed, it is unlikely that the average standard of living of natives increases at all.

What about President Bush's (and others') argument that immigrants perform "jobs Americans won't do?" It is probably untrue that there are *any* jobs some Americans won't do *if the wage is high enough*. That immigrants perform some jobs at wage rates lower than natives will accept just highlights the wage-lowering effect of immigration, which, as we have already discussed, is not a net benefit to natives.

Most of the arguments favoring immigration are incomplete or just wrong, like the above, but there is one valid argument that holds that there is a net gain for natives—that the losses in wages are more than offset by the gain to consumers and capital owners. This is difficult to explain (as any economics teacher can attest), but it turns on the fact that wages are equal to the *marginal* product of labor in competitive markets. All workers are evaluated as marginal workers, but if there is a large discrete increase in labor employed (as with immigration), the added output slightly exceeds the total wages paid to the additional workers (because the marginal product declines as more are employed). The excess is a net gain to natives, and it accrues (economists believe) to capital owners.

Although the way immigration produces this net gain may be obscure, economists are certain that it exists. Moreover, the magnitude can be roughly estimated, and the important point is that it is very small. The President's Council of Economic Advisers recently put this net gain at 0.28 percent of GDP, about $35 billion in 2005.[31] Therefore, the average American gains about $100 per year from immigration; however, not all share in this gain. Putting it in terms of our earlier figures, if immigration causes workers to lose $330 billion in wages then the gain to consumers and/or capital owners is equal to this $330 billion plus the extra $35 billion. The gains exceed the losses but only slightly.

Does this constitute an economic case for immigration? Yes, but only if you care solely about the total income of natives and are indifferent to its distribution. It remains true that lower-income natives lose substantially from immigration; the only thing added here is that the gain to higher-income groups is a little bit larger. The biggest effect is still the redistribution of income from native workers to other groups. And, it should be added, the small net gain identified here results from the reduction in wages of native workers. It is ironic that many immigration advocates stress the net gain from immigration and simultaneously deny that native workers receive lower wage rates. If there is no reduction in native wages from immigration (implausible, but some immigration advocates do hold this), then there is no net gain from immigration to natives as a group.[32]

Incidentally, if this net gain is to be the basis for guiding immigration policy, it calls for a very different type of policy than we have now. For a given number of immigrants, this net gain will be larger the more highly paid are the immigrants, so if we want to get as large a net gain as possible, we should let in only highly skilled workers. Current policy is virtually the exact opposite of this. Permitting only skilled immigration would have the added benefit of narrowing earnings inequalities rather than widening them, as existing immigration policy does.

All the foregoing discussion has concentrated on how *markets* respond to immigration and transmit gains and losses throughout the economy. There is another way in which immigration affects the economic standard of living of the native population that is also of importance. Immigration affects government tax, expenditure, and regulatory policies in ways that also bear on whether the native population benefits from immigration. Immigrants pay taxes and also receive services funded by tax revenues. The key question here is whether immigrants pay enough in taxes to cover the added cost of providing the government services and welfare benefits they receive. If they don't, then native taxpayers have to make up the shortfall, and this constitutes another way that immigration can harm the native population.

There have been several studies attempting to tabulate this fiscal effect of immigration. These studies have compared the taxes paid versus government services consumed by immigrants. But it isn't necessary to describe these studies in detail to understand why recent immigration has imposed a net fiscal cost on native taxpayers. After all, we have seen that the U.S. system transfers income from high-income families to low-income families. And immigrants, as suggested by their lack of skills, tend to have low incomes. In 2003, for example, median immigrant earnings were 26 percent lower than the median earnings of natives.[33] So we expect immigrants to pay less in taxes than natives and to receive more in taxpayer-funded benefits than natives. In addition, immigrants "typically have larger households, and their households typically contain a larger number of younger persons and older persons,"[34] which implies higher costs on school and medical care systems.

Thus, it is not surprising that most studies find that native-born households on average pay taxes to subsidize foreign-born households. The modest size of the estimated net cost on natives from this source may, however, be surprising. According to studies prepared for the National Academy of Sciences' National Research Council, the net cost on natives was in the range $11–20 billion per year in the mid-1990s.[35] Current costs would probably be at least double this, but at $22–40 billion this is still only about 0.2 to 0.3 percent of GDP. Effects in individual states with high immigrant populations (such as California) are, however, significantly higher than these nationwide totals suggest.

Let me sum up the discussion of the costs and benefits of immigration to this point. On average, native-born households receive a net gain from the increase in labor supply resulting from immigration, but that net gain is small, about 0.28 percent of GDP. Offsetting this is a net loss to native-born households resulting from immigrants' participation in government tax and expenditure policies, and that net loss is probably the same order of magnitude at 0.2–0.3 percent of GDP. Combining these two losses, and recognizing the uncertainties surrounding all such calculations, it is probable that the overall average economic effect on natives from recent immigration in the United States is close to zero.

That near-zero average effect, however, conceals the large redistribution of income produced by immigration, one that particularly harms less-skilled native workers and benefits the well-off. Related to this is the fact that immigration worsens just about every social problem you can name. Whether it is poverty, inequality, illegitimacy, people lacking health insurance, poor school outcomes, crime, terrorism, or the introduction and spread of communicable diseases—immigration disproportionately contributes to all of these. For example, of the 41 million without health insurance, 30 percent are immigrants or their children, and nearly 60 percent of the growth in the uninsured population between 1992 and 2001 came from immigrants.

We have not discussed an important, but less well-documented, potential consequence of immigration: There may be an indirect economic effect of immigration that results from its influence on the political determination of government policy. Immigration policy has dramatically changed the ethnic composition of the population, and that may create problems for political decision making as the various groups constitute interest groups fighting for their "piece of the pie." As William Easterly explains the possible outcome: "The existence of polarized interest groups that each act in their own interest is responsible for bad government policies. Societies that are more polarized have worse government policies than societies that are more unified. Any factor that breeds polarization will worsen policy, and thus cause lower growth."[36]

That immigration policy has created large, and growing, ethnic blocs is beyond dispute. In 1960, the U.S. population was approximately 90 percent white and 10 percent black. Today, the white share of the population is under 75 percent and continues to decline. Projections suggest that if immigration policy remains unchanged, whites will be in a minority shortly after the middle of this century, with three ethnic groups (blacks, Hispanics, and Asians) constituting nearly half of the population.

To many, this creation of a multicultural society seems a good thing, and perhaps it is, but evidence from the international scene suggests there are real dangers. From Easterly again: "Social scientists have documented extensive problems in economic policymaking when there is ethnic diversity.... [Economic] growth is two percentage points lower in the more ethnically diverse countries than in the least ethnically diverse countries."[37] Apparently, more homogeneous societies enjoy greater economic growth and more prosperity,[38] and if that holds true for the United States our future standards of living could be much lower as a result of our immigration policy.

Americans secure little if any net economic benefit from the mass immigration produced by immigration policy and may possibly bear long-run costs if economic growth suffers. But one thing we surely get and that is increased inequality. That egalitarians support an immigration policy with this result suggests once again how very elastic their concept of social justice must be.

Taxation

Up to this point, our emphasis has been on policies that transfer income to certain groups of people. Of course, transferring income *to* some implies that it is transferred *from* others, and in this chapter our attention shifts to the effects of the most important policies implicated in the taking side of the transfers, namely federal tax policies. Some government transfer programs do not directly involve taxation at all, but most of the larger transfer programs are government expenditure policies, and these policies must be financed by taxes. That is true, at least, unless the expenditure is funded through deficit finance, which we will discuss in the last section of the chapter.

WHO BEARS THE TAX BURDEN?

Do you know how large a share of your income goes to the federal government in the form of taxes? Few people do, although most people are sure they are paying too much while they believe that others, principally the rich, are avoiding paying their fair share. Before looking at the evidence, you might find it instructive to guess the federal tax burden as a share of income for the household income quintiles (fifths) we discussed in chapter 2. We will also be looking at the tax burdens for the top 10 percent and top 1 percent of households separately, to see how the so-called rich are treated. As a guide, keep in mind that federal taxes average about 20 percent of household income, so if some quintiles have a tax burden greater than this, others must have a lower burden.

What we will be looking at are estimates of what economists call *average tax rates*. The average tax rate is simply a ratio, calculated for each household or income class, where the numerator is the total tax burden and the denominator is total (before-tax) income. It indicates how much the tax reduces your disposable income, or as I earlier put it, the share of your income going to government.

Tax rates vary among income classes, and the way they vary forms the basis for classifying the tax as progressive, regressive, or proportional. When the average tax rate is higher for higher income classes, the tax is said to be progressive; when the rate is lower for higher income classes, the tax is regressive; and when it is the same at all levels of income, the tax is proportional. These terms have found their way into popular usage, but surprisingly few people understand the distinction between them. Even the *Wall Street Journal,* which you would think would know better, has characterized a progressive tax as one that "taxes the rich more than the poor."[1]

It is true that a progressive tax taxes the rich more than the poor, but so does a proportional tax and so do most real-world regressive taxes. Under a proportional tax that takes, say, 20 percent of everyone's income, a rich person with a million-dollar income will pay $200,000 in taxes, while a poor person with a $10,000 income will pay only $2,000 in taxes. The rich person is paying a hundred times as much in taxes as the poor person, but the tax is a proportional tax because it is the same percentage of income for both persons. For the tax to be progressive, the tax must take a larger *proportion* of the higher income, not just a larger absolute amount.

With these preliminaries out of the way, let's see who bears the burden of federal taxes. The figures in table 9.1 are from the Congressional Budget Office (CBO) and show average tax rates for households by income group (household quintiles, and the top 10% and 1% separately). There are four major federal sources of tax revenue.[2] In terms of revenue, from largest to smallest, they are individual income tax, Social Security payroll tax, corporation income tax, and excise taxes. Part A of the table aggregates the rates from these separate taxes into one overall tax rate for the federal tax system.

As you can see from the last column in table 9.1A, the overall federal tax system is, as of 2004, quite progressive. Households in the lowest-income quintile give up 4.5 percent of their incomes to federal taxes, with that rate rising steadily to 25.1 percent for the highest quintile. The table also separates out the top 10 percent and top 1 percent; they are, of course, already included in the highest quintile, but because many people are particularly interested in how the tax system treats the very well-off, these figures are shown separately. Progressivity continues within the highest quintile, with a tax rate for the top 10 percent of 26.9 percent, and 31.1 percent for the top 1 percent.

Because the table deals only with the federal taxes, these figures do not include state and local taxes. Add about 11 percentage points to each income class's tax rate to get a rough idea of the total tax burden.

TABLE 9.1A
Average Federal Tax Rates for All Federal Taxes

Income Category	1979	1985	1990	1995	2000	2004
Lowest Quintile	8.0	9.8	8.9	6.3	6.4	4.5
Second Quintile	14.3	14.8	14.6	13.4	13.0	10.0
Middle Quintile	18.6	18.1	17.9	17.3	16.7	13.9
Fourth Quintile	21.2	20.4	20.6	20.5	20.5	17.2
Highest Quintile	27.5	24.0	25.1	27.8	28.0	25.1
All	22.2	20.9	21.5	22.6	23.1	20.0
Top 10%	29.6	24.7	26.1	29.8	29.7	26.9
Top 1%	37.0	27.0	28.8	36.1	33.2	31.1

TABLE 9.1B
Average Federal Tax Rates for the Federal Individual Income Tax

Income Category	1979	1985	1990	1995	2000	2004
Lowest Quintile	0.0	0.5	−1.0	−4.4	−4.6	−6.2
Second Quintile	4.1	4.0	3.4	2.0	1.5	−0.8
Middle Quintile	7.5	6.6	6.0	5.3	5.0	2.9
Fourth Quintile	10.1	8.8	8.3	7.8	8.1	5.9
Highest Quintile	15.7	14.0	14.4	15.5	17.5	13.9
All	11.0	10.2	10.1	10.2	11.8	8.7
Top 10%	17.4	15.4	16.0	17.7	19.3	15.9
Top 1%	21.8	18.9	19.9	23.7	24.2	19.6

Source: Congressional Budget Office, "Historical Effective Federal Tax Rates: 1979–2004," December 2006, http://www.cbo.gov/ftpdocs/77xx/doc7718/EffectiveTaxRates.pdf.

Table 9.1A also shows how federal tax rates have varied since 1979. There have been a half dozen major changes in tax policy over this period, as well as changes in before-tax household incomes, that have combined to make the federal tax system more progressive today than in 1979. This may seem surprising because, accompanying all the policy changes (except for the one in 1993), there have been charges of unfair tax cuts for the wealthy presumably leaving too large a burden on the struggling middle class. Yet upper-income households are paying tax rates today that are higher relative to other groups than they did in 1979.

Every group's average tax rate is lower in 2004 than it was in 1979, but the declines have been greater for the lower income classes. Note that the top quintile in 1979 had an average tax rate that was 3.4 times as great as the lowest quintile (27.5 compared to 8.0), whereas in 2004 the rate for the top quintile was 5.6 times greater than that of the bottom quintile. Comparisons for other groups show the same pattern. This increased progressivity means that the tax system is having a greater equalizing effect on after-tax incomes than it did in the past.

We are interested in these facts, of course, because we want to know (among other things) whether the tax system is fair. As always, that judgment cannot be made objectively because it relies on differing individual values, but at least the figures in table 9.1 should help in arriving at such a determination. In one sense, however, I think it is misleading to rely on the figures in table 9.1A for the total federal tax system to determine whether people are sharing fairly in the burden of supporting the federal government. It is misleading because the figures in part A include tax rates for the Social Security payroll tax, and that tax differs from virtually all others and should be treated separately.

The Social Security payroll tax differs from other taxes in that individual taxpayers are scheduled to receive benefits in retirement that are related to their earlier tax contributions. For this reason, making a judgment about fairness for this tax requires considering the effects over people's entire lifetimes, both when they pay taxes and later when they receive benefits. It makes no sense to speak of the Social Security tax as unfair without also taking into account the promised later benefits.

We have already examined Social Security taxes and benefits in chapter 7. There, we saw that low-wage workers can expect to receive back more for each dollar of payroll taxes they pay than will high-wage workers (recall the higher rates of return for low-wage workers in table 7.1A). A judgment of fairness about the Social Security system should be based on its redistribution in favor of low-wage earners and other groups, including the way it favors earlier retirees and harms future generations.

For these reasons, I think it appropriate to focus on taxes other than Social Security payroll taxes when considering whether the tax burden is fairly shared. Specifically, I will concentrate on the federal individual income tax. That tax alone provides 80 percent of the revenues supporting all federal government spending programs except Social Security (and Medicare).

Part B of table 9.1 shows the CBO's figures for the average tax rates of the various household groups for the federal individual income tax. Looking at 2004, the first thing you may notice is that the two lowest quintiles have negative tax rates. How can anyone pay a negative tax? This is a reflection of the fact that the IRS treats refundable tax credits, such as the Earned Income Tax Credit (EITC), as negative taxes. The EITC is, of course, only one of many transfers to low-income families, but other transfers are defined as income and put into the denominator (before-tax income—if they are counted at all, as many aren't) of the ratio determining the average tax rate, rather than in the numerator as a negative tax. There is, therefore, an inconsistency in treatment between refundable tax credits and all other transfers, but as long as we understand what is being done that should not be an issue. The important general point is that most low-income households pay little or no federal income taxes.

The individual income tax is clearly much more progressive than the overall federal tax system. The top quintile in 2004 incurred a tax rate of 13.9 percent, almost five times as large as the 2.9 percent rate imposed on middle-income households. In contrast, when all taxes are combined in part A, the rate for the top quintile is less than twice the rate for the middle quintile.

It is also clear that the income tax has become more progressive in recent decades, as judged by the ratio of the tax rates in higher income classes to those in the lower income classes. Note, in particular, that the middle class, or middle quintile, in 2004 had a tax rate less than half the rate of 1979, 2.9 percent as compared with 7.5 percent.

The struggling, hardworking, beleaguered middle-income household is often portrayed as bearing a disproportionate share of the tax burden. As *New York Times* reporter David Cay Johnston put it in a recent book: "Since at least 1983 it has been the explicit, but unstated, policy in Washington to let the richest Americans pay a smaller portion of their incomes in taxes...while collecting more in taxes from those in the middle class."[3] Many people seem to believe this statement, but examination of table 9.1 shows the exact opposite to be the case: Tax rates are higher for the wealthy than in 1985[4] and lower for the middle class. Is the middle class, or middle quintile, overtaxed when it pays an income tax rate of 2.9 percent? In fact, the middle quintile devotes a larger share of its income to expenditures on entertainment (4.6% of income), dining at restaurants (5.8%), and gasoline (5.1%), than it contributes to income tax revenues.[5]

Another way to characterize the distribution of the tax burden is to consider the share of total tax revenues that is paid by the different income classes. In the same CBO study that produces the data in table 9.1, it is reported that in 2004 the highest quintile paid *85.3 percent* of all federal income tax revenues! Perhaps even more astounding is the fact that the wealthiest 5 percent of households paid more than half (58.4%) of all income taxes, whereas the lowest 60 percent of households (the lowest three quintiles) contributed only 0.9 percent of income tax revenues. What this way of looking at the distribution of taxes makes clear is that *higher-income households pay for almost everything the federal government does outside of Social Security, and a majority of taxpayers contribute almost nothing.*

As repeatedly pointed out in this book, facts such as these do not prove that a policy is fair or unfair, but they are clearly important factors to consider. Also relevant to consider is the fact that the public has a very distorted view of how tax burdens are shared. Surveys repeatedly show that most people believe the tax system imposes far smaller burdens on upper-income families than it really does. For example, one survey found that the median respondent thought that families with $200,000 incomes paid about $15,000, or 7.5 percent, in taxes at a time when the actual rate was nearly three times as high at 21 percent. Another survey found that people thought that 45 percent of millionaires paid no income tax at all, when the true figure was 2 percent.[6] Given these misconceptions, it is perhaps not surprising that other surveys repeatedly find that most people believe that upper-income people pay less than their fair share of taxes. Is 85.3 percent of all income taxes really less than their fair share?

Important as it is, fairness is not the only criterion important in evaluating the tax system, as we will see in the next section.

THE HIDDEN COSTS OF TAXATION

Do taxpayers receive a dollar in benefits for every dollar in taxes they send to Washington? Many people are inclined to answer this question in the negative, but the point I wish to emphasize in this section is that the question itself is incorrectly posed. *Even if* people do receive a dollar in benefits for each dollar of taxes, they will be harmed by the transaction. The reason is that taxes impose costs on taxpayers in excess of the amount of revenue collected. These indirect and hidden costs of taxation are referred to by economists as *excess burdens* to reflect the fact that the burden, or cost, of taxation is greater than the amount of revenue raised.

A simple example can clarify this important point. Suppose we place a tax on the sale of pizzas equal to $1,000 per pizza. My guess is that no pizzas would be sold because nobody would pay $1010 for a pizza. Production and consumption of pizzas would decline to zero. Thus there would be no tax revenue collected. Yet clearly people would be worse off even though they bear no *direct* tax burden. They are worse off because the tax leads them to consume fewer pizzas (and probably more hamburgers and tacos) than they would prefer. Economists would say that the tax *distorts* the consumption decisions of households. This burden is an excess burden because there is no direct burden of the tax—no revenue collected.

Most real world taxes produce both a direct burden, as measured by the tax revenue actually collected, and an excess burden. If the pizza tax, for example, was $10 per pizza, some pizzas would still be sold but perhaps at a price of $20 rather than $10. Tax revenue would be collected—$10 per pizza produced and sold—but consumers would bear an additional burden due to the reduction in the amount consumed at the higher price. In general, taxes discourage the economic activities that are subject to tax and thereby produce a distortion in the pattern of production and/or consumption; this distortion constitutes an excess burden. The total burden of taxation, the sum of the direct burden (equal to revenue) and excess burden, is therefore larger than the revenue collected. Note that the tax burdens measured in table 9.1

are defined to include only the direct burdens of taxes; the total burdens are larger than shown in that table.

How large the excess burdens of taxation are has been an important subject of economic research for decades. When I began studying economics in the 1960s, excess burdens were thought to be small compared to direct burdens, and they were mostly ignored in discussions of tax policy. An early attempt to estimate the excess burden of the federal individual income tax, for example, concluded that it was only 2.4 percent as large as the amount of tax revenue collected.[7] Today economists recognize that these hidden costs are much larger than that. Before considering exactly how large they are, let's examine the four most important ways the federal tax system produces these hidden costs.

The first of these "hidden costs" is not really so hidden, as many taxpayers are acutely aware of this cost. I am referring to the costs of complying with the tax laws: keeping records, reading and filling out tax forms, paying professional tax preparers, or purchasing tax preparation software. These costs add significantly to the burden placed on taxpayers. For instance, the IRS estimated that individual taxpayers spent 3.2 *billion* hours on tax compliance in 2000; it is as if all the workers in Minnesota did nothing but fill out tax forms for 40 hours each week all year long. In addition, taxpayers spent $19 billion for professional tax preparation assistance and computer software.[8]

Placing a monetary value on taxpayers' time, Joel Slemrod and Jon Bakija conclude that "our best estimate of the total annual cost of enforcing and complying with the federal corporate and personal income taxes in 2003 is $110 billion, or about 10 cents per dollar raised."[9] Or, as I would put it, each dollar of taxes collected places a burden of $1.10 on taxpayers due to the compliance costs they bear.

The other three types of excess burdens produced by taxes all reflect the way taxes adversely influence certain key economic decisions. Before discussing each type separately, it is worth stressing that it is the *marginal* rate of taxation that is responsible for these adverse effects. Under any tax other than a proportional tax, marginal and average tax rates will be different. The marginal rate is the tax rate that applies to a change in income from its current level, and in a progressive tax it exceeds the average rate. In the previous section, we were discussing exclusively average rates of taxation because they indicate how large the total (direct) tax burden is. But it is the marginal rate that is relevant for incentives. As the President's Council of Economic Advisers expressed it: "An individual's after-tax return from increased work effort, saving, or investment depends on the individual's *marginal tax rate,* the tax rate that applies to the last dollar of the individual's income."[10]

What really matters for economic incentives is the overall marginal tax rate that is the combined result of all taxes (federal, state, and local) and transfers (recall the marginal tax rates implicit in transfer policies). While the federal individual income tax by itself has marginal rate brackets that range from

10 percent up to 35 percent, the typical American family confronts an overall marginal tax rate that is considerably higher, in the range of 40 to 45 percent. At that level, it reduces substantially the reward from earning more income and adversely affects other economic decisions as well.

Returning to our main topic, high marginal tax rates produce excess burdens by distorting three types of economic decisions: how much to work; how much to save; and the form in which income is received and spent. Let's look at each of these in turn.

High marginal tax rates on earnings lead to reductions in the quantity of labor supplied to the economy, that is, to reductions in how much and how hard people work.[11] How large this negative impact on work incentives is has been, not surprisingly, the subject of myriad statistical studies by economists. Briefly summarizing these findings is difficult, but I think few economists would consider this characterization unreasonable: A 10 percentage point *reduction,* say from 45 to 35 percent, in the overall marginal tax rate on earnings would lead to an *increase* in the quantity of labor supplied of roughly 5 percent.[12] This is an average figure; obviously many persons would deviate from that average response.

Those who doubt that taxes have any significant effect on how much people work (and there are many, including some economists) would be advised to consider the experience of Iceland. Between 1987 and 1988, Iceland overhauled its income tax in a strange way that presented a rare opportunity to observe some of the effects of taxation. In the transition to the reformed income tax, workers' 1986 earnings were taxed in 1987, and their 1988 earnings were taxed under the new tax in 1988. Their 1987 earnings were not taxed at all—there was a one-year tax holiday! In that year, both labor supply and GDP increased about 4 percent. When the new tax was imposed in 1988, labor supply and GDP returned to their previous levels.[13] This suggests that taxes do significantly depress earnings and output, even if the effects often go unnoticed. And note that in Iceland we saw only the very short-run consequences of a tax change; the longer-run effects would likely be larger.

An even more striking bit of evidence is provided by the work of Nobel laureate Edward Prescott.[14] Prescott set out to explain the dramatic difference in work behavior between Europeans and Americans. There is a surprisingly large difference: Europeans (he focused on France, Germany, and Italy) work about *one-third less* than do Americans. What accounts for this? Prescott concludes that higher taxes on earnings are largely responsible for Europeans working less than Americans. According to Prescott, typical marginal tax rates on earnings in these European countries are about 60 percent, compared with around 40 percent for the United States.

Of course, there are many other possible explanations for this difference in work behavior. But what makes taxes look like the probable culprit is another fact reported by Prescott: In 1970, European and American labor supplies were almost identical. Moreover, in 1970 taxes on earnings were similar for these European countries and the United States. (The higher tax rates that we associate with these European countries are, in fact, a relatively recent development.) To sum up: When tax rates were the same, labor supplies were comparable; when tax rates rose in Europe and did not in the United States in the years after 1970, labor supply declined sharply in Europe relative to the United States. These figures are strong prima facie evidence that taxes have substantial effects on how much people work.

The third major type of excess burden produced by taxes (the first two being compliance costs and labor supply effects) is their effect on saving. Taxes falling on dividends, interest income, capital gains, and corporate and small business profits all have the effect of reducing the rate of return received by the saver/investor. Just as taxes on earnings can reduce work by reducing its remuneration, taxes that fall on capital income can reduce saving by making its payoff smaller. Insofar as people save less when they receive a lower rate of return, taxes on capital income will inhibit the flow of funds that finance capital investment and fuel economic growth. Just as we saw with Social Security, saving less means reduced capital accumulation and lower incomes in later years.

There is less of a consensus among economists regarding how much taxes affect saving: "In contrast to the evidence on labor supply, the evidence on how saving responds to incentives is subject to much greater uncertainty because of the lack of good data."[15] The confluence of higher taxes on capital income and lower saving in the United States than in many other high-income countries does, however, suggest that saving may be significantly affected by taxes.

In addition to possibly depressing saving by reducing the rewards savers receive (their after-tax returns), the tax system can reduce aggregate saving in a second way: by placing large tax burdens on people who tend to save high proportions of their income. It seems clear that high-income families save a larger proportion of their incomes, both in total and at the margin, than do lower-income families.[16] It then follows that a highly progressive tax system, which places a disproportionate burden on high-income families, will reduce national saving in comparison to a less progressive, or proportional, system. In effect, a progressive tax increases the tax burden on those who save and reduces it on those who consume, therefore reducing total saving.

The fourth significant way taxation can distort economic decisions and produce excess burdens is through use of an inappropriate definition of taxable income. Economists believe a comprehensive definition of income is more efficient (and equitable), yet the tax code is riddled with special provisions that exempt many types and uses of income from taxation. Exclusions, deductions, exemptions, and tax credits are the names for these provisions, often called *tax preferences* by those who approve of them or *tax loopholes* by those who disapprove. These tax loopholes (so you will know where I stand) eat up a large share of the potential income tax base. To be precise, income that is subject to taxation by the federal individual income tax is just *one-half* as large as total household income broadly measured.[17] As a result, taxpayers have incentive to channel too much of their income into forms that are not subject to taxation and that constitutes another excess burden.

How large the excess burden of federal taxes is cannot be estimated with precision, but in their annual report, the President's Council of Economic Advisers reference a study they consider representative: "A recent study estimated that the excess burden associated with increasing the individual income tax by one dollar is 30 to 50 cents. In other words, the total burden of collecting $1.00 in additional income taxes is between $1.30 and $1.50, not counting compliance costs."[18] Taking the midpoint of this estimate, $1.40, and adding in the 10 cents in compliance costs yields a reasonable estimate of $1.50 for each dollar of revenue for the total burden of raising tax revenue through the federal individual income tax. There are higher and lower estimates in the literature, but most economists would accept this as a plausible estimate.

I began this section with a question about whether taxpayers received a dollar in benefits for each dollar in taxes. We now see that if taxpayers are to benefit from government spending programs, they must receive at least $1.50 in benefits from each dollar in taxes, otherwise the hidden excess burden costs will leave them worse off. Note that this does not imply that government spending can't benefit taxpayers, for there are certainly expenditure programs that do provide more than $1.50 in benefits per dollar spent. But there are also many programs that do not provide this much benefit, and these programs have been enacted in part because taxpayers and politicians are not aware of how large the hidden costs of taxation are.

In Defense of the Rich

It is surprising the extent to which tax policy is shaped by a desire to soak the rich. It is not an exaggeration to say that a general animosity toward the rich and a suspicion that they get away with murder (i.e., not paying their "fair share") are a powerful political force that strongly influences our tax institutions. These attitudes are promoted in specious books with titles like *Perfectly Legal: The Covert Campaign to Rig Our Tax System to Benefit the Super Rich—And Cheat Everybody Else* and *Take the Rich Off Welfare,* which seem designed to provoke hostility and anger toward the rich.[19] Although the facts show that the wealthy bear a heavy tax burden and receive little back in the way of benefits from government expenditures, that hasn't stopped the unscrupulous from fomenting the opposite belief.

In this section I undertake the unpopular task of defending this vilified minority, the rich. I am not going to argue that they are, in any sense, better human beings than others, but only that they make important (and unappreciated) economic contributions to society.

First of all, who are the so-called rich? In contrast to poverty, there is no official definition to use. Opinion polls show that under 1 percent of Americans think of themselves as rich, and only about 7 percent even regard themselves as upper-income. Yet they also show that people believe that 21 percent of Americans are rich, but when asked to specify the actual income level that is necessary to be rich it turns out that there are only 4 percent of Americans who exceed that level.[20] In view of these contradictions, I will use a somewhat flexible standard to define the rich in this section—sometimes the top 20 percent and sometimes a smaller fraction.

At the outset, it is important to recall from the discussion in chapter 1 that the rich do not obtain their high incomes by oppressing or exploiting the poor and middle class. The rich, just like others, receive incomes that are determined by the productivities of the resources they supply to the market. Specifically, the prices of their labor and capital services are equal to the marginal productivities of these resources (with an important exception discussed below). They are rich by virtue of contributing a lot to the nation's output. So it is not just misleading, but completely wrong, to suggest that people become rich at the expense of others ("the rich get richer and the poor get poorer"). If a given rich person (and the nonlabor resources he owns) simply vanishes from the face of the earth, there wouldn't be any more income available to those of us remaining.

That said, there are at least four important ways the rich as a group make contributions that benefit the rest of society. First of all, they provide a large share of the capital that the economy utilizes in the production of myriad goods and services. Capital, recall, is the name for resources like buildings, equipment, vehicles, machinery, and computers that are used in the production of just about everything. The rich own a large share of these resources; they have accumulated these assets over a lifetime of saving and investing, or perhaps by inheritance. In fact, the wealthiest 10 percent own about 70 percent of all the capital in the American economy. They don't just sit on it, of course, but sell its services in various markets, receiving in return hundreds of billions of dollars each year in capital income (dividends, profits, interest, etc.).

The other 90 percent of the population, however, also receive a significant benefit from the provision of all this capital to the economy by the rich. Imagine that 70 percent of all the resources you use in your job (provided by your employer, aka the rich) simply vanished. You would be a lot less productive as a worker, wouldn't you? And, therefore, your wage would fall. As economists put it, the (marginal) productivity of workers depends in part on how much capital per worker there is: the less capital per worker, the lower the productivity and wage. And the rich provide the capital.

We cannot know exactly how much wages are dependent on the amount of capital provided by the rich, but economists have a standard way of arriving at an order of magnitude estimate. Applying this approach, I estimate that if the capital in the U.S. economy were reduced by 70 percent (the amount provided by the richest 10%), wage rates on average would decline by 26 percent.[21] That means that workers receive about $2.44 *trillion* in higher earnings annually thanks to the rich making their capital available for production.[22]

The rich also provide labor services to the economy. They work, and generally very hard: Families in the top quintile provide at least a third of all hours worked in the economy.[23] Moreover, the rich tend to provide highly skilled labor services; they are the doctors, scientists, entrepreneurs, engineers, lawyers, and college professors. They are highly paid for their efforts, but the question before us is whether by providing these services there are benefits to others. The answer is yes, and for the same reason that their provision of capital benefits others. Lesser-skilled workers' services are worth more when they cooperate in productive activities with more-skilled workers.

David Henderson makes the general point in this way: "Capital and highly skilled workers are typically what economists call 'complements' of low-skilled workers; that is, the more capital and high-skilled workers there are for low-skilled workers to work with, the more productive, and thus higher-paid, low-skilled workers become."[24] How much the provision of highly skilled labor by the rich enhances the productivity and wages of others is not known. There is no widely accepted way to get a rough idea. My conjecture is that the labor provided by the rich is even more important than the capital they provide, but that could easily be wrong. There is no doubt, however, about the direction of the effect; if the rich as a group work less, the wages of other people will be lower.

A more subtle contribution of the rich results from how they spend their incomes, their so-called conspicuous consumption. At any point in time there are many goods and services that can be afforded only by the rich. Often these goods, usually called luxuries, later become widely available at lower prices that can be afforded by everyone. We tend to forget that many items now regarded as necessities, and consumed even by the poor, like refrigerators, TVs, air conditioners, or dishwashers, were once consumed only by the very well-off. All of these goods were considered conspicuous, if not frivolous, consumption when first marketed, but today they are virtually necessities (at least to Americans).

The point is that the rich provided a market for these goods at a time when they were far too expensive to be purchased by everyone. That allowed businesses to operate and to learn how to provide these goods more cheaply so more could afford them. We have to consider the possibility that many of the goods and services that we take for granted today might not have become available at all had not the rich supported (through their purchases) these businesses in their early years. Or, if they did become available, they might have done so at a much later date. As Nobel laureate F. A. Hayek, to whom I think this argument can be credited, expressed it: "If we, in the wealthier countries, today can provide facilities and conveniences for most which not long ago would have been physically impossible to produce in such quantities, that is in large measure the direct consequence of the fact that they were first made for a few....A large part of the expenditure of the rich, though not intended for that end, thus serves to defray the cost of the experimentation that, as a result, can later be made available to the poor."[25]

I do not know how quantitatively important this benefit provided by the rich is, but I suspect it is more important than most of us realize.

The fourth major benefit provided by the rich is perhaps the most important of all. It relates to technological progress. As I explained in chapter 4, economists believe that improvements in technology are one of the most important determinants of increasing standards of living (economic growth) over time. These advances in technology do not just happen automatically with the passage of time, however much we take them for granted; they are created by real people. Who are these people? Who in recent years is responsible for the availability today of personal computers, anti-lock brakes, the Internet, cellular phones, microwave ovens, DVDs, CAT-scans, LASIK eye surgery, and so much more? I don't know the identities of the people responsible for these and innumerable other conveniences and necessities, but I do know this: they are to be found among the ranks of the rich.

Scientists, engineers, entrepreneurs, doctors, and other fantastically skilled and creative people are largely responsible for the prosperity we enjoy today, and they are the source of our hopes for continuing improvements in the future. Not all professionals in these fields make significant contributions to technological progress; in fact, probably only a tiny minority does this. Nor are they rich throughout their lives, as many come from humble backgrounds. But they end up rich.

In his recent book *They Made America,* Harold Evans chronicles the achievements of more than 50 pioneers in a variety of fields who contributed to our present prosperity.[26] They include Leo Hendrik Baekeland (inventor of plastic), George Eastman (Kodak cameras), Martha Matilda Harper (inventor of retail franchise networking), and of course Thomas Edison (incandescent light bulbs and much more). They come from diverse backgrounds, ethnicities, genders, religions—differing in many ways but with one thing in common: Virtually all became rich as a result of their economic contributions.

Even though these innovators are well paid for their contributions to technology, this is one instance where earnings are not equal to marginal value productivities; these creators often receive less than they contribute to the output of the economy. What they really produce is new and useful knowledge, and that knowledge can be used and reused over and over again by present and later generations, often without having to pay the original creator of this knowledge for the benefits they derive from using his or her creation. (Patents and copyrights often help the creators to be paid for their contributions but only for a limited time.) This is an instance of what economists call *positive externalities,* meaning that there are benefits to others in addition to those who engage in the initial transactions. Private markets may not produce enough activities that generate positive externalities, and that is the reason economists often support subsidies to research and development activities.

I think these four ways the economic activities of the rich benefit the rest of society are probably the most important, but they are by no means the only ways. We have already seen how much they contribute, through taxes, to financing the multitude of expenditure policies that mainly benefit other people. The rich also give more to nonreligious charities than those with lower incomes, both absolutely and as a percentage of income. Nor does this generosity stop at death: Estate tax returns show that charitable bequests are a sizeable share of the net estates of the wealthy. In 1995, those with estates under $1 million (and who filed estate tax returns)[27] made charitable bequests equal to 4 percent of their net estates,[28] and the fraction steadily increased until it reached 43 percent for those with estates over $20 million.[29]

All this means that the standards of living of the 80 or 90 percent of the population who are not rich owe a lot to the economic contributions of the past and present rich. The reverse is also true—the rich gain from the economic contributions of the nonrich. But there is a very great difference in magnitudes. To take an extreme case, if the poor vanished, the well-being of the rich would scarcely be affected, though a few might find that they have to mow their own lawns and clean their own homes. But if the rich didn't exist, not only would the wage rates of the poor be much lower but so too would their welfare benefits (remember where the taxes come from). And that is just the immediate, or short-run, effect: Economic growth would decline and the future poor would be even worse off.

What does this have to do with taxation? Taxation of the rich can reduce these economic contributions, and that results in some hidden costs on the rest of us. If taxation reduces their saving (and hence accumulated capital), work effort, or innovations, that will in time be reflected in lower wages across the board, as well as in less tangible losses. I am not arguing that existing taxation of the rich has already produced calamitous outcomes, as I think that is obviously false, but it is clear (as explained in the next section) that it has already had some harmful consequences. What should be recognized is the potential for damage to all of us from heavy taxation of the rich. It would be a step in the right direction if we stopped demonizing the rich and acknowledged the crucial economic roles they play in preserving and augmenting our prosperity.

A Proportional Tax

Dissatisfaction with the federal income tax has grown to such an extent that many call for a complete overhaul of the tax rather than the minor tinkering that has characterized recent reforms. Let's take a look at one possibility.

Suppose we replace the income tax with a proportional tax on a comprehensive measure (without any tax loopholes) of income (or consumption).[30]

Currently, the federal income tax has (marginal) rate brackets of 10, 15, 25, 28, 33, and 35 percent applied to successively higher chunks of income. What single rate, if applied to all income, do you think could replace these graduated rates and still raise the same amount of revenue?

The answer to that question is surprising to most people: a proportional tax with a rate of about 10 percent would yield the same revenue as the present income tax. That this is true can be seen from the CBO estimates in table 9.1B. Look at the row labeled "All" there for 2004, and you will see that the rate given is 8.7 percent. The "All" row is the overall average tax rate, that is, total taxes divided by total income, so it is the rate that if applied to total income would yield the same revenue. I will refer to the required rate as 10 percent because it is unlikely that the tax base could be quite as comprehensive as total household income as defined by the CBO. A 10 percent rate would, however, impose a burden equal to 8.7 percent of broadly measured household income.

Thus, it is feasible to use a surprisingly low rate if the federal income tax is replaced by a proportional tax. This reform option is very easy to describe, but its consequences would be widespread. Let's look at them briefly.

First, such a tax would be much simpler than the present tax and have lower compliance costs. It is not clear how much the current $110 billion in compliance costs would be reduced, but I think they would clearly decline by at least half, or $55 billion. Most of the other benefits of a proportional tax are linked to the substantial reduction in marginal tax rates it achieves. As pointed out earlier, marginal tax rates are the source of a number of distortions (excess burdens) produced by the current tax. With nearly one-third of taxpayers currently in marginal brackets of 25 percent or more, and around 75 percent in brackets of 15 percent or more, a reduction to a single marginal rate of 10 percent would represent a substantial decline. That can be expected to have a significant effect in encouraging labor supply, saving, and entrepreneurship, and in discouraging attempts to remove income from taxation by converting it into nontaxable forms (to the extent that there are any tax loopholes remaining).

Exactly how large the economic gains from such a tax reform would be is not known exactly, but there is no shortage of estimates available. Representative of the best of these studies is the recent paper by David Altig et al.[31] They conclude that a proportional tax would increase GDP by nearly 10 percent (primarily from increasing labor supply and capital accumulation).[32] It is important to understand that this gain does not occur instantly, but gradually grows to that level over a period of years. In fact, according to Altig et al., it takes nearly 50 years for the full 10 percent gain to be realized, but more than two-thirds of the improvement is realized in the first 13 years.

Thus, average before-tax incomes of Americans would ultimately be about 10 percent higher if we replaced the federal income tax with a proportional tax with a single rate of 10 percent. Note that this is equivalent to saying that the present federal tax has depressed incomes by about 9 percent below the level they would now be had we been using the more efficient tax system all along. The potential gain from tax reform is large precisely because the actual loss from current taxation is large. We have had the oppressive and inefficient federal income tax in much like its present form for half a century, so ample time has passed for the full negative effects to be realized. That average incomes in America are 9 percent lower is perhaps the best way to conceptualize the overall inefficiency of the federal income tax system—the hidden cost of the tax system. That a 9 percent loss in income (GDP) is produced by a tax that raises only about 9.7 percent of GDP[33] in tax revenue may suggest just how harmful this tax is per dollar of revenue raised. For each dollar of revenue, before-tax income (GDP) is reduced by nearly a dollar, so disposable income is two dollars lower per dollar of revenue raised.[34]

Why would anyone oppose a tax reform that would greatly simplify the system, remove inequities due to tax loopholes, improve efficiency in several important ways, and ultimately lead to a 10 percent increase in average income? The answer is simple: Egalitarians oppose this reform because of its distributional effects. Replacing the *progressive* federal income tax with a *proportional* tax increases tax burdens on low- and middle-income households and reduces tax burdens on the well-off. It makes the after-tax distribution of income more unequal, and to egalitarians any change in this direction is unacceptable.

There are, to be sure, other objections to proportional taxation, but without doubt the major one is that it is unfair to increase tax burdens on the poor and middle class. Frankly, I have never felt that it was particularly unfair to have everyone pay the same proportion of their income to support the federal government. I see this reform as rectifying some inequities in the present system, such as the fact that about 30 percent of the population pays no federal income tax at all. But egalitarians will fixate on the unfairness of increasing tax burdens on the poor and middle class, so let's confront this issue head on.

In one sense, a proportional tax on total income (or consumption) is clearly more equitable than the present tax. That concerns how it treats people who are equally situated, that is, have equal incomes. They would pay the same tax, as they should. But under the present tax, with its myriad loopholes and special provisions, very often taxpayers with equal incomes pay quite different taxes, a violation of the equity principle that equals should be treated equally.

But the equity issue that egalitarians are most concerned about is how the tax affects people at different income levels. It is true that replacing the income tax with a proportional tax will increase tax burdens on the poor and middle class and reduce tax burdens on the well-off. We can get an idea of exactly how it would do so from the last column in table 9.1B, showing the current average tax rates for different income classes. With a proportional tax, all of these rates would be 8.7 percent, unless we treat the EITC as a negative tax as the CBO does. Thus, the top quintile would see its rate decline from 13.9 percent to 8.7 percent, the middle quintile would see its rate rise from 2.9 to 8.7 percent, and the lowest quintile would see its rate (as the CBO calculates this, with the EITC as a negative tax) rise from –6.2 percent to 2.5 percent. In fact, note that the bottom four quintiles, 80 percent of the population, bear a heavier tax burden under a proportional tax.

These figures should be understood to indicate only the immediate, or very short-run, effects of shifting to a proportional tax. They make no allowance for any of the beneficial economic consequences of the tax. We will return to this point below, but first let's be a little more precise about exactly how much various income groups would be affected in the short run. Other data from the CBO make it possible to determine the magnitudes of changes in tax burdens and show that the current tax (relative to a proportional tax) increases the tax burden on the top quintile by 3 percent of total household income, while reducing it on the lowest four quintiles by that amount. In other words, in comparison to a proportional tax, the federal income tax redistributes 3 percent of total household income from the top quintile to the bottom four.

But the distribution of these benefits (reduced tax burdens) to the bottom four quintiles does not go predominantly to the poor. In fact, the lowest quintile receives only about 20 percent of the total amount redistributed downward. Nearly 80 percent of the reduced tax burdens due to the progressive income tax goes to the second, third, and fourth quintiles—the 60 percent of the population in the middle of the income distribution. The big gainers from the present income tax are not the poor; each of the three middle quintiles receives a bigger tax break than the lowest quintile. The federal income tax is, in fact, a massive middle-class subsidy, with only a small share trickling down to the lowest quintile. This is not so easy to defend from an equity perspective, unless you are a diehard egalitarian who wants to penalize the upper class to benefit the middle class.

As mentioned, the sizeable losses to the middle class from moving to proportional taxation are only the temporary, or short-run, effects. As we have seen, over time the improvement in productive incentives results in a 10 percent increase in incomes (GDP), and that will more than offset the losses for many of those who are initially harmed. Indeed, the Altig et al. paper estimates that after the economy has fully adjusted to a proportional tax, 60 or 70 percent of the population will be better off than they would be under the current tax.[35] These are, of course, those in the upper part of the income distribution; those at the bottom are worse off even in the long run. But the harm done to them is also much lower than in the short run because of the productivity gains. In fact, Altig et al. estimate that the lowest quintile bears a long-run loss of around 2 to 3 percent of their income,[36] far smaller than the 8.7 percent immediate loss and small enough that they might bear no loss if the economic response is a bit more favorable than estimated by the authors. The reason why low-income households are not permanently harmed by an amount equal to 8.7 percent of their income is that their wage rates rise as a result of the improved economic growth.[37]

Thus, a proportional tax would end up benefiting a large majority of households, with only the lowest 20 percent or so bearing any additional burden and that burden is only 2 or 3 percent of their income. It can be objected that this is the long-run effect, while the immediate effect is a greater burden on a larger number of people. This is quite true, and politicians and the media often tend to stress the short-run and obvious consequences over the long-run and hidden consequences. Before you conclude that this is entirely appropriate, remember that we are now living with the long-run consequences of exactly that way of assessing tax (and other) policies. The Altig et al. conclusions can be restated thus: Today 70 percent or so of Americans are worse off than they would have been had we adopted a proportional tax 50 years ago, with an average loss of about 10 percent in income. The only beneficiaries are those in the bottom quintile, and they gain an amount only equal to 2 or 3 percent of their income (or under 0.2 percent of GDP).

The evidence, of which the Altig et al. paper is representative, suggests that we are today paying a heavy price for the redistribution produced by the progressive income tax. Yet the best alternative (in my opinion), a proportional tax, still rankles because it imposes that 10 percent tax on the poor and near poor. Perhaps it is okay to tax the middle class at 10 percent, but can we in good conscience place such a burden on the poor? I think that is what stops a lot of people from favoring a proportional tax, and it reflects an approach to the evaluation of tax (and other) policies that is the cause of a lot of mischief.

The approach I am referring to is the one that insists that every single individual policy must have an immediate egalitarian outcome, preferably benefiting the poor or at a minimum not harming them. The mistake here is that it is neither necessary nor desirable for *every* policy to individually have egalitarian consequences, even if that is the overall goal. What matters is the impact of all policies together. Because there are many different policies that can be used to benefit the poor, we should utilize only those that do so effectively, and a progressive income tax is not such a policy. Consider that by not taxing those with low incomes at a 10 percent rate, someone with a $20,000 income realizes $2,000 in tax saving, but a much poorer person with an income of $5,000 gains only a fourth as much. The bigger gains go to the less needy, exactly the opposite of what we want. (This is why the middle class is the big winner in the short run from progressive taxation.)

Transfers are potentially much more effective in targeting benefits on the most needy, and in adjusting the size of benefits to the degree of need, than any tax. Because transfers can do the job better, they should be the focus of antipoverty policy. In fact, they already are, as we saw in discussing the $620 billion in welfare programs in chapter 6. Even if we adopted a 10 percent tax, households in the bottom quintile would still be receiving in transfer benefits an amount four or five times as large as the taxes they pay. And if the

10 percent tax is still thought to be too heavy a burden, it would be simple to increase welfare benefits under the programs deemed the most effective to compensate for the tax increase.

It is simply not sensible to saddle the federal income tax with the job of helping the poor. Once that is understood, we may be able to adopt a tax that will greatly increase our prosperity, such as a proportional tax or something similar. Only a misguided egalitarianism that emphasizes the short-run benefits from progressivity for the middle class stands in the way.

DEFICITS

Government has two principal ways of paying for its expenditure programs: It can tax the public or borrow money to cover its expenditures. In 50 of the 57 years since 1950, the federal government has run a deficit, that is, it has spent more than it collected in taxes and borrowed to make up the shortfall. Moreover, the deficits have been gradually getting larger. In the 1950s and 60s, deficits averaged under 1 percent of national income (GDP), in the 1970s a little over 2 percent, but since the 1980s they have averaged nearly 3 percent. Is this something we should be worried about?

In understanding why the answer is yes, we need to think about why deficits may be worse than the alternative, higher taxes.[38] After all, higher taxes are not good for the economy, as we have seen. The relevant question is whether deficits are worse than higher taxes since both have negative consequences.

Deficits are worse. To see this, let's consider the government borrowing money to pay for an expenditure program this year instead of raising taxes. The first thing to note is that we have not avoided raising taxes; we have only postponed the tax increase into the future. When the government borrows, it incurs the obligation to pay interest on the government securities in future years, as well as perhaps to retire (pay off) the debt at some future date. So deficit finance today means higher taxes in the future. We do not avoid the adverse effects of taxation (including the excess burdens) by borrowing to pay for government.

At this point, it might seem that there is no difference in the real costs of deficits and taxation; it is just a question of whether we bear those costs now or in the future. But deficits have a second effect that differs from taxes: Deficits tend to reduce capital accumulation more than do taxes. When government borrows to finance a deficit, it absorbs some of the funds provided by savers, and these funds would otherwise have been channeled into financing private investments. Thus, government borrowing crowds out private investments. Of course, taxation will also reduce capital accumulation to a degree, but it does so much less dollar for dollar than does government borrowing. (People pay taxes primarily by reducing consumption; deficits primarily divert saving to the government, leaving less available for private investment.)

This effect of reducing capital accumulation and economic growth, combined with the other adverse effects of higher future taxes, means that deficit finance has higher overall economic costs than does tax finance. If raising a dollar in taxes costs $1.50, as argued earlier, then raising a dollar by government borrowing costs even more than this.[39] That is why economists generally prefer taxes to deficits as a way of financing government expenditures: Taxes, bad as they may be, are less bad than deficits.

Implicit in this discussion is another major effect of deficits: They tend to redistribute income from future generations to the present generation. Under deficit finance, the costs—both taxes and reduced future output and incomes—fall on people in the future, but the benefits of government spending accrue (generally) to the present generation. In this respect, deficit finance has effects quite similar to those we saw with PAYGO Social Security. There may be circumstances in which this is appropriate,[40] but in most cases it is difficult to defend on equity grounds imposing costs on our children and grandchildren so that we can enjoy the benefits of more government spending today.

A study by Douglas Elmendorf and N. Gregory Mankiw estimates how large the costs of reduced capital accumulation from past deficits really are; in the late 1990s, GDP was roughly 3.5 percent lower as a result of past deficits.[41] The loss would probably be a bit larger today.

Thus, there are two good arguments against the use of deficit finance. First, it is more costly when all the costs are counted than tax finance. Second, it shifts the costs into the future. A third consideration is political: When deficits can be used to pay for government spending, it is an invitation to irresponsible government spending and/or tax cuts. Politicians can win votes by providing benefits (government spending or tax cuts) to today's voters without imposing any costs on them. The costs are well hidden and fall on voters in the future who don't get to vote in today's elections. The political temptation to use deficits, which politicians obviously can't resist, is one reason why some favor an amendment to the constitution requiring a balanced budget.

All this is not to say that deficits should never be tolerated. In some cases, they may actually have some beneficial consequences. One is that they may have stimulative effects on the economy when it is operating well below capacity, as during recessions. Whether they actually do much to hasten recovery from a recession is debated by economists, but they certainly may have this effect. Nonetheless, this factor hardly justifies the persistent deficits of the past half century.

Everyone knows about the budget deficit because it is one of the most widely reported economic statistics. Yet few people realize that there are hidden deficits in government accounts that have exactly the same consequences we have traced out for the official deficit. Economist Laurence Kotlikoff has spent years arguing that the official deficit greatly understates the scope of the real problem, and he has tried to get the government to measure deficits in a more meaningful way.[42] Where are these hidden deficits that are not being properly measured? The most important are in the PAYGO Social Security system.

To see how Social Security accounting procedures conceal what is really deficit finance, note that the essence of deficit finance is the government obtaining funds in return for debt instruments—which are government promises to repay these funds at a later time. A government bond or treasury bill is just a promise from the government to repay a certain sum in the future. Now think of the taxpayer whose current payroll taxes finance Social Security retirement benefits. The taxpayer does not receive an outright bond in return for paying his taxes, but he receives a promise that the government will pay him a certain sum when he retires. In effect, taxpayers receive *implicit* government bonds in return for their taxes that can be cashed in when they retire. In a meaningful sense, government is borrowing from current payroll taxpayers and using the proceeds to pay retirement benefits to current retirees. It is true that these implicit obligations of the government are not perfectly equivalent to outright government bonds—they can't be cashed in before retirement, for example—but they produce the same economic effects as outright deficit finance.

Social security is a shrine to the political appeal of deficit finance—financing expenditures by promising those who provide the funds that they will be repaid in the future. It is no coincidence that the economic effects of deficit finance—reduced capital accumulation and economic growth, with earlier generations benefiting at the expense of later generations—are exactly the same as with Social Security.

There is one difference between outright deficits and the hidden deficits in the Social Security system: The hidden deficits are much larger than the official budget deficit. Indeed, as suggested above, all of the spending on Social Security and Medicare can be thought of as financed by borrowing from young workers. Another way of seeing this is to focus on the amount of debt outstanding. Deficits, of course, are annual excesses of spending over taxes, while the national debt is the sum of all past deficits and surpluses. In other words, the national debt is the value of all outstanding bonds, treasury bills, and other obligations. The official national debt is about $8 trillion. What is the comparable figure for Social Security and Medicare? That is, how much has been promised to taxpayers based on the taxes they have already paid into the system?

This sum is called the *unfunded accrued liability* of the Social Security system, and it has been estimated at $32 trillion, four times as large as the national debt! It is analogous to the official national debt in that it is what government has promised to pay in the future. The only way to meet this unfunded liability is out of future taxes, just as is the case with the official national debt. Given the similarities, it is not really so surprising that the economic effects of PAYGO Social Security closely resemble those of deficit finance.

It is, however, ironic that many people become almost hysterical over the dangers of deficit finance and the national debt without recognizing that the hidden deficits and debt in Social Security have the same effects. If the official deficit is bad for the economy, it is difficult to avoid the conclusion that Social Security is bad for the economy. Yet often the same people who warn of the dangers of the smaller official deficit want to continue the much larger hidden deficits by preserving PAYGO Social Security.

The (Many) Costs
of Transfers

When economists discuss redistributive (transfer) policies, the first, and very often the only, disadvantage they will emphasize is the loss in efficiency. This treatment is enshrined in the oft-noted point that transfers involve a trade-off between equity and efficiency. We get more of one good thing, equity (aka equality), and less of another good thing, efficiency. It's up to each person to decide whether on balance the outcome is desirable.

That approach is instructive as far as it goes, but it overlooks the fact that there are a number of other costs of transfer policies in addition to the loss in efficiency. In this chapter I will enumerate what I believe are the most important of these costs. Some of these have been alluded to in earlier chapters, while others are discussed for the first time here. Taken together, these costs constitute the case that redistribution by government is undesirable. I don't claim to prove that case, for in the end desirability, like social justice, is very much in the eye of the beholder, but I do contend that the costs of transfers are much greater than is generally acknowledged.

Intentionally missing from this discussion is any evaluation of the arguments favoring government redistribution. This is not because I think there are no good arguments for redistribution (there are),[1] but most readers of this book will have been exposed to the case for egalitarianism ad nauseam already. Today, as Thomas Sowell points out, "the reigning dogma of our time is equality,"[2] and at least 90 percent of what is written concerning transfer policies, academically and in the news media, is penned by committed egalitarians. What is missing is "the rest of the story," and I try to fill that gap here.

It's Stealing

Among the Ten Commandments, one admonishes us against theft: Thou shalt not steal. A prohibition against stealing is not, of course, unique to Christianity and Judaism but can be found in all the major religions. So universal is the understanding that stealing is wrong that "all societies condemn and punish theft."[3] Most people do not require academic demonstrations of the pragmatic advantages of prohibiting stealing if we are to have a civilized society—they know instinctively that theft is immoral.

What does this have to do with government transfer programs? Government transfers produce the same result as theft. What belongs to one person or group ends up in the pockets of another person or group. That description accurately describes both government transfer programs and theft, which suggests the crucial question: How can an action that is universally decried as wrong when undertaken by an individual be right when carried out by government?

To some (especially libertarians) this question has a simple answer: It can't. Redistribution by government is equivalent to theft, and that suffices to demonstrate that it is immoral. I do not fully agree with this position, but the libertarians have a point that deserves serious consideration.

The argument that government redistribution is a form of theft and therefore immoral has been countered in several ways. One is to argue that the fact that recipients of government transfers are needier (have lower incomes) than those who pay the taxes means these government transfers improve equity and are therefore moral. But that can't be right. No one argues that stealing is moral when the thief has a lower income than the victim of the crime. Nor would we think of teaching our children that it is okay to take the toys of other children if the latter have more. A difference in economic conditions does not make stealing moral.

Another tack is to hold that government redistribution achieves legitimacy by virtue of resulting from a democratic political process. But legality should not be confused with morality. There is no shortage of instances from our own history where government has instituted lawful policies that are now universally perceived as immoral. Slavery, restricting the right to vote to males, and segregated schools come to mind. Even today there are many policies of government the morality of which is widely disputed, like abortion rights and affirmative action. For all its virtues, a democratic political process does not guarantee that its policies are moral; the morality of a policy must be decided based on the content of the policy.

Neither of these positions provides a very good basis for holding that redistribution by government differs from stealing in a way that makes redistribution moral. There is one argument, however, that does accomplish this. It holds that government transfers are a form of collectivized charity, with those who give up resources (taxpayers) choosing to do so in order to help other people. In this view, government redistribution is not a case of *taking* from unwilling taxpayers but of taxpayers using the instrumentality of government to more efficiently organize *giving* to groups deemed in need of assistance. How this can be, and why government can be more efficient from the standpoint of the taxpayers than relying on private charities, forms the basis for one of the prominent arguments (among economists, at least) for government redistribution.[4]

The problem with this argument is that it applies, at best, to *some* of the taxpayers. It is true that some taxpayers do approve the use of their taxes to finance transfers to other people, and for them these transfers do not resemble stealing. But what about the taxpayers who do not want to see their taxes used in this way? For them the analogy to stealing seems to be fully appropriate. The fact that some taxpayers approve of transfers they pay for does not make it any less immoral to appropriate the resources of those who disapprove of the policy.

The argument that redistribution is immoral because it represents legalized stealing is weakened, I would suggest, to the degree that those who give up resources (or income—normally but not always taxpayers) want to transfer these resources to the recipient groups. But for others, who may or may not be in the majority (it doesn't matter), redistribution of their resources seems fully analogous to stealing. That is why there is more than a germ of truth in H. L. Mencken's famous dictum: "Every election is a sort of advance auction sale of stolen goods."[5]

THE MORALITY OF THE MARKET

While the efficiency of the market is often conceded, it is unfashionable to defend the morality of the market; it is most often viewed as an amoral, if not immoral, method of determining incomes. Henry Aaron suggests how egalitarian scholars view the market in his comment on a paper by Irving Kristol (1977): "Kristol then comes close to defending a view not seriously advanced by any reputable economist for a few decades, that the distribution of income generated by the capitalist marketplace enjoys some kind of moral status."[6] In contrast, I think Aaron's implication that there is *no* moral basis for supporting markets goes way too far. There is, in fact, much to admire about markets from a moral perspective.

There are two quite distinct ways of assessing the moral attributes of the market, or capitalism. One is to focus on the results, or outcomes, that are produced. In our case, that means examining the actual incomes that people earn in their market transactions. The other is to evaluate the process used by the market to determine incomes. Basically, the point is that morality concerns both the ends (the outcomes, or incomes) and the means (the process) that produce those outcomes. Let's first consider the outcomes-based approach.

As we saw in chapter 1, the central point concerning how incomes are determined in a market setting is that they tend to equal the contributions people make to society's total output. Those who add more to society's output receive higher incomes, and those who add less receive lower incomes. It is this result of markets that we wish to evaluate. Is it moral (or equitable, or just—which I take to mean roughly the same thing) that incomes are tied to productivities in this way?

As repeatedly emphasized, there is no objective moral (or ethical) standard that is universally accepted that would permit us to resolve this issue. But surely it is too much to say, as Aaron seems to, that there is no moral content to incomes determined in this way. After all, for people who are roughly equally situated (have similar abilities and opportunities), having incomes linked to productive contributions seems perfectly fair. Those who work harder will make more, and that is moral. It would be decidedly unjust to pay two people the same if one toiled long hours and the other chose not to work. And recall that the market also tends to reward other attributes like thrift, honesty, and perseverance in addition to hard work; being rewarded for having good values also accords with most concepts of justice.

When people are dismissive of the justice in market outcomes, they invariably select examples of those with extremely high or extremely low incomes to make their case. I agree that in the extreme tails of the income distribution instances can be found that convince most of us that we do not want to rely totally on markets to determine how well everyone lives. But suppose we restrict our attention to the broad middle range of income, excluding those with exceptionally high and low incomes. How do you feel about the morality of market determined incomes within this range?

To be more specific, consider the distribution of income among the 60 percent of families in the middle three quintiles of the distribution. Based on annual incomes, families at the very top of this range (the 80th percentile) have incomes about four times as large as those at the bottom (the 20th percentile). However, in distributions of lifetime income, the top only has incomes of about twice as high as the bottom, and that, as argued in chapter 2, is a better measure of economic inequality. There is, then, relatively little inequality within this group comprising three-fifths of the population. Moreover, those at the top of the range will tend to have higher incomes for reasons related to the choices they have freely made. There will be more dual-earner families at the top; they will be working longer hours; they will have saved more; they will have stayed in school for more years and worked harder while they were there. In short, there is a reasonable expectation that they deserve their higher incomes. For this group of people, I suggest that market-determined incomes are more morally justified than is likely to be true of any alternative method of determining incomes.

I used the phrase "*more* morally justified" to emphasize that I am not claiming that markets are perfect, even within this limited range. I am saying that I expect the market to do at least as well as the alternative, which is to have the government redistribute incomes. Governments are not especially good arbiters of morality, if indeed morality plays any role in determining who benefits from redistributive politics.

The morality of linking incomes to productive contributions for those at the very top and bottom is more problematic. Personally, I do not believe that morality calls for redistribution from the wealthy to the middle class, but perhaps it does call for redistribution from the wealthy *and* the middle class to the poor.

Turning to the process-based approach to evaluation of the market distribution of income, let me begin with an analogy to a sporting event. Consider a football game that ends with a score of 42 to 0. How do we evaluate the fairness, or morality, of this game? If we look at the results, it is clear that one team did immensely better than the other—there was great inequality in the score. Does this mean that the game was unfair? Obviously not. To make a determination of fairness, we need to look at the rules of the game and their application to the two teams in this particular instance. Only if we judge the rules to be unfair, or unfairly applied, would we conclude that the outcome was unfair.

According to an influential book by philosopher Robert Nozick, the same point applies in judging the equity of market outcomes.[7] We cannot, or should not, judge the market distribution of income to be unfair based just on observing the final results (incomes received, that is, the score). In reaching judgments of fairness, how do we describe the market process that Nozick urges us to focus on? It is a process built upon voluntary exchanges. Both parties to an employment contract, for example, agree to the terms in the expectation of mutually benefiting. Income is not taken from the employer by the employee; it is given to the employee in exchange for his labor services. Nozick views voluntary exchanges as a morally just process and concludes that whatever emerges from that process (including the distribution of income) should be judged as just. One can quarrel with this conclusion on a number of levels, but that the market process, based as it is on the free choices of all participants, deserves some respect as a fair process seems apparent.

Closely related to this position is the venerable one that emphasizes the connection between markets and individual freedom.[8] Freedom is desirable both as an end in itself and as an indispensable means in achieving our individual ends. In the economic sphere, markets exemplify freedom. People are free to purchase or not purchase a product; to work at this job or that one, or none at all; to start a business and produce whatever they want. All this, of course, is subject to the proviso that others have the same rights—you are free to offer your services to any employer, but the employer is free to accept or reject your offer.

Given the importance of freedom in the history of this country and its founding, it is remarkable how rarely people today oppose government actions on the grounds that they diminish our economic freedoms. Take the minimum wage. This policy clearly violates the freedom of workers and employers to consummate employment contracts on terms they find mutually agreeable. I have discussed this policy in numerous classes over my teaching career and have been struck by the fact that no student has ever made the argument that this policy is wrong because it reduces the freedom of employers and employees. Similarly, popular and academic discussions of the minimum wage almost never address this aspect of the issue.

Except perhaps in the case when redistribution represents collectivized charity and benefits those who bear the costs, altering the market's distribution of income with redistributive policies always reduces freedom. Indeed, Richard Pipes is surely correct in observing that "the main threat to freedom today comes not from tyranny but from equality,"[9] at least within the United States. Of course, egalitarian policies may have beneficial results that make it worthwhile to give up a bit of our freedom, but the loss in freedom should still be acknowledged as a real and significant cost of the policies.

A final process-oriented virtue of the market concerns equality of opportunity. Equality of opportunity, which relates to the process that generates incomes, and equality of results, which concerns the incomes that are received, must be sharply distinguished. If we have equality of opportunity, there is certain to be inequality of results (incomes) as some people will utilize the opportunities more effectively than others. Similarly, if we impose equality of results we cannot have equality of opportunity because those who make the most of their opportunities would have to be denied the fruits of their endeavors.

The original conception of equality of opportunity held that there should be no artificial or man-made impediments to people making the most of their abilities and skills. It recognized that people would have different abilities and so some would be more likely to succeed than others. Equal opportunity is satisfied if all are free to offer their services in any job market, for example, even if only a few have the talents necessary to be hired. Similarly, it is no violation of equal opportunity to observe that only those with adequate resources can start a business, for resources are a *natural* requirement of this endeavor, not an obstacle unnecessarily placed in one's way. Examples of impediments that believers in equal opportunity wanted to see removed were things like restricting access to an occupation to those with licenses or to those who were of a certain ethnicity, gender, or religion.

A free market is quite consistent with this concept of equal opportunity. Unfortunately, the concept of equal opportunity has been appropriated by egalitarians who have given it a very different meaning. In much modern usage, equality of opportunity is taken to mean that all should have the same probability of succeeding. James Coleman illustrates this usage: "The fact that each person begins life with a set of private resources, genetic and environmental (the first from his parents and the second largely so), means that in the absence of public resources, children will have unequal opportunities."[10] This concept of equality of opportunity is, in fact, virtually indistinguishable from equality of results. For if everyone were supposedly given the same probability of success, and the results turned out to be unequal, that would simply be evidence that the probabilities were not equal to begin with: Only actual equality of results would demonstrate equal opportunity in this sense.

Equality of opportunity interpreted as equal chances of succeeding is, of course, impossible to achieve. There is no way that one who is 5 feet 6 inches tall can have the same chance of succeeding in professional basketball as one a foot taller, just as there is no way that one with an IQ of 75 can have the same chance of becoming a doctor as one who has an IQ of 125. Equality of opportunity in the old-fashioned sense takes people as they are, with widely differing abilities and talents, and lets all try to make the most of what they have. It is a realizable goal and is broadly consistent with the level playing field in a free market. Equality of opportunity in the modern egalitarian sense is just a backdoor way of arguing for equality of results and is inconsistent with free markets.

I conclude that both market outcomes and market processes have many virtues that are consistent with most people's conception of morality or justice. When government overrides the market with its redistributive policies, it will to some degree diminish rather than enhance justice even in the best of circumstances. In many cases, it may do a great deal worse than the market, as we will see in the next section.

EQUITY AND GOVERNMENT REDISTRIBUTION

If there is one belief that unites those who support the redistributive policies of government, it is probably that these policies produce a more equitable, or fair, result than does the market. Is this really true? Let's look at a few examples of the justice produced by government transfer policies.

The minimum wage transfers income from consumers in general to (among others) the teenage children of middle- and upper-income families. More poor people are harmed by the policy (from the higher prices and reduced employment opportunities) than are benefited. Is this fair?

Farm subsidies transfer income from nonfarm households to farm households, and farm households have incomes on average higher than nonfarm households. Around 60 percent of the farm subsidies go to farm households with incomes of more than twice the national average. Is this fair?

Affirmative action policies apply different standards to various ethnic groups in an attempt to transfer income among the groups. In effect, many institutions employ quotas that are based on ethnicity. In both college admissions (which we discussed) and employment, whites and Asians often must be better qualified to have the same chance of success as blacks or Hispanics. Is this fair?

Immigration policy leads to lower wage rates, especially for the least skilled of American workers, and higher returns to capital. It therefore redistributes income from low- and middle-income households to high-income households. Is this fair?

Social Security provided large windfall benefits to retirees in the early years (the start-up phase) of the program. These returns come at the expense of lower standards of living for all later generations. Both poor and wealthy retirees in the start-up years benefited, but in terms of absolute dollars (rather than relative to their incomes), the wealthy gained far more than the poor. Is this fair?

Social Security also redistributes income within the same generation, that is, among those retiring at the same time. One provision in the law that does this is called the *dependent spouse option,* according to which a married couple can receive benefits based on their individual earnings histories *or* choose to receive 150 percent of the benefits due to the higher-earning spouse, even if the other spouse did not work and pay taxes at all. As a result, single-earner couples often receive larger benefits than two-earner couples with the same total earnings. Is this fair?

These examples have been taken from redistributive policies that are not normally thought of as welfare programs. Even within the group of welfare programs, there are many instances whose implications for equity are unclear.

Medicaid, the largest welfare program, covers (among other things) the cost of long-term care, such as nursing home care for the elderly. (Medicare does not normally cover this.) This benefit is intended to be limited to those with low incomes *and* assets. But provisions in the law allow much income and assets to be exempt. For example, one's home and furnishings, no matter how valuable, are exempt. Even a privately owned business can often be exempt. The rules are complicated, however, so it is not surprising that there has evolved a thriving industry that instructs middle- and high-income elderly persons how they can shelter their assets and achieve eligibility for Medicaid. The result is that the heirs of many upper-income persons can preserve their inheritances with the taxpayers picking up the cost of providing long-term care for their parents. Is this fair?

Issues of fairness also arise in the heart of the welfare system, even when the benefits go to those with very low incomes. As we saw in chapter 6, a large share of welfare benefits goes to never-married women with children. Many of these women have made the decision to have children they know they cannot support. Such actions are certainly irresponsible, if not immoral. Yet our welfare system transfers income from those who have children only when they can provide for them to those who choose to be dependent. Is this fair?[11]

Or how about the provision of welfare benefits (and other tax-financed benefits, like schools) to immigrants, legal and illegal? Because large majorities of Americans have for decades wanted to reduce the number of immigrants, especially illegal immigrants, is it fair to make them pay taxes to provide welfare and other benefits to people who they do not want in their country?

These examples are intended, as is probably obvious, to make the point that redistributive policies often do not promote what most people think of as equity. Indeed, they often introduce inequities where none existed before. Many more examples could be given, as anyone familiar with the plethora of actual transfer policies knows. For example, in chapter 1 I discussed how some inequalities in market-determined incomes are necessary to achieve equity ("Just Inequalities"). Government policies that produce greater equality in annual money incomes tend to produce inequities in all these cases, as for example when those who work harder and longer are taxed more heavily (or subsidized less generously) than those who prefer more leisure.

Discussions of redistributive policies often make the claim that giving up some efficiency is a small price to pay for the compensating gain in fairness, or social justice. But do we really get greater equity as a result of redistributive policies? While acknowledging (once again) that people have differing views of what constitutes equity, these examples certainly are suggestive that the answer is not obvious.

If one's view of fairness is that anything that narrows differences in annual incomes is fair, and that seems to be close to the view of many egalitarians, then it is probably true that *overall* the redistributive state promotes fairness of this sort. There are many policies that do not even achieve that, as we have seen, but I suspect that all together they do work to achieve greater relative equality. But fairness-as-equality is a very inadequate basis for a principled view of equity; many equalizing measures are not fair at all.

Even if overall the system is more fair than not, it should be acknowledged that the many inequities of actual policies weaken the case for government redistribution. And it is not enough to claim, as some in effect do, that the only implication of this is that we need more good redistribution and less bad redistribution, for we don't really have the luxury of picking and choosing in that way. Once government is empowered to redistribute income, it is predictable that there will be good and bad policies, and the bad policies should be considered as part of the cost of getting the good policies. Richard Epstein makes a similar point: "The only moral case for redistribution is to overcome differences of wealth in the service of those with real human needs. Once redistribution becomes a legitimate function of government, it is likely to be unleashed in ways that flatly contradict this purpose."[12] And so it has, as I hope the examples in this section may suggest.

EFFICIENCY AND GOVERNMENT REDISTRIBUTION

Most people don't understand what economists mean by the terms *efficiency* and *inefficiency*. They are not synonyms for good and bad but have technical meanings that are, in truth, difficult to explain succinctly. Inefficiency, for example, is often said to involve reducing the size of the income pie, providing benefits less than costs, introducing waste in the use of resources, reducing the average income, and distorting the allocation of resources. These are all plausible descriptions of inefficiency, but they do not provide much help in explaining how the concept applies in evaluating policies that transfer income among people.

Arthur Okun has provided a metaphor for the role of inefficiency in redistributive policies that clarifies its significance. If income is redistributed from rich to poor, Okun suggests imagining that "the money must be carried from the rich to the poor in a leaky bucket. Some of it will simply disappear in transit, so the poor will not receive all the money that is taken from the rich."[13] Money does not literally disappear, of course, but inefficiencies produce results that can often be accurately characterized in this way. When there is no inefficiency, there is no leak in the bucket and a dollar less for the rich means a dollar more for the poor. With inefficient policies, the bucket leaks and the size of the leakage measures the magnitude of the inefficiency. With a 20 percent leakage, for example, a $1 cost to the rich becomes an 80¢ benefit to the poor.

Importantly, note that saying there is an inefficiency (a leakage) is not tantamount to concluding that the policy is bad. We may conclude that an 80¢ benefit for the poor justifies placing a cost of $1 on the rich; undoubtedly, egalitarians feel this way. But, except for extreme egalitarians, certainly the size of the leakage is important in evaluating the policy. We are likely to feel very differently about a policy that provides a 10¢ benefit to the poor at a cost of $1 to the well-off than one that provides an 80¢ benefit at that cost.

So, exactly how porous is the leaky bucket? There is no simple answer, as it depends on many factors, including the specific policies used to effect the redistribution. But it is possible to get a rough idea that is consistent with the empirical literature by following a dollar on its journey from the taxpayers to low-income recipients. As we saw in the last chapter, to acquire $1 to spend the government imposes a cost of around $1.50 on taxpayers. Of this 50¢ inefficiency, 40¢ is due to distortions in economic incentives and 10¢ is due to compliance costs.

Armed with a dollar from taxpayers, the government spends it on a welfare program. The administrative cost of welfare programs absorbs part of this dollar, probably about 10¢. Thus, 90¢ worth of resources actually goes to recipients. But they do not receive benefits that they value as 90¢ because of the inefficiencies in the welfare program. In particular, because of the high marginal tax rates implicit in welfare programs and the restrictions on how the sums can be spent (in the case of in-kind programs), 90¢ in welfare benefits are probably worth only about 60¢ to recipients. (The size of this leakage, I should say, is less well established in the economics literature than on the tax side of the redistribution, but I believe this magnitude is probably typical for welfare programs.) We are not quite finished, however, because just as taxpayers incur compliance costs, so do transfer recipients. I am not aware of any studies evaluating these compliance costs and will simply assume they are of similar magnitude (per dollar) as for taxpayers, so they produce a leakage of another 10¢.

Thus, a transfer that places a cost of $1.50 on taxpayers provides a benefit worth $0.50 to recipients. In terms of the leaky bucket, two-thirds of the contents have leaked out due to the inefficiencies in the tax and transfer programs. Alternatively, we could say that it costs taxpayers $3 to provide a benefit worth $1 to recipients. Needless to say, I don't suggest this is an exact measure, but I think most economists familiar with the relevant literature would agree that it is in the right ballpark.

Actually, I think this estimate of the leakage is likely to understate its true magnitude. This is because the literature it is based on has not evaluated all of the types of inefficiencies known to be produced by transfer policies. For example, no account is made of the extent to which the welfare system has encouraged the formation of female-headed families. (It is, in fact, not clear how policies that affect family structure and size, even if the magnitudes are known, can be fit into this leaky bucket framework.) Another inefficiency that is known to result from transfer programs is that they lead to lower private charitable contributions. (The evidence suggests that a dollar spent on social welfare policies reduces charitable contributions by between 5 and 10¢.) This means that those who benefit from charities, which may include the recipients of the government transfer, bear another cost that should be attributed to the leaky bucket.

Perhaps the most significant reason why the bucket may be leakier than the empirical evidence suggests, however, is that this evidence is based on a one-year snapshot evaluation of the results. In other words, a dollar transferred has a cost of $1.50 for the person who has a higher income this year and a benefit of $0.50 for the person who has a lower income this year. But, as we saw in chapter 2, people do not remain at the same income positions throughout their lives. There is a great deal of mobility, which means that in some years a person may be a recipient of transfers and in other years a taxpayer.

To see what this means for the leaky bucket, let's examine an extreme case. Suppose there are only two persons, one with high and one with low income. Each year a dollar is transferred from the high- to the low-income person. However, they switch positions each year—next year the low-income person has a high income, and vice versa. What this means is that both persons receive a benefit worth $0.50 in one year and bear a cost due to the tax of $1.50 the next, a net loss of a dollar over any two-year period. Even though it looks like someone benefits when we look at the evidence for each year separately, everyone is harmed when we take a longer run viewpoint.

In this example, the lifetime incomes of the two people are equal, although they differ in each year, with the result that redistribution based on annual incomes harms everyone. Lifetime incomes are, of course, not equal, but as we saw in chapter 2 they are much more equally distributed than are annual incomes. An example shows how this implies that the leakage will be greater when evaluated from a long-run perspective.

Consider a scenario in which person A spends four years with a low income and one year with a high income, whereas person B has a high income for four years and a low income for one year. Person A has a significantly lower average income over the five-year period, but the 67 percent annual leak in the transfer bucket implies that A gains only 50¢ for the five-year period as a whole while person B loses $5.50. (A gains 50¢ for four years and loses $1.50 in one year, while B loses $1.50 for four years and gains 50¢ for one year.) When the leaky bucket is evaluated for the five-year period as a whole, more than 90 percent of the bucket has leaked out.

Insofar as people move around the income distribution over their lifetimes, spending some years as net beneficiaries of government redistribution and other years as net losers, it is certain that fewer people end up benefiting from the policies over their lifetime than suggested by focusing on a single year. In a sense, it is much as if they are stealing from themselves using a leaky bucket—not an attractive proposition. The leaky bucket may be virtually a sieve when evaluated from the relevant long-run perspective.

Efficiency matters, and matters greatly, in evaluating the costs of transfer programs. Okun's leaky bucket analogy helps convey why this is so, and the evidence suggests that efficiency losses are substantial when evaluated properly.

THE POLITICS OF REDISTRIBUTION

How does the political process function when dealing with redistributive issues? Politics is, I believe, intrinsically more difficult to understand than markets, and I have no expertise in political analysis. Nonetheless, I suggest that the political consequences of having the government virtually unconstrained when it comes to its power to benefit some people at the expense of others are possibly among the most important of the costs of the welfare state.

Although it is something of an oversimplification, let us think of political outcomes as determined by a process of majority voting. This process is sometimes described as one that gives the majority what it wants, but that characterization is misleading. There is not one majority that agrees among itself and always gets what it wants, but different majorities that support various policies. This is particularly true for transfer policies, and the results are somewhat surprising.

When the distribution of income is subject to political determination by majority voting, the predicted result is basically that we can't be sure what will happen. Whatever set of policies currently exists, it is always possible to propose new policies that will benefit a majority (by imposing costs on a minority) and thereby secure majority approval. Economists would say that there is no equilibrium to majority voting as applied to distributional issues, so we can't know where the political process will lead. Perfect equality, even if it could be achieved, is not a stable result because there would always be a majority who believe they deserve higher incomes than other people and who would support policies producing that outcome.

What we can be fairly certain of is that there will be constant change in government policies as politicians continue to propose and enact policies to benefit their constituents. Moreover, it won't always be the same constituents; sometimes the poor will benefit, sometimes the middle class, and sometimes the well-off. The likely result is crisscrossing and offsetting redistributive policies, which as we have seen certainly describes the policy landscape. This instability in government policies is itself a bad thing because people need a predictable and stable framework of rules and institutions within which they can plan and live their own lives.

Another implication of majoritarian determination of redistributive policies is that it will invariably produce highly inefficient policies. A policy does not have to produce overall benefits greater than its costs to secure majority approval. If a majority of voters secures net benefits of, say, $10 billion from some policy, they can be counted on to vote for this policy even if it imposes costs of $50 billion on a minority. When many such policies are enacted, with different people comprising the majority and minority for the various policies, it becomes possible that everyone ends up losing: They get benefits from the policies when they are in the majority but lose more from the policies when they are in the minority. This possibility is enhanced when the costs are often hidden and fall on people in the future, which as we have seen is often the case.

In actuality, policies do not require support by a majority of voters to be enacted by Congress. A policy that has substantial benefits for a small minority, like farm subsidies, can secure approval in Congress. Partly, this is because politicians are not elected based on their stands on individual policies. Rather, they can favor a set of policies, each of which benefits a minority but all together the minorities add up to a majority. It also helps if the benefits are obvious and concentrated while the costs are diffused over a large group and are often hidden. This is the conventional explanation for the existence of so-called special interest policies that benefit only a minority.

The prospect of using the political system to benefit oneself at the expense of others introduces a type of inefficiency we have not yet discussed. Clearly, people are willing to invest time and resources in an effort to use government to further their interests. Consider a proposal for a policy that would transfer $100 billion from group A to group B. Group B may be expected to support a lobbying effort in favor of the policy, make political donations to politicians who will vote in its favor, or conduct a public relations campaign to influence public opinion. But group A has the same incentive to use its resources to oppose enactment of this policy. Both groups end up using resources trying to alter or retain the way the economic pie is sliced. As James Gwartney and

Richard Wagner express this point: "Resources that would otherwise be used to create wealth and generate income are wasted fighting over slices of a shrinking economic pie."[14]

This type of inefficiency, called *rent-seeking costs* by economists, was not evaluated in our leaky bucket example in the previous section. That is because there is little credible evidence concerning exactly how large these costs are. There is, however, evidence that these costs have been growing in recent decades. For example, the number of lobbyists registered with the federal government was 3,420 in 1976 but grew *tenfold* to 34,750 in 2005. But lobbying is only the most obvious form of these costs. Businesses frequently, for instance, employ lawyers, accountants, publicists, and expert witnesses to further their public policy goals. CEOs often have to travel to Washington to defend their so-called ill-gotten profits when they could have been devoting their efforts to producing more and better products.

One of the less obvious political costs of redistributive policies is that they deflect attention from the other issues dealt with by government. As elected officials spend more of their time promoting, reforming, enacting, and over-seeing the myriad transfer programs, they have less time to spend on other, arguably more essential, policies. The result is poorer policies all around. As former Senator Phil Gramm (an economist) put it: "A government that tries to do everything can't do anything very well."[15]

The danger is that politicians spread themselves so thin that not only are redistributive policies poorly conceived and executed but other policies end up suffering from relative neglect. It is no secret that many politicians consider it their mission in life to use government to provide benefits to their varied constituencies (at the expense of other people, of course) and that many politicians have built a career doing just that. What Dick Morris said of President Bill Clinton's approach to terrorism is true of many others: "On another level, I just don't think it was his *thing*. You could talk to him about income redistribution and he would talk to you for hours and hours. Talk to him about terrorism, and all you'd get was a series of grunts."[16]

There are also less tangible consequences arising from a political process that routinely and ubiquitously transfers income back and forth. By their nature, transfer programs ensure that people have diametrically opposed interests, and opposing interests are often divisive. Social Security pits the young against the old, the federal income tax positions the wealthy against the middle class, affirmative action sets whites against minorities, and so on. The political maneuvering surrounding these and other redistributive issues exacerbates or even creates conflict among groups, and antagonisms and distrust become more common. As Robert Higgs expresses it: "People lose their sense of belonging to a common political community. Instead, fellow citizens regard each other as either patsies or moochers, and feel personal hostility toward those who appear to be net gainers from the system."[17]

People become so inured to seeing groups receiving special benefits from government programs that they can easily rationalize securing benefits for themselves in this way. After all, "everyone does it" and "I have paid my taxes, and I deserve to get something back." In the end, everyone is stealing from everyone else, and it is not clear who really benefits from the smaller economic pie. It is not surprising that we get crisscrossing and offsetting transfer policies that are riddled with inequities and inefficiencies. It's just what you expect from the political process when it embarks on the pursuit of social justice where people have necessarily conflicting interests.

DOES THE WELFARE STATE HARM THE POOR?

In chapter 6, I briefly discussed an argument that welfare programs might actually harm the poor. This argument depended on dropping the conventional economic assumption that recipients of transfers know the consequences of their choices, for otherwise they would always benefit from transfers that they have chosen to receive. But in this section I am going to retain the conventional assumption and explain how even if we assume that recipients of transfers know the consequences of their choices, the welfare state actually harms many if not most of the poor.

The key difference between this and the discussion in chapter 6 is that in chapter 6 I considered only the effects of welfare programs. In this section, I will be examining the combined effects of welfare programs and other welfare-state policies like Social Security and the tax system, which are, of course, not considered as welfare programs. When all the consequences of the welfare state are evaluated, it is clear that many, if not all, of the poor are injured.

With more than $600 billion a year spent on welfare programs, is it possible that the negative effects of other welfare-state policies offset this vast sum for low-income households? Could the hidden costs of other transfer policies and taxes that fall on the poor be large enough to offset the welfare benefits, leaving them worse off? For most of my professional life, I have not thought that was possible. I am now not so sure. What I now realize I overlooked was the varied ways low-income households are affected by the welfare state at different points in their lifetimes.

Most evaluations of welfare-state policies are based on examining annual data, toting up the gains and losses to people in a given year. We have repeatedly seen how that can be misleading, as people don't stay in the same income categories year after year. A household may receive welfare for several years, then circumstances change and they depend on earnings for several years. What matters is how the welfare-state policies affect them over this entire period, not just when they are on welfare.

At the risk of oversimplifying, we might think of a typical low-income household's life cycle as featuring three distinct phases. In the first phase, a low-income household has children and can sometimes be eligible for myriad welfare programs. But children grow up, and welfare programs are not nearly as generous for those without young children. Thus, in the second phase, these households become more dependent on their own labor earnings. The third phase, of course, is retirement, with Social Security becoming the major source of income. The way the welfare state affects a low-income household will be quite different in these three phases, and we need to consider all three together to determine whether the household truly benefits. Of course, not all low-income households follow this simple life cycle pattern, but the important point is that most low-income households are dependent on earnings for part of their lives, and on Social Security at the end.

What I will argue is that in the first phase, welfare does improve the living standards of low-income households, but that the welfare-state policies that affect them in the other two phases lower their living standards enough to offset to a large degree, if not totally, the benefits received in the first phase. The welfare-state policies that inflict costs on low-income households in the last two phases of their lifetimes are numerous, but I will concentrate on three where there is evidence of substantial costs: federal income taxation, Social Security, and immigration policy.

All three of these policies have the effect of lowering the before-tax wage rates available in unskilled jobs. This is their long-term effect, but that is the relevant one to evaluate how the poor are affected today because these policies have been around long enough for their full effects to be realized. Taking all three of these policies together, based on the analyses discussed in previous chapters, I estimate that wage rates for unskilled workers are approximately 25 percent lower due to these redistributive policies of the welfare state. That is a substantial loss. Recall that the median earnings of a male high school dropout were about $27,000 in 2005. If wage rates had been a third higher (so $27,000 is 25 percent lower), median earnings would be $36,000. Thus, the median male high school dropout bears a cost of about $9,000 a year. For the median female high school dropout, with earnings of about $20,000, the loss is around $7,000 a year. For low-income households who are dependent on their earnings for part of their lives, this is a substantial offset to the gain they receive while on welfare.

Low-income households in their retirement years bear a different sort of cost attributable to Social Security. As we saw in chapter 7, even low-income persons receive a very low rate of return from Social Security. Indeed, I explained there that they would now be receiving pensions perhaps twice as large had they saved their tax dollars privately, or had we been using a well-designed privatized system. Thus, the poor are harmed during this period of their lives as well as when they are working.

These costs on the low-income population from government transfer policies are not incorporated in the leaky bucket estimates discussed earlier: They are in addition to the costs emphasized there. The empirical work on the leaky bucket has utilized only the one-year perspective, and therefore the work misses effects that occur at different periods of the life cycle.

It is evident that these costs on low-income households are large enough to substantially reduce the lifetime benefits they receive from the welfare state as a whole. Moreover, there are many costs (higher prices due to agricultural subsidies and the minimum wage, for example) that I have not evaluated quantitatively for lack of evidence, but taken as a whole they probably substantially add to the negative effects on the low-income population. In some cases, there is no doubt that overall these costs are large enough to leave low-income households worse off on a lifetime basis than they would be if there were no welfare-state policies at all. Perhaps this is true in most cases, but there are too many uncertainties and unknowns to be confident of the exact consequences. One can hope that researchers will address this question using an appropriate lifetime framework and provide firm evidence. But it is clear that the bucket is a lot leakier than the one-year perspective implies.

As the discussion throughout this chapter suggests, there are many reasons why we should be skeptical of egalitarians' claims that the welfare state promotes social justice, or even the well-being of the poor themselves.

Just Say No

All critiques of social policy end with the author's prescription to solve the identified problems, and this book is no different. However, I will not argue for implementation or reform of specific government policies but rather that we adopt a general principle to guide us in our evaluations of all federal policies. The principle is simple: The federal government shall not adopt any policies that transfer income (resources) from some Americans to other Americans. Put more concisely, the federal government should not redistribute income.

In a sense, the last chapter has already made the case for adherence to this principle by pointing out all the costs resulting from having no such rule constraining the government. In this chapter I will make the argument more specifically, but in doing so I will tend to emphasize primarily the *economic costs* of redistributive policies. Although there is no doubt that the injustices produced by redistributive policies, the infringements on individual freedom, and the strains on the political process are all important costs of the welfare state, they are difficult to quantify. Without intending to downplay the importance of these issues, here I will focus on the potentially measurable effects on people's real incomes since this is what the economics literature has attempted to evaluate.

THE ECONOMIC COST OF THE WELFARE STATE

What have the welfare-state policies of the federal government done to the collective income of Americans, that is, roughly, to GDP? I have presented quantitative estimates of the effects of three important components of the welfare state in previous chapters: Social Security, federal income taxation, and deficit finance. As you may recall, these estimates suggest that Social Security has reduced GDP by about 10 percent, the federal income tax (compared to a proportional tax) by 9 percent, and past deficits by 3.5 percent. Taken together, these three policies have reduced GDP by perhaps 22.5 percent.

How to account for other welfare-state policies is less clear. These other policies include all welfare programs, the policies discussed in chapter 8, and a number of other policies not discussed in this volume at all, like farm subsidies. Although I have seen a few scattered estimates in the economics literature dealing with some of these policies individually, there is little firm basis for an evaluation of their overall effect. There is no doubt, as should be clear from our analyses of some of these programs, that their overall effect is to reduce economic productivity and the incomes of Americans. Some account should clearly be taken of these policies, so I will bite the bullet and conjecture that their combined effect is to reduce GDP by 2.5 percent. I believe this is a pretty conservative estimate.

Therefore, I conclude that the federal welfare-state policies in the aggregate have reduced GDP by around 25 percent. Needless to say, this is not presented as a definitive estimate; it might be better to say that the available evidence suggests that GDP has been reduced by 25 percent plus or minus 10 percentage points. But the figure of 25 percent is certainly in the right ballpark, and it is the one I will refer to, with the previous caveat noted.

This is a huge cost borne by the American people. Unfortunately, it is also largely what I have referred to as a hidden cost, which is not so easy to explain or document. After all, it is composed of effects cumulated over the past 50 or 75 years including economic growth *not* achieved, saving and investment *not* undertaken, innovations *not* realized, medical progress *not* achieved, and labor effort *not* supplied. That these costs are not easy to see and associate with their ultimate cause is a major reason why Americans (and others) have acquiesced to so many unwise welfare-state policies. And it doesn't help that the evangelical egalitarians who dominate academia and the news media ignore or dismiss the evidence confirming these large costs.

If we are truly concerned about the well-being of the American people, reform of our dysfunctional welfare state should be a top priority.

PRINCIPLES VS. EXPEDIENCY

I was fortunate early in my career to be taught by two remarkable economists, James Buchanan and Leland Yeager. They both have emphasized throughout their long and fruitful careers the importance of using general principles as a guide not only to the evaluation of public policies but also in our daily lives.[1]

Most of us reflexively and unthinkingly rely on principles to guide our behavior every day. For example, in every conversation we face the choice of lying or telling the truth, and most of us automatically adhere to the principle that we should tell the truth. We don't systematically evaluate each potential statement on a case-by-case basis, weighing the advantages and disadvantages of potential lies compared to the truth. We know our interests will be better served over the long term by relying on a general principle that has proven its worth over generations.

As Yeager reminds us: "the logic of heeding principles rather than acting on case-by-case opportunism carries over from everyday life into the realm of government economic policy."[2] The alternative to using principles as a guide (and constraint) in the evaluation of government policies is to evaluate each on a case-by-case basis. A case-by-case approach attempts to identify, qualitatively and quantitatively, the good and bad consequences of any potential policy and then weigh them carefully in making a decision. As proponents of this approach might put it, we should evaluate each policy on its merits.

What is wrong with this case-by-case approach? Aside from the fact that it is precisely this approach that has given us today's welfare-state policies, a central difficulty is that we never can know all the important consequences produced by a policy. Every policy has unanticipated and unintended consequences (often harmful and hidden costs) that are not apparent until years after the policy is implemented, if they are ever recognized. We are more likely to select beneficial policies if we rely on principles that we have reason to believe work in most cases, even if that means that some good policies are occasionally rejected.

As an indication of how the case-by-case approach works in practice for government decision making, political scientist James Payne carefully scrutinized 14 Congressional hearings evaluating a variety of government spending programs. Does Congress hear a balanced selection of supporters and opponents of these programs, and weigh the costs and benefits of each policy carefully? On the contrary, Payne found that: "One thousand and fourteen witnesses appeared in favor of the spending; only seven could be counted as opponents.... In other words, pro-spending witnesses outnumbered anti-spending witnesses 145 to one!"[3] In a more recent study in which he examined the actual comments made in Congressional hearings, Payne came up with these numbers: "Comments in favor of spending constitute 96 percent of all evaluative remarks about [government expenditure] programs. Overall, positive program comments outnumbered negative ones by an enormous margin, 748 to 31, a 24-to-1 ratio."[4]

Committed big-government advocates may choose to believe that this gross imbalance in what Congress hears reflects the truth, but public choice economists have long understood that it will occur regardless of whether the expenditure programs are worthwhile. Any expenditure program, and especially a redistributive one, creates a powerful constituency that can be counted on to promote its continuation and expansion. Not only the beneficiaries (and their lobbyists) will rush to pressure Congress (with promises of campaign contributions and votes), but employees of the government agencies that administer the programs can be counted on to proclaim their worth. Those who stand to lose from these policies lose so little individually from each of the hundreds of separate programs that it is not worthwhile to become informed or testify—if indeed they are even aware of the existence of the programs in the first place. This is, of course, just an example of the so-called special interest bias that infects government processes, as mentioned in the last chapter.

Americans should require no lengthy defense of principles over expediency because our very country was founded on a belief in the primacy of the principles articulated in the Constitution. The Constitution is based on the general principle of limited government and attempts to produce that outcome by specifying swaths of activities that are out of bounds to the federal government. The Constitution reserves many activities to the states and to the people. That the restraints on the federal government that the founders tried to build into the Constitution have not been adequate to control the explosive growth of government in the twentieth century is unfortunately all too apparent.

It is in the spirit of constitutionally limited government that I am arguing for a principle that denies to the federal government the power to redistribute income. How we could implement such a principle is unclear; it might be helpful to have a Constitutional amendment. But that may not be necessary or sufficient, for it can be argued that the Constitution already prohibits redistribution.

The Fifth Amendment to the Constitution contains the clause (known as the "takings clause"): "Nor shall private property be taken for public use, without just compensation." Legal scholar Richard Epstein has devoted an entire book to the argument that this clause was intended to, and should, prohibit redistribution by the federal government.[5]

On the surface, this is certainly reasonable. A person's earnings are undoubtedly his private property. While the takings clause permits government to appropriate private property, it can do so only under two conditions: that the appropriation be for "public use" and that the person receive "just compensation." It is difficult to interpret programs that provide benefits to a small subset of the population, whether they be farmers, the elderly, or welfare recipients, as constituting a public use—that is, that benefit the public generally. Economists refer to goods that provide benefits to the entire public as "public goods" and there are many examples, including national defense, medical research, and environmental improvements. But redistributive policies hardly fit this category.

Similarly, redistributive policies provide no "just compensation" to the people who have to pay for them. There are few if any *tangible* benefits to the taxpayers who bear the costs of welfare and other redistributive programs, and those that exist certainly fall far short of full compensation for the costs.

Egalitarians might argue that we all get the intangible benefit of social justice from more equally distributed incomes, but I think few people would view social justice (whatever it means) as adequate compensation for a 25 percent lower income.

I am no Constitutional scholar, and so my opinion that the takings clause should be interpreted to prohibit redistribution carries no legal imprimatur. On the other hand, it is evident that *something* acted to restrain the federal government from redistributing income over the first 140-odd years of its existence. It is a notable feature of our history that the federal government engaged in very little that could be called redistribution up until the advent of Franklin Roosevelt's New Deal. If not the Constitution, it must have been the good sense of the American electorate that concluded the federal government had no business taking money from some people and giving it to others.

Whatever its Constitutional merits, there is much evidence that a large part of the American people agree with the principle I am espousing. A 2003 survey found that nearly half the public (47%) disagreed strongly (29%) or somewhat (18%) with the statement: "It is the responsibility of government to reduce the differences in income between people with high incomes and people with low incomes."[6] Another survey found that while two-thirds of the public thought there was "too much inequality," fewer than one-third thought the government ought to do anything about it.[7] Yet another amazingly found that "Only 65 percent of American adults thought the federal government should do *anything* to help the poor."[8]

In a volume examining many surveys assaying attitudes toward inequality, Everett Ladd and Karlyn Bowman conclude: "Americans are not inclined to a politics of envy. They are inclined to the idea that opportunity is present to those who avail themselves of it. As a result, they are unsympathetic to government redistribution of wealth."[9] Yet government supplies us with a massive amount of redistribution. If more Americans come to understand the harmful effects of these policies and take a *principled* stand against them, we will all be better off.

GOVERNMENT SANS REDISTRIBUTION

What would the federal government look like if it were somehow constrained from adopting redistributive policies? We can't know for sure, but because nearly two-thirds of all federal spending today is on redistributive policies, it is clear a nonredistributive regime would have to be dramatically different. Let's speculate a little on how federal policies today might look if no redistribution had been permitted over the last three quarters of a century.

First, consider Social Security and Medicare. These policies could not exist in their current form because they transfer income from workers to retirees (that is, operate on a pay-as-you-go basis). But, and this is the important point, they could exist in a different form, one that did not entail redistribution. For example, the privatized form of Social Security that I sketched in chapter 7 would be permissible. Recall that this policy involved requiring people to put 10 or 12 percent of the first $12,000 of earnings into accounts to provide for their cash and medical care needs in retirement. Of course, many variations on this theme would also be permissible.

The central point is that we could have nonredistributive forms of Social Security and Medicare that place a floor under standards of living for virtually all the elderly if we wish. Similarly, unemployment insurance, and perhaps some other programs, could be reformed to accomplish many of their intended goals without involving redistribution.

Apart from social insurance programs, most other redistributive programs would simply have to go, implying substantially lower federal spending. This includes all the welfare programs (with federal spending now of about 3.5 percent of GDP) and also other programs like farm subsidies and the noxious "earmarks" (formerly, and more accurately, called pork barrel spending) that add up to roughly 1 percent of GDP. Thus, federal spending (outside the social insurance area) would be lower by about 4.5 percent of GDP.

Turning to the tax side of the federal budget, what sort of taxation is nonredistributive when used to finance public goods like national defense and medical research? Because everyone benefits from these programs, everyone should pay some taxes to finance them—in sharp contrast to the federal income tax now, which exempts about a third of the population from any tax at all. How the tax burden should vary among the people is a more difficult issue. However, many people have concluded that the closest approximation to nonredistributive taxation is a proportional tax of the sort discussed in chapter 9.[10] The basic idea is that people probably benefit from national defense (for example) roughly in proportion to their incomes (or consumption): People with higher incomes have more to protect and are willing to pay more (in proportion to their incomes or consumption) for this protection.

Thus, a proportionate system of taxation is probably the best approximation of nonredistributive taxation. As we saw in chapter 9, a tax rate of 10 percent would be required to raise the same revenue as the current federal income tax raises, or about 12 percent if the proportional tax also replaces the corporation income tax. And the corporate tax would surely have to go since it clearly places a disproportionate burden on those who receive income from capital.

However, a nonredistributive federal government would be spending less, and so the required proportional tax rate would be lower than 12 percent. With redistributive spending equal to 4.5 percent of GDP eliminated, the required tax rate would be about 6 percent. (It falls by more than 4.5 percentage points because GDP is a broader measure than the potential tax base, whether it be personal income or consumption.)

So this is the situation: If the federal government had adopted only non-redistributive policies, we could pay for it with a tax rate of 6 percent, and there would be no payroll (or corporate) tax atop that. Contrast that with the actual federal taxes we pay for the redistributive state: rates that range from about 15 percent (payroll taxes for the lowest earners who don't pay any income taxes[11]) to marginal tax rates of 30–40 percent for most middle-and upper-income taxpayers. *Federal marginal tax rates would be more than 75 percent lower than they are today for most taxpayers!*

That would only be the obvious difference in federal budgetary policy. More important would be the effect on the performance of the economy. Based on the analysis developed throughout this book, a nonredistributive federal government would permit more of the productive potential of the American people to be realized. If we use my earlier estimate—that GDP is 25 percent lower as a result of welfare-state policies—then GDP today would be one-third higher than it currently is. That's about $4 *trillion* in additional output. This also means that personal incomes—yours, mine, and everyone else's (at least on average)—would be a third higher.

This comparison is based on what we could have had today if the federal government had not adopted the welfare-state policies it did. We can't undo the past, and if these policies and their consequences were irreversible, there wouldn't be much point in dissecting them. But happily, these things are reversible. We can in the future have a federal government with smaller spending and much lower marginal tax rates, resulting in substantially higher personal incomes. All we need to do to achieve this is to keep the federal government out of the business of redistributing income.

I have tended to emphasize the narrow economic benefits of a nonredistributive state, and there are, to be sure, other benefits and other costs. In defense of my narrow focus on so-called crass material things—as egalitarians are apt to dismiss the advantages of having incomes a third higher—let us consider a bit further why higher incomes are beneficial.

A higher GDP (higher incomes) provides the means to a great many different ends. Invariably, higher incomes are associated with better health and greater longevity, more education, greater artistic as well as scientific achievements—it's not just about "things." Many of the so-called social problems that we confront would be much more manageable, and might not even be problems, if people had incomes a third higher. Consider college tuition costs, energy costs, housing costs, or the costs of health insurance, health care, and prescription drugs—all would be far less burdensome if we were a third wealthier. Nor should we forget that the technological progress that accompanies growth in incomes might produce more effective solutions to problems like global warming. We simply have more and better options when we have more income.

When egalitarians defend the welfare state, they incessantly remind us that one of its alleged benefits is security, the certainty that government will take care of us if unfortunate events occur. For example, they often point out that Social Security benefits are indexed to, and therefore protect the elderly from, inflation. I am not sure how secure those planning to retire in 20 or 30 years feel, but given the impending problems confronting Social Security and Medicare and the political uncertainties concerning how they will be dealt with, I am a bit dubious about government-provided security. In any event, I think most people would be happy to incur a bit more insecurity if their incomes were a third higher; for those who value security highly, private insurance and private savings can provide a substantial amount of it.

But whatever security some individuals get from the welfare state, it is clear that another type of security—collective security—suffers as a result. Our collective security as a nation depends heavily on our productive capacity, our potential GDP. When national emergencies arise, whether man-made or natural, our ability to deal with them is directly proportional to our productive capacity. Think about World War II. We won that war in large part because our productive capacity was greater than that of our enemies—our greater productive capacity provided us with greater collective security.

Collective security is furthered not just by greater military might. It is perhaps true that we won the Cold War partly as a result of using our productive capacity to strengthen our military capabilities. But our stronger economic system (higher GDP per person) also played a central role as it became apparent to people living in communist regimes that their systems were inherently inferior to ours. Communism, after all, imploded without a single shot being fired.

The experience of the Cold War provides an important lesson for the current War on Terror. Even more so than with the Cold War, the War on Terror is unlikely to be won by military power alone given the nature of our enemy. But if our economy pulls further and further ahead of their antiquated economic systems, it becomes more and more likely that their systems will crumble from within. Higher GDP thus not only provides the means to finance necessary military and internal security safeguards, it also acts as a demonstration of the superiority of our economic arrangements, in both ways furthering our collective security.

Apart from providing security from external enemies, higher GDP also is a protection against natural disasters like epidemics or hurricanes—we have greater capacity to respond effectively and quickly with a more productive economy. It is interesting to speculate how Hurricane Katrina, which devastated New Orleans and the Gulf Coast in 2005, might have had different results under a nonredistributive federal regime. Had residents of Louisiana and New Orleans been responsible for construction and maintenance of their own levees (rather than dependent on earmarks in the federal budget), would they have been better protected? Would the residents have been better able to evacuate had they had incomes a third higher, implying (among other things) that more would have owned automobiles? Would the houses have been better constructed to withstand the water and winds? We cannot know for certain, but higher incomes unquestionably would have provided the capacity to achieve greater security.

Economists thus emphasize so-called crass material things like GDP and incomes for very good reasons. It is only a failure of imagination that leads people to cavalierly dismiss their importance.

If this makes the advantages of a nonredistributive federal government sound too good to be true, in one sense that is correct. The benefits from embracing the nonredistributive principle would not occur immediately. It has taken a half century or more for the full costs of the welfare state to be realized, and it will take a similarly long period to fully reverse those consequences. Realistically, moving toward a nonredistributive federal regime might add 0.5–1.0 percentage points to the annual rate of growth in real GDP per capita; it would take several decades for most of the benefits to be realized. During the transition period, many people would find their incomes lowered as a result of scaling back the welfare-state policies.

The welfare state arose in large part because we sacrificed the long-term good for short-term political and economic benefits. It is time we rethink our priorities and focus on what is in our long-term interests.

WHAT ABOUT THE POOR?

Any proposal that suggests dismantling the federal welfare state will be dismissed out of hand by egalitarians. They will play their usual trump card, that any such movement would devastate the most vulnerable and poorest members of society and is therefore unthinkable. Recall some of the words that were used to describe the moderate cutback in only *one* welfare program (the 1996 welfare reform): *cruel, heartless, draconian, unconscionable.* I shudder to think of how my proposal, which involves elimination of *all* federal welfare programs, would be characterized. Yet I don't shrink from consideration of how the poor would be affected.

A key element in my proposal is that it applies only to *federal* welfare-state programs. State and local governments could continue any amount of redistribution they wish. Thus, my proposal is based squarely on the genius of the founding fathers in creating a federal system of government, one in which different levels of government are assigned the tasks they can best perform. There are good reasons for believing that a system in which states (and, to a lesser extent, local governments) have the responsibility for assisting the poor will be more effective than one in which the federal government plays the dominant role.

Let's consider first how total government welfare spending would be affected. Currently, welfare program expenditures by state and local governments are about 1.5 percent of GDP, while federal expenditures are about 3.5 percent. Thus, if there are no offsetting changes, eliminating federal welfare spending would reduce total welfare spending from 5 percent to 1.5 percent of GDP. There would likely be some offsetting changes, but for the moment suppose total spending on welfare programs did decline to 1.5 percent. Would that be catastrophic for the poor?

One and a half percent of GDP is a very large sum, currently equal to about $200 billion a year. That would finance a transfer of about $7,000 to each person in the bottom 10 percent of the income distribution, or about $28,000 for a family of four (40% above the poverty line for a family of four). That would seem to be sufficient to provide for the truly needy among the American population, at least unless more than one-tenth of our fellow citizens are incapable of providing for themselves.

Another way to evaluate just how large 1.5 percent of GDP devoted to welfare is to compare it to the historical record. As pointed out earlier, total government welfare spending did not exceed 1 percent of GDP for the first 175 years of our history (up to the mid-1960s).[12] During this period the poor not only survived but most became not poor. In fact, our nation became the richest on earth during this period. With the improved circumstances and opportunities available to the poor today, is it so farfetched to believe that welfare expenditures that are 50 percent higher as a share of a much larger national income would be enough to provide a reasonable safety net?

One of the prominent effects of government welfare spending is that it tends to crowd out (i.e., reduce) other forms of assistance. Correspondingly, a reduction in federal welfare spending can be expected to lead to an increase in nongovernmental assistance to the poor. This includes assistance from family and friends of the poor, private charities, and religious organizations. While these offsets to reduced federal spending would not be dollar for dollar, there is no question that nongovernmental assistance to the poor would rise substantially in response to a reduced federal role. In addition, state and local governments might also respond by increasing their expenditures. However, it would be unrealistic to anticipate these reactions to fully offset the decline in federal spending, so we should expect total resources devoted to welfare programs to fall, but by less than the reduction in federal spending.

Welfare programs operated by state, local, and nongovernmental entities can also be expected to be more effective per dollar spent than welfare administered at the federal level. Not only are the former entities closer to and more familiar with the problems faced by the poor but they also have greater flexibility in designing and carrying out programs of assistance. One of the virtues of a decentralized approach, as in a federal system, is that different states and organizations will utilize different approaches and can learn from both the successes and failures realized. It should not be forgotten that the welfare reform of 1996, widely regarded as one of the few successes among welfare policy reforms, was built upon the experiences of several states experimenting with different approaches. These states had to receive waivers from the federal government just to try alternative approaches, but with the federal government out of the picture there would be a great deal more experimentation, which would lead over time to more effective policies.

From a long-run perspective, one of the most important policies affecting the poor is the public school system. Although not often thought of as a welfare program (and not included in the 1.5% figure), it does redistribute a large quantity of resources to the poor, primarily financed by state and local taxpayers. (With expenditures per pupil of nearly $10,000, a poor family with two children in school receives an annual subsidy costing taxpayers $20,000—a much larger subsidy than provided by any of the explicit welfare programs.) It is a testament to the generosity of American taxpayers that this large redistribution is not controversial; it reflects our commitment to providing opportunity to all people, including the children of the poor.

In a 1999 Gallup survey, people were asked "In what ways do you think the government should help the poor?" Among a dozen possible responses, the two receiving the highest percentages were "Better education" (38%) and "More skill training" (29%).[13] There is little doubt that *potentially* the long-run poverty-reducing effects of better equipping the poor with job skills is a more effective (and acceptable, to taxpayers) strategy than relying on the transfer programs that now dominate the (federal) agenda. *Actually,* of course, the performance of the school system in preparing disadvantaged children for productive lives has been dismal. It is not too much to hope that eliminating the federal redistributive role would lead to increased attention to this crucial area. Egalitarian efforts to transfer more and more money to the poor are responsible, at least in part, for the neglect of this traditional state and local government function.

Overall, however, it is likely that total welfare assistance would decline if the federal government did not engage in redistribution. Although egalitarians will see the decline of welfare as a decisive drawback, it does not imply that the poor will necessarily be worse off. Current welfare programs are a great impediment to work, saving, and the formation of stable families, and a reduction in welfare spending would have positive effects in all these areas. But we have not yet considered what may be the greatest benefit to the poor if there was a reduction in the redistributive state: The wage rates for workers with limited skills would rise substantially.

As I explained at the end of the previous chapter, welfare-state policies have probably reduced the wage rates for unskilled workers by about a fourth. Elimination or reform of these policies along the lines suggested above could be expected to produce a substantial increase in these wage rates, probably on the order of a third. This implies male high school dropouts could be earning $36,000 a year rather than $27,000, and female high school dropouts could be earning $27,000 rather than $20,000.

So how would a movement to a nonredistributive federal government affect the poor? The bottom line is that it means smaller government welfare assistance but higher wage rates. For many, if not most, of the poor, I believe this would represent a clear net improvement.

I, along with most Americans, would not wish to live in a society that did nothing to provide for our neediest fellow citizens, but there is no danger of that happening if we restrict the federal government to its traditional functions. State and local governments and nongovernmental entities are capable of providing adequate assistance and would probably do a better job than the federal government. Surprisingly, most Americans already seem to agree with this sentiment. A 1997 CBS News Poll asked the question: "Would you rather welfare programs like food stamps and aid to dependent children be the responsibility of state government, or of the federal government?" By a margin of nearly two to one (60% to 32%), Americans preferred that the state governments have this responsibility.[14]

However we evaluate the net effect on the poor, it should not be forgotten that the other 90 percent or so of the population will certainly benefit from prohibiting the federal government from redistributing income.

Egalitarians lionize the legendary Robin Hood, who robbed from the rich and gave to the poor. Although this practice may be laudable when carried out by a mythical individual, it loses much of its luster when executed by the federal government. We have much to gain if we can learn to just say no to federal redistribution; just say no to stealing from each other.

Notes

INTRODUCTION

1. Richard A. Musgrave, "Cost-Benefit Analysis and the Theory of Public Finance," *Journal of Economic Literature* 7 (September 1969), pp. 797–806.

2. The apposite phrase *big-government conservatism* is used by Michael Tanner. See his *Leviathan on the Right: How Big-Government Conservatism Brought Down the Republican Revolution* (Washington, DC: The Cato Institute, 2007).

3. R.S.J. Tol and G. W. Yohe, "Review of the Stern Review," *World Economics* 7 (October–December 2006), pp. 233–50. The figures I give are approximate; they are read from a graph (Figure 1, p. 235) in the Tol and Yohe paper.

CHAPTER 1: EGALITARIANISM AND THE MARKET

1. "Egalitarianism: Threat to a Free Market," *Business Week*, December 1, 1975, p. 62.

2. Thomas Sowell, "The Equality Dogma," syndicated column, February 17, 2004.

3. Aaron Wildavsky, *The Rise of Radical Egalitarianism* (Washington, DC: The American University Press, 1991), p. xxviii.

4. Milton and Rose Friedman, *Free to Choose* (New York: Avon Books, 1980), p. 131.

5. Wildavsky, *Rise of Radical Egalitarianism*, p. xxx.

6. This is the phrase Michael Parkin uses in his *Microeconomics*, 4th ed. (Reading, MA: Addison-Wesley, 1998), p. 16.

7. Thomas J. Stanley and William D. Danko, *The Millionaire Next Door: The Surprising Secrets of America's Wealthy* (Atlanta: Longstreet Press, 1996), p. 16.

8. N. Gregory Mankiw, *Principles of Microeconomics* (Fort Worth, TX: The Dryden Press, 1997), p. 392.

9. Abigail Thernstrom and Stephan Thernstrom, *No Excuses: Closing the Racial Gap in Learning* (New York: Simon & Schuster, 2003). The Thernstroms cite several studies supporting this position on p. 193.

10. The 2002 NSSE annual report is available at http://www.indiana.edu/~nsse/.

11. Richard J. Herrnstein and Charles Murray, *The Bell Curve: Intelligence and Class Structure in American Life* (New York: The Free Press, 1994).

12. Linda S. Gottfredson, "Mainstream Science on Intelligence," *The Wall Street Journal*, December 13, 1994, p. A18.

13. Mark Snyderman and Stanley Rothman, *The IQ Controversy, the Media and Public Policy* (New Brunswick, NJ: Transaction Books, 1988), p. ix.

14. Charles Murray, "IQ and Economic Success," *The Public Interest* 128 (Summer 1997), pp. 21–35.

15. For a discussion of the major twin study in the United States, see William Wright, *Born That Way* (New York: Routledge, 1999). This engaging book is a non-technical but highly informative discussion of the twin studies and the nature vs. nurture debate.

16. Linda S. Gottfredson, "The General Intelligence Factor," *Scientific American* 9(4) (Winter 1998), p. 24.

17. David J. Armor, *Maximizing Intelligence* (New Brunswick, NJ: Transaction Publishers, 2003), p. 10.

18. Ibid., p. 97. In comparison with the original list of eight, it will be noticed that several have been combined in this shorter list.

19. Ibid., p. 97.

20. Nothing said here, or nothing in science, implies that in the future environmental interventions may not be found that produce larger effects than those now known. Genetic engineering comes to mind.

CHAPTER 2: INEQUALITY

1. *Parade*, April 15, 2007, pp. 4–14.

2. The calculation is done as follows. For average income in the top fifth, multiply its share, 48.1, divided by 20, times the overall average income of $73,304; the result, $176,296, is the average income of families in the highest fifth (except for rounding error). For average income in the bottom fifth, multiply its share, 4.0, divided by 20, times the overall average income, yielding $14,661 as the average income in the bottom fifth. The reason for dividing by 20 is that if a quintile share is 20, that fifth has exactly the national average income. Put differently, the bottom quintile's average income is 4/20 of the national average, and so on.

3. This is a bit of an overstatement because the Census Bureau's figures already reflect the indirect taxes paid by businesses before they compensate workers (such as the employer portion of payroll taxes). Only direct taxes must be subtracted to obtain after-tax incomes.

4. Edgar K. Browning and William R. Johnson, "Taxes, Transfers, and Income Inequality," in *Regulatory Change in an Atmosphere of Crisis*, ed. Gary M. Walton (New York: Academic Press, 1979), pp. 129–52.

5. Robert Rector and Rea Hederman, Jr., "Two Americas: One Rich, One Poor? Understanding Income Inequality in the United States," The Heritage Foundation Backgrounder (no. 1791) (Washington, DC: The Heritage Foundation, 2004).

6. U.S. Bureau of Labor Statistics, *Consumer Expenditures in 2005* (Washington, DC: U.S. Government Printing Office, 2007), table 1.

7. Nicholas Eberstadt, "The Mismeasure of Poverty," *Policy Review* (August–September 2006), http://www.hoover.org/publications/policyreview/3930481.html.

8. Attributed to Gary Burtless's commentary on a presentation by Gary Solon in "Earnings Variability: Transitory or Persistent?," American Enterprise Institute, September 2000, p. 2.

9. Andrew J. Rettenmaier and Donald R. Deere, "Climbing the Economic Ladder," National Center for Policy Analysis, May 2003.

10. Bruce Bartlett, "Income Picture out of Focus," *The Washington Times,* July 14, 2003.

11. Sidney Verba and Gary Orren, *Equality in America: The View from the Top* (Cambridge, MA: Harvard University Press, 1985), p. 5.

12. Don Fullerton and Diane Lim Rogers, *Who Bears the Lifetime Tax Burden?* (Washington, DC: The Brookings Institution, 1993), p. 17.

13. Edgar K. Browning and Jacquelene M. Browning, *Public Finance and the Price System,* 3rd ed. (New York: Macmillan Publishing Company, 1987), table 8-9, p. 247.

14. Fullerton and Rogers, *Lifetime Tax Burden,* table 4-10, p. 114. They do not give these figures, but they can be calculated from those in the table.

15. Ibid., p. 26.

16. Data from table P-24, available at the Census Bureau Web site at http://www.census.gov/hhes/www/income/histinc/p26.html. I have not included all the educational classifications covered in this table. For example, I do not include those with less than a ninth-grade education (median earnings of $22,330) because this group is only 4 percent of the labor force and is disproportionately composed of immigrants, including illegal immigrants. (All of the numbers reported include illegal immigrants.)

17. Verba and Orren, *Equality in America,* pp. 155–56.

18. Fullerton and Rogers, *Lifetime Tax Burden,* table 4-14, p. 123.

19. Alan Reynolds, *Income and Wealth* (Westport, CT: Greenwood Press, 2006) and Gene Epstein, *Econospinning: How to Read between the Lines When the Media Manipulates the Numbers* (Hoboken, NJ: John Wiley & Sons, 2006).

20. These figures are calculated from table F-3 of the Historical Income Tables—Families, which is available at the Census Bureau Web site: http://www.census.gov/hhes/www/income/histinc/f03ar.html.

21. Eberstadt, "The Mismeasure of Poverty," table 2.

22. Daniel T. Slesnick, *Living Standards in the United States: A Consumption-Based Approach* (Washington, DC: The American Enterprise Institute Press, 2000). The figures cited in the text are calculated from tables 3 and 5.

23. Claudia Goldin and Lawrence F. Katz, "Decreasing (and Then Increasing) Inequality in America: A Tale of Two Half-Centuries," in *The Causes and Consequences of Increasing Inequality,* ed. Finis Welch (Chicago: University of Chicago Press, 2001).

24. Frank Levy, *Dollars and Dreams: The Changing American Income Distribution* (New York: Russell Sage Foundation, 1987), table 9.2, p. 196.

25. Edgar K. Browning, "The Trend toward Equality in the Distribution of Net Income," *Southern Economic Journal* 42 (July 1976), table IV.

26. The culprits are the second, fourth, and fifth factors listed earlier, all of which require much larger adjustments to the data today than in 1950.

27. Mervyn King, "Overview," *Income Inequality: Issues and Policy Options*, A Symposium Sponsored By The Federal Reserve Bank of Kansas City, Jackson Hole, Wyoming, August 27–29, 1998, p. 371.

28. Gary S. Becker and Kevin M. Murphy, "The Upside of Income Inequality," *The American*, May/June 2007, pp. 20–23.

29. Steven Pinker, *The Blank Slate: The Modern Denial of Human Nature* (New York: Penguin, 2002).

30. Mark Kramer, ed., *The Black Book of Communism: Crimes, Terror, Repression* (Cambridge, MA: Harvard University Press, 1999).

31. Irving Kristol, *Neoconservatism: The Autobiography of an Idea* (New York: The Free Press, 1995), p. 166.

CHAPTER 3: GROUP INEQUALITIES

1. The figure for Jewish families is for 1980 and is reported in Christopher Jencks, "Discrimination and Thomas Sowell," *New York Review of Books* 35 (October 1988), p. 34.

2. It might be thought that the influx of black workers to the nondiscriminating firms would decrease wages there, but it won't. Firm A will have to replace its lost black workers with white (or other) workers hired away from the nondiscriminating firms, so while the nondiscriminating firms are employing more black workers, they will end up employing fewer white workers; the reverse is true for firm A. Total employment among the firms is unaffected, and that is what will guarantee that the going market wage will remain at $40,000 for all workers.

3. James J. Heckman and Peter Siegelman, "The Urban Institute Audit Studies: Their Methods and Findings," in *Clear and Convincing Evidence: Measurement of Discrimination in America*, ed. Michael Fix and Raymond J. Struyk (Washington, DC: Urban Institute Press, 1993).

4. Calculated from table 1 in James J. Heckman, "Detecting Discrimination," *The Journal of Economica Perspectives* 12 (Spring 1998).

5. This is the ratio of median family income received by each group. Calculated from table FINC-01, Selected Characteristics of Families by Total Money Income in 2005. Available at the Census Web site. See http://pubdb3.census.gov/macro/032006/faminc/new01_003.htm for white families, and http://pubdb3.census.gov/macro/032006/faminc/new01_006.htm for black families. Other family income comparisons cited below also come from this source.

6. This figure is for 2001. I couldn't locate the figure for 2005 on the Census Web site.

7. Actually, it would be preferable to focus on hourly wage rates because markets determine wage rates, not annual earnings. Earnings are influenced also by how much one works, and even among full-time year-round workers there are variations in hours worked. Much data, however, is available only for annual earnings, but unless black and white full-time workers differ significantly, this should be reflective of wage rate differences.

8. Campbell R. McConnell, Stanley L. Brue, and David A. Macpherson, *Contemporary Labor Economics*, 6th ed. (Boston: McGraw-Hill, 2003), p. 468.

9. George J. Borjas, *Labor Economics*, 3rd ed. (Boston: McGraw-Hill, 2005), table 7.1, p. 236.

10. William R. Johnson and Derek Neal, "Basic Skills and the Black-White Earnings Gap," in *The Black-White Test Score Gap*, ed. Christopher Jencks and Meredith Phillips (Washington, DC: The Brookings Institution, 1998).

11. Census Bureau, *Children's Living Arrangements and Characteristics: March 2002*, Current Population Report P20–547, table A-1.

12. Kate Antonovics and Robert Town, "Are All the Good Men Married? Uncovering the Sources of the Marital Wage Premium," *The American Economic Review* 94 (May 2004), p. 317.

13. Ibid., p. 317.

14. Ronald G. Ehrenberg and Robert S. Smith, *Modern Labor Economics*, 2nd ed. (Glenview, IL: Scott, Foresman and Company, 1985), p. 445.

15. June O'Neill, "The Role of Human Capital in Earnings Differences between Black and White Men," *The Journal of Economic Perspectives* 4 (Fall 1990), p. 33.

16. Abigail Thernstrom and Stephan Thernstrom, *No Excuses: Closing the Racial Gap in Learning* (New York: Simon & Schuster, 2003, p. 13.

17. Thernstrom and Thernstrom, pp. 36–37.

18. O'Neill, "Role of Human Capital," pp. 40–41.

19. James J. Heckman, "Detecting Discrimination," *The Journal of Economic Perspectives* (Spring 1998) pp. 101–16.

20. Thernstrom and Thernstrom, *No Excuses*, p. 38.

21. Ibid., p. 130.

22. James J. Heckman and Amy L. Wax, "Home Alone," *The Wall Street Journal*, January 23, 2004.

23. Ibid.

24. Ibid.

25. Thernstrom and Thernstrom, *No Excuses*, p. 132.

26. Diana Furchtgott-Roth and Christine Stolba, *The Feminist Dilemma* (Washington, DC: The American Enterprise Institute, 2001), p. 28.

27. Ibid., pp. 26–27.

28. Ibid., p. 65.

29. Borjas, *Labor Economics*, p. 386.

30. Steven E. Rhoads, *Incomparable Worth: Pay Equity Meets the Market* (Cambridge: Cambridge University Press, 1993), p. 13.

31. Historical Income Tables—People, table P-32: http://www.census.gov/hhes/www/income/histinc/p32.html.

32. Furchtgott-Roth and Stolba, *Feminist Dilemma*, pp. 48–49.

33. Steven E. Rhoads, *Taking Sex Differences Seriously*. (San Francisco: Encounter Books, 2004), p. 214.

34. Furchtgott-Roth and Stolba, *Feminist Dilemma*, pp. 68–69.

35. David Neumark and Sanders Korenman, "Sources of Bias in Women's Wage Equations: Results Using Sibling Data," *Journal of Human Resources* xxix (1994), pp. 379–405.

36. Steven Pinker, *The Blank Slate: The Modern Denial of Human Nature* (New York: Penguin, 2002), p. 347.

37. Rhoads (2004), p. 28.

38. Ibid., p. 25.

39. Pinker (2002), p. 357.

40. Ibid., p. 356.

41. Furchtgott-Roth and Stolba, *Feminist Dilemma*, p. 79.

42. Victor R. Fuchs, Alan B. Krueger, and James M. Poterba, "Economists' Views about Parameters, Values, and Policies: Survey Results in Labor and Public Economics," *The Journal of Economic Perspectives* 36 (September 1998), pp. 1387–1445. The survey did not contain any questions about other group disparities.

43. Quoted in Diana Furchtgott-Roth, "Still Hyping the Phony Pay Gap," *On the Issues* (American Enterprise Institute for Public Policy Research, March 2000), p. 1.

44. You can see a video of her speech containing these remarks at http://www.hillaryclinton.com/video/13.aspx

Chapter 4: Incomes around the World

1. I take this striking example from Jeffrey D. Sachs, *The End of Poverty* (New York: The Penguin Press, 2005), p. 1.

2. The data are from the World Bank, *World Development Report 2005* (New York: The World Bank and Oxford University Press, 2004), especially table 1. Data for other countries are converted to U.S. dollars (2003) using purchasing power parity conversion factors, which are thought to be more accurate than relying on official exchange rates.

3. Specifically, the World Bank ranks households on the basis of household income per capita (rather than total household income for the Census Bureau) and constructs quintiles containing 20 percent of the population (rather than 20% of the households).

4. To be more specific, using a widely used summary measure of inequality calculated by the World Bank (the Gini index) the United States is the 70th most unequal nation out of the 134 listed by the World Bank.

5. The World Bank recalculated the $1 threshold as $1.08 using 1993 prices, and I have adjusted this using the consumer price index to the corresponding 2003 level.

6. The figures are from Peter H. Lindert, *Growing Public: Social Spending and Economic Growth since the Eighteenth Century* (New York: Cambridge University Press, 2004), table 6.1, and refer to 1999. The table includes only 28 countries, but they are most of the high-income countries of the world.

7. Richard Lynn and Tatu Vanhanen, *IQ and the Wealth of Nations* (New York: Praeger Publishers, 2002).

8. Garrett Jones and W. Joel Schneider, "Intelligence, Human Capital, and Economic Growth: A Bayesian Averaging of Classical Estimates (BACE) Approach," *Journal of Economic Growth* 11 (March 2006), pp. 71–93.

9. James Gwartney and Robert Lawson (with Erik Gartzke), *Economic Freedom of the World: 2005 Annual Report* (Vancouver, BC: The Fraser Institute, 2005).

10. World Bank, *Doing Business in 2006* (Washington, DC: The World Bank and the International Finance Corporation, 2006).

11. World Bank (2004), table A2, gives the estimates reported in this paragraph. In this tabulation, "low income" means countries with per capita incomes below $765, very poor indeed.

12. Robert E. Lucas, Jr., "The Industrial Revolution: Past and Future," *The Region* (Federal Reserve Bank of Minneapolis, 2003) available at www.minneapolisfed.org/pubs/region/04-05/essay.cfm.

13. Elsa Vila-Artadi and Xavier Sala-i-Martin, "The Economic Tragedy of the Twentieth Century: Growth in Africa," NBER Working Paper No. 9865, July 2003.

14. The figures for 1960 cited in this and the previous three paragraphs are from the Penn World Table at the Center for International Comparisons of Production, Income and Prices, which gives values in 1996 prices (http://pwt.econ.upenn.edu/). I have updated to 2003 dollars to make them comparable to the figures from 2003, taken from the World Bank (2004, table 1).

15. Googling this statement and Lucas's name generates several sites where this quotation (or a paraphrase of it) is attributed to him, but none of the ones I have looked at give a specific reference.

16. These quotations are taken from Jim Garaghty, "How Debates Get Settled," *National Review Online,* June 8, 2004. Garaghty also gives several other similar quotations from other people.

17. This example is discussed in Sachs (2005), chap. 6. Sachs says that Spain's GDP per capita was nearly four times Poland's in 1989, but according to the Penn World Table the ratio was two to one.

18. David Osterfeld, *Prosperity versus Planning: How Government Stifles Economic Growth* (New York: Oxford University Press, 1992).

19. Robert Heilbroner, "The Triumph of Capitalism," *The New Yorker,* January 23, 1989, p. 98.

20. Richard Pipes, *Communism: A History* (New York: Modern Library, 2001), p. 154.

21. Vito Tanzi and Ludger Schuknecht, *Public Spending in the 20th Century: A Global Perspective* (New York: Cambridge University Press, 2000), table 1.1. The 17 countries include the major European economies as well as Australia, Canada, Japan, New Zealand, and the United States.

22. The data in this and the next two paragraphs are from U.S. Department of Labor, Bureau of Labor Statistics, *Comparative Real Gross Domestic Product Per Capita and Per Employed Person Fifteen Countries 1960–2004,* July 22, 2005, tables 2 and 6. http://www.bls.gov/fls/

23. The figures for Germany are somewhat misleading because the 1982 figure is for West Germany, while the 2004 figure is for reunified West and East Germany. In 1991, the first year for which data is available for reunified Germany, incomes were 81.0 percent of the American level.

24. William Easterly, *The Elusive Quest for Growth* (Cambridge, MA: The MIT Press, 2002), p. 14.

25. Easterly (*Elusive Quest,* p. 33) gives the figure $1 trillion in 1985 dollars.

26. Michael Mandelbaum, *The Ideas That Conquered the World* (New York: Public Affairs, 2002), p. 297.

27. Lucas, "Industrial Revolution."

CHAPTER 5: POVERTY

1. Mollie Orshansky, "Counting the Poor: Another Look at the Poverty Profile," *Social Security Bulletin* 28 (January 1965), pp. 3–29.

2. More precisely, this is the weighted-average poverty line for a family of four because a four-person family's poverty line varies with the number of children and adults in the family.

3. Rose D. Friedman, *Poverty: Definition and Perspective* (Washington, DC: The American Enterprise Institute, 1965).

4. I am referring to the utility theory of consumer choice. According to this theory, consumers allocate their budgets so that the marginal utility per dollar of expenditure on all items is the same and is equal to the marginal utility of income. If enough food is consumed to meet an objective poverty standard, then the consumer will be getting an equal benefit per dollars worth from other goods as well, implicitly defining other needs in terms of marginal utility.

5. An example: "Liberals also object to the continuing use of the 1963 'food multiplier'.... Today [1998], American households allocate less than one-fifth of their budgets to food purchases. Were the same methods used to construct poverty lines today, the food-cost multiplier would be five, not three." Bradley R. Schiller, *The Economics of Poverty and Discrimination,* 8th ed. (Upper Saddle River, NJ: Prentice-Hall, 2001), p. 36.

Of course, the "same methods" were logically incorrect in 1963, and applying them today would be quantitatively an even worse error.

6. Nicholas Eberstadt, "The 'Poverty Rate': America's Worst Statistical Indicator," *On the Issues* (Washington, DC: The American Enterprise Institute, March 2002).

7. Mary Jo Bane and David Ellwood, "Slipping into and out of Poverty: The Dynamics of Spells," *Journal of Human Resources* 21 (Winter 1986), pp. 1–23.

8. Greg Duncan, *Years of Poverty, Years of Plenty* (Ann Arbor: University of Michigan Press, 1984); Richard Coe, "Dependency and Poverty in the Short and Long Run," in *Five Thousand American Families: Patterns of Economic Progress,* vol. 6, ed. Greg J. Duncan and James N. Morgan (Ann Arbor, MI: Institute for Social Research, 1978), pp. 273–96; Rebecca M. Blank, *It Takes a Nation* (Princeton, NJ: Princeton University Press, 1997).

9. Daniel T. Slesnick, *Consumption and Social Welfare* (Cambridge, MA: Cambridge University Press, 2001), p. 162.

10. Ibid., p. 167. This figure does use the personal consumption expenditures (PCE) price index to adjust the poverty thresholds rather than the official consumer price index (CPI). I discuss this issue further later in this chapter.

11. Slesnick, *Consumption and Social Welfare,* p. 178.

12. There is one important cash-welfare program, the Earned Income Tax Credit, that is also not counted because it is defined as a tax, and the poverty thresholds are based on before-tax incomes.

13. Why then didn't the original definition of poverty take account of in-kind transfers? The probable reason is that most of these transfers didn't exist or were of negligible magnitude when the poverty lines were formulated. It was taken for granted that the poor would have to use cash to acquire food, housing, and medical care.

14. Table RD-REV POV01 RS, available at http://pubdb3.census.gov/macro/032006/altpov/newpov01rs_001.htm.

15. Edgar K. Browning and Jacquelene M. Browning, *Public Finance and the Price System,* 4th ed. (New York: Macmillan Publishing Company, 1994), p. 260.

16. At least, this seems to be the case from the heading in the last column of the table cited in note 14. It says that this column adds in "noncash, *nonmedical* (my italics) transfers that can be measured and evaluated." In earlier years, (some) medical transfers were included.

17. If the $700 apartment is worth only $400 to the recipient, why doesn't the government give the recipient the $700 cost of the subsidy as cash and therefore increase

their income by $300 more? It must be that the government (or the taxpayers) believe the apartment reduces poverty by at least $700 worth regardless of how the recipient values the transfer.

One common objection to the use of market value for medical transfers runs like this: If a person has $200,000 in medical expenses paid for by Medicaid, we certainly don't want to count that sum as income and conclude that the person is really rich! This is correct, but the way market value should be used for medical care subsidies is to estimate the cost of insurance coverage for a given population and use that amount rather than the actual outlays (if any) on medical expenses. For a mother with two children, for example, medical insurance coverage comparable to Medicaid might cost about $4,000, and that would be taken as the market value of Medicaid, whether the family had actual medical expenses of $200,000 (or zero).

18. W. Michael Cox and Richard Alm, *Myths of the Rich and Poor* (New York: Basic Books, 1999), p. 21.

19. Bruce D. Meyer and James X. Sullivan, "Measuring the Well-Being of the Poor Using Income and Consumption," NBER Working Paper No. 9760 (June 2003), p. 34.

20. As one piece of evidence that correction of the problems discussed here would substantially reduce the adjusted rate of 8.2 percent, consider that for several years in the 1980s the Census produced estimates of the effect of including in-kind transfers using a market valuation approach as well as its flawed recipient valuation method. When counted at market value, the inclusion of in-kind transfers (some of them; not all were included) reduced the poverty rate by 5.0 percentage points. When counted at recipient value, the reduction was only 2.4 percentage points. (These figures are averages over a seven-year period.) So using the recipient value methodology understates by more than half (2.6 percentage points for these years) the effect of in-kind transfers on the poverty rate. For the yearly data, see Edward N. Wolff, *Economics of Poverty Inequality and Discrimination* (Cincinnati: South-Western College Publishing, 1997), table 4.5, pp. 114–15.

21. Robert E. Rector and Kirk A. Johnson, "Understanding Poverty in America," *The Heritage Backgrounder* (no. 1713) (Washington, DC: The Heritage Foundation, January 6, 2004). This paper is a must read for anyone concerned with how the poor really live in America. Available online at www.heritage.org/Research/Welfare/bg1713.cfm.

22. Douglas J. Besharov, "We're Feeding the Poor as if They're Starving," *The Washington Post*, December 8, 2002.

23. Richard J. Herrnstein and Charles Murray, *The Bell Curve: Intelligence and Class Structure in American Life*. (New York: The Free Press, 1994), p. 146.

24. The mean score of those who haven't completed high school on the National Adult Literacy Survey was 218, below the level-one cutoff score of 225 (usually taken to indicate functional illiteracy). See the National Institute for Literacy Web site at http://www.nifl.gov/nifl/facts/NALS/html.

25. Table POV22 at the Census Web site: http://pubdb3.census.gov/macro/032006/pov/new22_100_01.htm.

26. Lawrence M. Mead, *The New Politics of Poverty: The Nonworking Poor in America* (New York: Basic Books, 1992).

27. Ibid., p. 66.

28. Table POV24 at the Census Web site: http://pubdb3.census.gov/macro/032006/pov/new24_100_01.htm.

29. Isabel V. Sawhill, "The Behavioral Aspects of Poverty," *The Public Interest* (Fall 2003), pp. 83–84.

30. Table POV29 at the Census Web site: http://pubdb3.census.gov/macro/032006/pov/new29_100_01.htm.

31. These figures are for 2003 from the Census Web site, table C-8, which is apparently no longer online.

32. Calculated from table POV38 at the Census Web site: http://pubdb3.census.gov/macro/032006/pov/new38_000.htm.

33. From Senator Joe Lieberman's campaign Web site.

34. Michael Novak (Chairman of the Working Seminar on Family and American Welfare Policy), *The New Consensus on Family and Welfare* (Washington, DC: The American Enterprise Institute, 1987), p. 5.

35. Sawhill, "Behavioral Aspects of Poverty," p. 83.

36. From the 1971 book by that title: William Ryan, *Blaming the Victim* (New York: Pantheon Books, 1971).

37. Sawhill, "Behavioral Aspects of Poverty," p. 82.

38. Christine Ross, Sheldon Danziger, and Eugene Smolensky, "The Level and Trend in Poverty, 1939–1979," Institute for Research on Poverty, University of Wisconsin–Madison, June 1985. This estimate is based on comparing only earnings in 1939 with the poverty thresholds and therefore probably overstates the poverty rate to a degree.

39. Welfare spending did start to rise sharply around 1965, but even this had little to do with the decline in poverty in the late 1960s because the spending on cash welfare (which is counted in measuring poverty) increased only slightly whereas the spending on in-kind programs (not counted) grew substantially.

40. Table HINC-05 at the Census Web site: http://pubdb3.census.gov/macro/032006/hhinc/new05_000.htm

41. The Census notes that about 17 percent of the poverty population is foreign born, but this figure counts the children of immigrants who are born in this country as native born, and if we think of them as part of immigrant families the percentage would be greater than 17 percent. I have been unable to find the exact number and am guessing that it would be around 20 percent based on some indirect evidence.

42. The 2005 figure is from table RD-REV POVO1 at the Census Web site: http://pubdb3.census.gov/macro/032006/altpov/newpov01_001.htm. The 1965 rate is from Charles Murray, *Losing Ground: American Social Policy 1950–1980* (New York: Basic Books, 1984), p. 64.

CHAPTER 6: OUR TRILLION DOLLAR WELFARE SYSTEM

1. U.S. Congress, Committee on Ways and Means, *2004 Green Book* (Washington, DC: U.S. Government Printing Office, March 2004), pp. K1–K13.

2. This number is extrapolated from the $583 billion figure for 2004 by assuming welfare expenditures are the same percentage of GDP in 2005 as in 2004. The source for the 2004 figure is Karen Spar, "Cash and Noncash Benefits for Persons with Limited Income: Eligibility Rules, Recipient and Expenditure Data, FY2002–FY2004," Congressional Research Service, March 27, 2006.

3. The estimates are made as follows. The lowest quintile of families contains 22.3 percent of all children under 18, so it is assumed that 22.3 percent of public school

spending benefits this quintile. The lowest quintile contains 38.5 percent of those over 65, so it is assumed that they receive 38.5 percent of Medicare spending. For Social Security, which is related to previous earnings that are lower for those in the bottom quintile, I assume that the lowest quintile receives half the average benefit. The figure for charity is from Sheryl Sandberg, "The Charity Gap," *The Wall Street Journal*, April 4, 2007, and pertains to only that fraction of total charitable donations that targets those in need. The figure for uncompensated care is equal to 2 percent of total health care spending, which is the share found in a study for New York, Randall R. Bovbjerg et al., *Caring for the Uninsured in New York* (October 20, 2006), http://www.urban.org/url.cfm?ID=311372

4. Aaron S. Yelowitz, "Evaluating the Effects of Medicaid on Welfare and Work: Evidence from the Past Decade" (Washington, DC: Employment Policies Institute, December 2000), table 1.

5. The Earned Income Tax Credit is the only major welfare program where benefits increase as earnings rise, and it only does this over a range of low earnings. At higher earnings levels, its benefits decline with further increases in earnings, as do the benefits from all the other programs.

6. At $10,000 in earnings, welfare benefits would be $15,000; at $20,000 in earnings, benefits would be $10,000; at $30,000 in earnings, benefits would be $5,000; and so on.

7. One program, the Earned Income Tax Credit, is an exception since it acts to increase net pay at low levels of earnings (but not at higher levels). However, when that program is combined with other welfare programs and taxes, the overall effect is to reduce net rates of pay, as suggested by the example in the previous section.

8. Robert A. Moffitt, "The Temporary Assistance for Needy Families Program," in *Means-Tested Transfer Programs in the United States,* ed. Robert A. Moffitt (Chicago: University of Chicago Press, 2003), p. 317.

9. Barbara Steinberg Schone, "Estimating the Distribution of Taste Parameters of Households Facing Complex Budget Spaces: The Effects of In-kind Transfers," Agency for Health Care Policy and Research, unpublished manuscript, 1994, as cited by Edgar O. Olsen, "Housing Programs for Low-Income Households," in Moffitt *Means-Tested Transfer Programs,* p. 415.

10. Jagadeesh Gokhale, Laurence J. Kotlikoff, and Alexi Sluchynsky, "Does It Pay to Work?" National Center for Policy Analysis Policy Report, No. 258, March 2003, p. 16.

11. I use the word *suggests* because economists believe that not all reductions are necessarily inefficient. Reductions produced by *income effects* (the size of the transfer) are not inefficient, whereas those caused by *substitution effects* (the marginal tax rate effect) are inefficient.

12. Robert A. Moffitt, ed., *Welfare, the Family, and Reproductive Behavior: Research Perspectives* (Washington, DC: National Academy Press, 1998), p. 53.

13. Charles Murray, "Help the Poor: Abolish Welfare," in *American Perestroika: The Demise of the Welfare State,* ed. Richard M. Ebeling, Lissa Roche, and Lorna Busch (Hillsdale, MI: Hillsdale College Press, 1995), p. 50.

14. Barbara Downs, *Fertility of American Women: June 2002* (Washington, DC: U.S. Census Bureau, 2003), Current Population Reports, P20–548, p. 5.

15. Moffitt, *Welfare,* p. 3.

16. Maggie Gallagher and Linda Waite, *The Case for Marriage* (New York: Random House, 2000), p. 125.

17. Susan E. Mayer, *What Money Can't Buy* (Cambridge, MA: Harvard University Press, 1997), p. 1.

18. Ibid., p. 14.

19. Moffitt, *Welfare,* p. 5.

20. Scott Beaulier and Bryan Caplan, "Behavioral Economics and Perverse Effects of the Welfare State," *Kyklos* (forthcoming).

21. Ibid., manuscript p. 8.

Chapter 7: Social Security and Medicare

1. The rates reported are the combined employer and employee tax rates for Social Security and Medicare (after 1965 when Medicare was enacted) together. The tax rate today, 15.3 percent, is nominally composed of equal rate levies of 7.65 percent on the employee and the employer. Economists are in agreement that despite this use of separate taxes on employer and employee, the employee bears the full burden of this tax. In other words, the wage workers are paid by their employers would be 7.65 percent higher if the employer did not have to remit this sum to the government.

2. The figures for the years after 2020 are based on the assumption that tax rates will be increased to finance benefits. The necessity of this or some other change in the system will be discussed in a later section.

3. The annual pension is computed assuming a rate of return of 3 percent, and based on a 20-year remaining life span. (Life expectancy at age 65 for females in 2003 was 19 years while for males it was 16 years.)

4. The very high returns shown in table 7.1 for the earlier years must be interpreted with some caution. They do not imply that the pensions were large in absolute amounts, but only large relative to the taxes paid. Early retirees paid much lower tax rates during their working years.

5. Jeremy J. Siegel, *Stocks for the Long Run,* 3rd ed. (New York: McGraw-Hill, 2002), pp. 12–13.

6. Martin Feldstein and Andrew Samwick, "The Economics of Prefunding Social Security and Medicare Benefits," National Bureau of Economic Research, Working Paper No. 6055, June 1997, p. 120.

7. Fuchs, Krueger, and Poterba (1998), cited in chapter 3 regarding their survey of labor economists, also surveyed economists specializing in public finance, the field dealing with Social Security. Question 17 asked them what the personal saving rate would have been if Social Security had never been enacted. The median response was that the saving rate would have been 60 percent higher. Twenty-five percent of those surveyed thought it would be at least double the actual rate.

8. Feldstein and Samwick "Economics of Prefunding"; Jeffrey C. Edwardson, *Social Security Money's Worth Measures in a Life Cycle Context* (Ph.D. diss., Texas A&M University, College Station, Texas, 2000); Laurence J. Kotlikoff, "Privatization of Social Security: How It Works and Why It Matters," *Tax Policy and the Economy* 10 (Cambridge, MA: The MIT Press, 1996), pp. 1–32; Isaac Ehrlich and Jinyoung Kim, "Social Security, Demographic Trends, and Economic Growth: Theory and Evidence from the International Experience," National Bureau of Economic Research, Working Paper No. 11121, February 2005; Laurence J. Kotlikoff, Kent A. Smetters, and Jan Walliser, "Finding a Way Out of America's Demographic Dilemma," National Bureau of Economic Research, Working Paper No. 8258, April 2001 are

representative. Some of the relevant studies estimate how much GDP would rise if Social Security were completely privatized. That, of course, approximates how much Social Security has previously depressed GDP.

9. Moreover, for reasons we need not go into, this reduction in the growth rate is not permanent. After the economy fully adjusts to Social Security, the growth rate should gradually revert to its former level.

10. Edwardson, *Social Security Money's Worth Measures*.

11. The data cited in this section are from various publications by the Board of Trustees of Social Security and Medicare, especially *A Summary of the 2007 Annual Reports*, available at http://www.ssa.gov/OACT/TRSUM/trsummary.html.

12. This is true for the cash pensions of Social Security. It will not be true for Medicare, which requires higher tax rates to cope with rising costs of medical treatments.

13. These estimates are from Social Security and Medicare Boards of Trustees (2004), chart B and p. 5.

14. These are called the "three most common" rationales by Martin Feldstein and Jeffrey B. Liebman, "Social Security," in *Handbook of Public Economics*, ed. A. J. Auerbach and M. Feldstein (Amsterdam, The Netherlands: Elsevier Science, 2002), vol. 4, pp. 2251–54. The three rationales discussed in the 2004 *Economic Report of the President* (pp. 130–31) delete one of the Feldstein-Liebman arguments and add a new third one: Private annuity markets have certain defects. It is not a very convincing argument for Social Security and obviously suffers from the main defect in the three arguments discussed in the text.

15. Actually, in 2002, 56 percent of people reaching age 62 began receiving Social Security rather than waiting until they were 65. Early retirement is permitted, but the annual Social Security pension is 25 percent smaller for retirement at 62 rather than at 65. Another 23 percent retired at age 63 or 64 on reduced benefits. Retired people are often depicted as financially strapped, but how strapped can the nearly 80 percent of them who accept lower Social Security benefits to avoid a couple years more work really be?

16. It also increases poverty among workers because of the reduced wage rates associated with lower GDP.

17. President's Council of Economic Advisers, *Economic Report of the President, 2004* (Washington, DC: U.S. Government Printing Office, 2005), p. 131.

18. For those who do not earn as much as $12,000 a year, the pension would be smaller, but note that the $12,000 ceiling is only slightly above what a minimum-wage job provides for those who work full time. For those who are unable to work, a welfare program would be required.

19. Peaks and troughs from "Are We There Yet?," *Wall Street Journal*, August 5, 2002. The calculations of the 35-year total returns for the S&P 500 were provided by the Private Enterprise Research Center at Texas A&M University.

20. For an accessible treatment of the transition issues and one proposal for phasing in a privatized plan, see Martin Feldstein, "A New Era of Social Security," *The Public Interest* (Winter 1998). The 2 percent figure refers to Social Security alone; if Medicare were privatized also, the costs on some would probably be on the order of 4 or 5 percent of income.

21. Henry J. Aaron, "Social Security: Tune It Up, Don't Trade It In," in *Should the United States Privatize Social Security?*, ed. Henry J. Aaron and John B. Shoven (Cambridge, MA: The MIT Press, 1999), p. 55.

22. See Feldstein and Liebman, "Social Security," pp. 2250–51, and references cited there.

CHAPTER 8: MORE TRANSFERS

1. These numbers are all averages for the decade of the 1990s, calculated from table B-44, *Economic Report of the President, 2005* (Washington, DC: U.S. Government Printing Office, 2005).

2. This example is based on the discussion in Jonathan Gruber, *Public Finance and Public Policy* (New York: Worth Publishers, 2005), pp. 374–75.

3. George J. Borjas, *Labor Economics,* 3rd ed. (Boston: McGraw-Hill, 2005), p. 512.

4. Daniel Hammermesh, "Transfers, Taxes, and the NAIRU," NBER Working Paper No. 548, September 1980; Martin S. Feldstein, "Unemployment Insurance: Time for Reform," *Harvard Business Review,* March/April 1975.

5. See Alan B. Krueger and Bruce D. Meyer, "Labor Supply Effects of Social Insurance," in *Handbook of Public Economics,* vol. 4, ed. A. J. Auerbach and M. Feldstein (Amsterdam, The Netherlands: Elsevier Science B.V., 2002), pp. 2327–91.

6. Feldstein, "Unemployment Insurance," p. 231. The data are for 1970. For more recent data that show the same pattern, see the *2004 Green Book,* table 4–4, pp. 4–15.

7. Alida J. Castillo-Freeman and Richard B. Freeman, "When the Minimum Wage Really Bites: The Effect of the U.S.-Level Minimum on Puerto Rico," in *Immigration and the Work Force: Economic Consequences for the United States and Source Areas,* ed. G. J. Borjas and R. B. Freeman (Chicago: University of Chicago Press, 1992), pp. 177–211.

8. David Neumark and Olena Nizalova, "Minimum Wage Effects in the Longer Run," NBER Working Paper No. 10656, July 2004.

9. Richard V. Burkhauser and Joseph J. Sabia, "Why Raising the Minimum Wage Is a Poor Way to Help the Working Poor," Employment Policies Institute, July 2004, p. 3.

10. Two other prominent possibilities are that the wages of higher-paid workers will be lower, or the return to capital will be lower. In either case, the costs are spread throughout society, falling on both high- and low-income families.

11. Donald R. Deere, Kevin M. Murphy, and Finis R. Welch, "Examining the Evidence on Minimum Wages and Employment," in *The Effects of the Minimum Wage on Employment,* ed. Marvin Kosters (Washington, DC: The AEI Press, 1996), p. 36.

12. Richard V. Burkhauser and Joseph J. Sabia, "Raising the Minimum Wage: Another Empty Promise to the Working Poor," Employment Policies Institute, August 2005. Both of the Burkhauser-Sabia papers are available online at http://www.epionline.org/index.cfm.

13. In making this estimate, I assume that employment among poor workers affected by the minimum-wage increase declines by 5 percent, that the poor bear 5 percent of the costs (from higher prices) of the minimum wage, and that the overall marginal tax rate applicable to their earnings is 50 percent. Under these conditions, the aggregate disposable real income of the poor is slightly reduced. Of course, some poor people are benefited, but the losses to other poor people are larger.

14. Robert Lerner and Althea K. Nagai, "Pervasive Preferences: Racial and Ethnic Discrimination in Undergraduate Admissions across the Nation," Center for Equal Opportunity, http://www.ceousa.org/multi.html.

15. Data from "The Expanding Racial Scoring Gap between Black and White SAT Test Takers" from the Web site of *The Journal of Blacks in Higher Education* at www.jbhe.com.

16. Stephan Thernstrom and Abigail Thernstrom, *America in Black and White* (New York: Simon & Schuster, 1997), p. 408.

17. Stephan Thernstrom and Abigail Thernstrom, "Reflections on the Shape of the River," *UCLA Law Review* 46 (1999), p. 1605.

18. Richard H. Sander, "A Systemic Analysis of Affirmative Action in American Law Schools," *Stanford Law Review* (November 2004), pp. 367–483.

19. Ibid., p. 443.

20. Ibid., p. 373.

21. Ibid., pp. 371–72.

22. The May 2005 issue of the *Stanford Law Review* contains several articles criticizing Sander's paper, as well as Sander's response to his critics. I think Sander demolishes his critics in this exchange.

23. George J. Borjas, "The Labor Demand Curve Is Downward Sloping: Reexamining the Impact of Immigration on the Labor Market," *Quarterly Journal of Economics* (Fall 2003), pp. 1335–74.

24. This is a rough estimate, arrived at as follows. Total labor earnings are about 70 percent of GDP, so with GDP at $12.5 trillion in 2005, workers receive around $8.75 trillion. Immigrant workers, however, receive about 10 percent of this $8.75 trillion, leaving around $7.9 trillion in earnings of natives. A 4 percent reduction implies natives would have received $330 billion more in the absence of immigration.

25. A qualification to this statement is discussed later in this section.

26. This is documented in some detail in George J. Borjas, *Heaven's Door: Immigration Policy and the American Economy* (Princeton, NJ: Princeton University Press, 1999), chapter 2.

27. Congress of the United States, Congressional Budget Office, "The Role of Immigrants in the U.S. Labor Market," November 2005. Calculated from table 4.

28. Recall, from chapter 2, that the HiLo ratio is the ratio of the average (family, in this case) income for the top quintile to that of the bottom quintile. The HiLo ratios reported here are from Jared Bernstein et al., *Pulling Apart: A State-by-State Analysis of Income Trends* (Washington, DC: Center on Budget and Policy Priorities/Economic Policy Institute, January 2000), table 2.

29. Two other high-immigrant states, Texas and Florida, were ranked the 7th and 13th most unequal states.

30. Linda Chavez, "After the 'Minutemen,'" column of May 4, 2005. Available at www.lindachavez.org.

31. Council of Economic Advisers, "Immigration's Economic Impact," June 20, 2007, http://www.whitehouse.gov/cea/cea_immigration_062007.html.

32. Borjas (*Heaven's Door*, p. 96) emphasizes this point.

33. *Economic Report of the President*, 2005, p. 100.

34. Borjas, *Heaven's Door*, p. 112.

35. See James P. Smith and Barry Edmonston, eds., *The New Americans: Economic, Demographic, and Fiscal Effects of Immigration* (Washington, DC: National Academy Press, 1997), chaps. 6 and 7.

36. William Easterly, *The Elusive Quest for Growth* (Cambridge, MA: The MIT Press, 2002), p. 59.

37. Ibid., p. 270 and p. 272.

38. Alberto Alesina and Eliana La Ferrara, "Ethnic Diversity and Economic Performance," NBER Working Paper No. 10313, February 2004, point out that "Several

subsequent papers confirmed these results (i.e., that racially fragmented countries grow less) in the context of cross country growth regressions" (p. 8).

CHAPTER 9: TAXATION

1. "Edwards for Tax Reform," *Wall Street Journal,* October 7, 2004, p. A18.

2. There are some other smaller taxes, such as tariffs and estate taxes, that are not included in the table.

3. David Cay Johnston, *Perfectly Legal: The Covert Campaign to Rig Our Tax System to Benefit the Super Rich—And Cheat Everybody Else* (New York: Portfolio, 2003), p. 18.

4. The same statement is correct if we use 1983 tax rates, which are referred to by Johnston; although they are not shown in table 9.1 they are available from the CBO study. 1985 and 1983 tax rates are virtually identical.

5. These figures are calculated from the Consumer Expenditure Survey for 2005. This survey is discussed in chapter 2.

6. These surveys are reported in Joel B. Slemrod, "The Economics of Taxing the Rich," in *Does Atlas Shrug?,* ed. J. B. Slemrod (Cambridge, MA: Harvard University Press, 2000), p. 8.

7. Arnold C. Harberger, "Taxation, Resource Allocation, and Welfare," in *Taxation and Welfare,* ed. A. C. Harberger (Boston: Little, Brown, 1974), pp. 25–62. (The paper was originally published in 1964.)

8. *Economic Report of the President* (2005), pp. 73–74.

9. Joel B. Slemrod and Jon Bakija, *Taxing Ourselves: A Citizen's Guide to the Debate over Taxes,* 3rd ed. (Cambridge, MA: The MIT Press, 2004), p. 160.

10. President's Council of Economic Advisers, *Economic Report of the President,* 2005 (Washington, DC: U.S. Government Printing Office, 2005), p. 74.

11. Technical note: Economists will recognize that I am referring to the compensated response to the taxation of earnings here. That means, roughly, how taxpayers would respond if the marginal tax rate were changed but in such a way that we continue to collect the same amount of revenue. This is relevant in evaluating tax reform proposals that are so-called revenue neutral.

12. There are studies, of course, that imply this change would produce either smaller or larger increases than the 5 percent figure I give. This 5 percent estimate is based on a survey (Fuchs, Krueger, and Poterba, 1998) that I have used before to make sure estimates I emphasize are in the mainstream.

13. This example is based on Marco Bianchi, Bjorn Gudmundsson, and Gylfi Zoega, "Iceland's Natural Experiment in Supply-Side Economics," *American Economic Review* 91 (December 2001), pp. 1564–79. With regard to the effect on GDP, it would be more accurate to say that the growth rate of GDP in 1987 was 4 percentage points higher than normal because GDP was growing both before and after 1987.

14. Edward C. Prescott, "Why Do Americans Work So Much More than Europeans?," *Federal Reserve Bank of Minneapolis Quarterly Review* 28 (2004), pp. 2–15.

15. Slemrod and Bakija, *Taxing Ourselves,* p. 130.

16. Although whether this is true has long been in dispute, recent evidence seems to support this conclusion. See Karen Dynan, Jonathan Skinner, and Stephen P. Zeldes, "Do the Rich Save More?" *Journal of Political Economy* 112 (April 2004), pp. 397–444.

17. The broadest measure of income available in the National Income and Product Accounts is called Personal Income, and it has been for many years twice as large as taxable income under the federal individual income tax.

18. *Economic Report of the President* (2005), p. 77.

19. David Cay Johnston, *Perfectly Legal: The Covert Campaign to Rig Our Tax System to Benefit the Super Rich—And Cheat Everybody Else* (New York: Portfolio, 2003), and Mark Zepezauer, *Take the Rich Off Welfare* (Cambridge, MA: South End Press, 2004). That many people do become angry at the rich as a result of reading books like this is abundantly clear from the readers' reviews (highly favorable) of these two books on Amazon.com.

20. Slemrod, "Economics of Taxing the Rich," p. 6.

21. Technical note: For this calculation I used a Cobb-Douglas production function with a labor share of 0.75 and a capital share of 0.25. A 70 percent reduction in capital reduces labor's marginal product by 26 percent.

22. That workers benefit from the provision of capital by the rich may seem to contradict the marginal productivity theory that says each person gets exactly what he adds to production, with nothing left over to benefit other people. That is true for a small (marginal) change in labor or capital, but a 70 percent change is not a small change, and the marginal productivities of both inputs will be significantly affected by a change of that magnitude.

23. Edgar K. Browning and William R. Johnston, "Taxes, Transfers, and Income Inequality," in *Regulatory Change in an Atmostphere of Crisis*, ed. Gary M. Walton (New York: Academic Press, 1979), p. 143. This figure is from the mid-1970s, and there is little doubt that the top quintile's share of all hours worked is even higher today.

24. David R. Henderson, *The Joy of Freedom: An Economist's Odyssey* (Upper Saddle River, NJ: Prentice-Hall, 2002), p. 226.

25. F. A. Hayek, *The Constitution of Liberty* (Chicago: University of Chicago Press, 1960), pp. 43–44.

26. Harold Evans, *They Made America* (New York: Little, Brown and Company, 2004).

27. Estate tax returns do not have to be filed at all for most decedents who have small estates, so those who did file with estates under a million had significant estates, averaging $712 thousand.

28. By net estate, I mean the total estate less the amount left to surviving spouses.

29. Gerald E. Auten, Charles T. Clotfelter, and Richard L. Schmalbeck, "Taxes and Philanthropy among the Wealthy," in Slemrod, *Does Atlas Shrug?*, table 12.6. There were only 272 estates of over $20 million.

30. Many economists have come to favor consumption as the tax base rather than income. The main difference is that taxing consumption rather than income favors saving and capital accumulation because the return to saving is not taxed under a consumption tax. Because most people save very little, that is, they consume most of their income, the difference between the two would be slight for them. In the interest of brevity, I will not devote any space to a comparison of the two alternatives.

31. David Altig, Alan J. Auerbach, Laurence J. Kotlikoff, Kent A. Smetters, and Jan Walliser, "Simulating Fundamental Tax Reform in the United States," *The American Economic Review* 91 (June 2001), pp. 574–95. Slemrod and Bakija, *Taxing Ourselves*, p. 266, refer to this study as "perhaps the most useful exercise along these lines." The estimates developed in this paper seem to be quite close to the average value found in other studies, and I will rely on them as the best available evidence.

32. Specifically, this refers to a proportional tax on consumption that replaces both the federal individual income tax and the corporation income tax. The exact figure they give is a 9.4 percent increase, but they make no allowance for reduced compliance costs or increased innovation and entrepreneurship from the greatly reduced taxation of the so-called affluent.

33. This 9.7 percent figure is the share of both the individual and corporate income taxes because the study I am citing replaces both with a proportional tax in generating the estimated 9 percent loss in GDP.

34. This does not mean that the excess burden cost is a dollar per dollar of revenue, for part of the loss is that people are working less and so gain leisure time in compensation. The excess burden cost is probably closer to 50 cents per dollar of revenue, as we saw in an earlier section.

35. Based on table 7.2 in Slemrod and Bakija, *Taxing Ourselves*, which credits Altig et al., "Simulating Fundamental Tax Reform," for the information. (This table apparently did not make it into the final version that was published.) What this table shows is that those within the 40th–50th percentiles of the income distribution and all higher up gain. It does not show what happens to people in the 20th–40th percentile, but based on the figures given I would guess that the upper half of this quintile gains, also.

36. Specifically, the table cited in the previous footnote shows a loss equal to 1 percent of potential lifetime earnings for the 10th–20th percentiles. *Potential lifetime earnings* includes the value of nonwork (leisure) time as well as actual earnings, and I have expressed the loss as a percentage of actual earnings to avoid confusion, following the Altig et al. ("Simulating Fundamental Tax Reform," pp. 587–88) statement that their measure of lifetime earnings is "more than twice the size of remaining *actual* lifetime earnings."

37. Another reason is that with a 10 percent higher GDP, the 10 percent tax rate can be reduced to 9 percent and still yield the same revenue.

38. I am assuming that the level of government spending is taken as given, and we are deciding whether to raise taxes to cover the expenditures or run a deficit. Some conservatives argue that when the government operates at a deficit this will restrain government spending, and to this extent deficits are good.

39. The classic technical analysis of this argument is Martin Feldstein, "Debt and Taxes in the Theory of Public Finance," *Journal of Public Economics* 2, 8(2) (November 1985), pp. 233–45.

40. A major war is one example. Future generations secure benefits from successful completion of war, and deficit finance is one way to have them share in the costs.

41. Douglas W. Elmendorf and N. Gregory Mankiw, "Government Debt," in *Handbook of Macroeconomics*, vol. 1C, ed. J. B. Taylor and Michael Woodford (Amsterdam: Elsevier, 1999), pp. 1615–69.

42. Laurence J. Kotlikoff, *Generational Accounting: Knowing Who Pays, and When, for What We Spend* (New York: The Free Press, 1992), and Laurence J. Kotlikoff and Scott Burns, *The Coming Generational Storm* (Cambridge, MA: The MIT Press, 2004).

Chapter 10: The (Many) Costs of Transfers

1. See Harvey S. Rosen, *Public Finance*, 7th ed. (New York: McGraw-Hill, 2005), pp. 148–56, for a discussion of the most common arguments favoring income redistribution by government.

2. Thomas Sowell, "The Equality Dogma," syndicated column, February 17, 2004.

3. Richard Pipes, *Property and Freedom* (New York: Vintage Books, 1999), p. 77.

4. This is the so-called public good argument for redistribution. See Rosen, *Public Finance,* for a brief discussion.

5. H. L Mencken, *Minority Report: H. L. Mencken's Notebooks* (New York: Alfred A. Knopf, 1956), p. 325.

6. Henry J. Aaron, "Commentaries," in *Income Redistribution,* ed. C. D. Campbell (Washington, DC: American Enterprise Institute, 1977), p. 50.

7. Robert Nozick, *Anarchy, State, and Utopia* (New York: Basic Books, 1974).

8. See, for example, Milton Friedman, *Capitalism and Freedom* (Chicago: Phoenix Books, 1963).

9. Pipes, *Property and Freedom,* p. 283.

10. James S. Coleman, "Equality of Opportunity and Equality of Results," in *Against Equality,* ed. W. Letwin (London: Macmillan, 1983), p. 195.

11. Of course, many people reluctantly conclude that these transfers should be made in the interest of the children, who are blameless. But the transfers go to the mothers.

12. Richard A. Epstein, *Skepticism and Freedom: A Modern Case for Classical Liberalism* (Chicago: University of Chicago Press, 2004), p. 61.

13. Arthur M. Okun, *Equality and Efficiency: The Big Tradeoff* (Washington, DC: The Brookings Institution, 1975), p. 91.

14. James D. Gwartney and Richard E. Wagner, "Public Choice and the Conduct of Representative Government," in *Public Choice and Constitutional Economics,* ed. J. Gwartney and R. Wagner (Greenwich, CT: JAI Press, 1988), p. 22.

15. Quoted by Steven Moore in "Misplaced Trust," *National Review Online,* October 16, 2001.

16. Quoted in Bryon York, "Clinton Has No Clothes," *National Review Online,* December 17, 2001, http://nationalreview.com.

17. Robert Higgs, "Nineteen Neglected Consequences of Income Redistribution," *The Freeman,* December 1994, p. 654.

CHAPTER 11: JUST SAY NO

1. For example, see Leland B. Yeager, "Economics and Principles," *Southern Economic Journal* 42 (April 1976), pp. 559–71; and James M. Buchanan and Roger D. Congleton, *Politics by Principle, Not Interest* (Indianapolis: Liberty Fund, 2003).

2. Yeager, "Economics and Principles," p. 559.

3. James L. Payne, "The Congressional Brainwashing Machine," *The Public Interest* (Summer 1990), p. 100.

4. James L. Payne, "Budgeting in Neverland," *Policy Analysis* (Washington, DC: The Cato Institute, July 26, 2006), p. 7.

5. Richard A. Epstein, *Takings: Private Property and the Power of Eminent Domain* (Cambridge, MA: Harvard University Press, 1985).

6. Reported by the Roper Center at http://www.ropercenter.uconn.edu/cgi-bin/hsrun.exe/Roperweb/pom/StateId/RPQbmAsgrFEThDlltvuQ7la9Z9spm-UsKe/HAHTpage/Summary_Link?qstn_id=489568.

7. From the 1996 General Social Survey administered by the National Opinion Research Center.

8. Bradley R. Schiller, *The Economics of Poverty and Discrimination*, 8th ed. (Upper Saddle River, NJ: Prentice-Hall, 2001), p. 2.

9. Everett Carll Ladd and Karlyn H. Bowman, *Attitudes toward Economic Inequality* (Washington, DC: American Enterprise Institute Press, 1998), p. 114.

10. For example, Epstein (*Takings,* pp. 295–303) makes this case.

11. The reduction in the overall marginal tax rate confronting low-income families would be even greater than suggested here (looking at taxes only) because of the elimination of the federal welfare programs that contain (see chapter 6) implicit marginal rates of their own.

12. Except for a few scattered years, principally during the 1930s.

13. Schiller (*Economics of Poverty,* p. 2). The response "Financial aid; more money" was in a distant fourth place with 12 percent.

14. From the Roper Center for Public Opinion Research, University of Connecticut, http://www.ropercenter.uconn.edu.

Index

Aaron, Henry, 171
Affirmative action policies, 1, 136, 139, 170, 175, 182
African Americans: Armed Forces Qualification Test, 45; children's early environmental influences, 47–48; hours worked by, 44; levels of discrimination against, 39–40; low test scores, 45–46; median income levels, 37, 38–48; mismatching students with colleges, 137–39; poverty estimates, 76; and SAT scores, 137–39; *vs.* whites: income levels, 43, 44–45; test scores, 45–46
African nations, average income, 64
Age: influence on income, 12–13; and IQ, 17, 47–48; and productivity, 43–44; and Social Security benefits, 12, 110, 113, 121, 123
Aid to Families with Dependent Children. *See* Temporary Assistance for Needy Families (TANF)
Armed Forces Qualification Test (AFQT), whites *vs.* black scores, 45, 46–47
Armor, David, 16–17
Asian families, poverty estimates, 76
Asian Indian families, median income levels, 38
Asian Tigers (Hong Kong, Singapore, Taiwan, South Korea): economic growth in, 64–65, 66

Audit study determination of wage rates, 39
Average income: in Central African Republic, 64; in China, 56; in India, 56; in Japan, 64; in Mexico, 64; in Soviet Union, 67; in Taiwan, 64; in United Kingdom, 63; in U.S., 55; in Venezuela, 64
Average tax rates, 148, 150, 151, 153, 161, 162

Bane, Mary Jo, 76
Behavioral choices and poverty, 84–85
The Bell Curve (Herrnstein & Murray), 14
Bowman, Karlyn, 191
Browning-Johnson study, 23–24, 28
Buchanan, James, 188–89
Bush, George W., 142
Business Week, 2

Capitalism: misperceptions of, 7; *vs.* Communism, 3, 67, 68, 69; *vs.* socialism, 68, 69
Causes of poverty, 82–85
Census Bureau, 19–22; before-tax income statistics, 22; Browning-Johnson study, 23–24; consumption *vs.* income measurement, 24; corrections made for in-kind transfers, 78–79; family income ranking, 20; HiLo ratio, 20–21, 23–24, 28.29;

About the Author

EDGAR K. BROWNING is Professor of Economics at Texas A&M University. He has published extensively on issues related to government expenditure and tax policies and is the co-author of two bestselling economics textbooks. In 1987, he was elected President of the Southern Economics Association.

LaVergne, TN USA
23 December 2009
167967LV00001B/3/P